Advertising and Consumer Society

Advertising and Consumer Society

A Critical Introduction

Nicholas Holm
Lecturer in Media Studies, Massey University, New Zealand

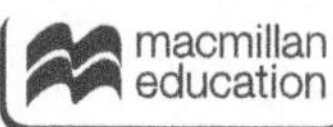

palgrave

First published 2017 by
PALGRAVE

Palgrave in the UK is an imprint of Macmillan Publishers Limited, registered in England, company number 785998, of 4 Crinan Street, London, N1 9XW.

Palgrave Macmillan in the US is a division of St Martin's Press LLC, 175 Fifth Avenue, New York, NY 10010.

Palgrave is a global imprint of the above companies and is represented throughout the world.

ISBN 978-1-137-47174-1 paperback

This book is printed on paper suitable for recycling and made from fully managed and sustained forest sources. Logging, pulping and manufacturing processes are expected to conform to the environmental regulations of the country of origin.

A catalogue record for this book is available from the British Library.

A catalog record for this book is available from the Library of Congress.

Printed and bound by CPI Group (UK) Ltd, Croydon, CR0 4YY

Contents

CHAPTER 1

Introduction: Why study advertising?

On 20 February 2011 over 15,000 people (by most accounts) lined a train track to celebrate the opening of the Kyushu Shinkansen: the latest section of the Japanese high-speed 'bullet train' that was to service the Southern island of Kyushu. Some were dressed in costumes; others took part in synchronised dancing; many simply jumped or waved at the passing train which was recording footage that would later serve as the basis for 'The 250km Wave': a commercial to advertise the opening of the new train line. Set to the catchy, upbeat soundtrack of Maia Hirasawa's 'Boom', the commercial presented an endearing image of regional unity and offbeat exuberance. It would eventually go on to win three awards at the 2011 Cannes Lions International Festival of Creativity, including a gold 'Outdoor Lion' for the use of stunts in an advertisement (Engine Films, 2011).

'The 250km Wave' was first broadcast on Japanese television on Friday 9 March, only two days before the Great East Japan Earthquake struck off the coast of Tōhoku. The strongest earthquake ever recorded in Japan, the Great East Japan Earthquake killed over 15,000 people and displaced over 225,000 more. Given the mood of national mourning following the unprecedented natural disaster, the advertisement was pulled from television screens as it was felt that its celebratory tone was inappropriate during that time. However, the commercial was still available online on YouTube and over the following months became the subject of intense online interest. Within three months the Japanese video had logged over two million views (Johnny, 2013), and by the time the official account closed the video had recorded over three and a half million views: more than any other non-music or earthquake-related video (Clegg, 2016). Rather than turn away from the joyful imagery of the commercial, the people of Japan had embraced the advertisement as an 'uplifting message of national solidarity' (Creativity Online, 2011). As a result of its popularity in that moment, over the coming years 'The 250km Wave' would remain an important cultural touchstone and a message of hope for rebuilding the Japanese nation.

'The 250km Wave' demonstrates the power of advertising to shape and influence our lives in often unexpected ways. Advertising across all media is a vitally important part of our media landscape and we too frequently overlook the ways in which commercials can shape our lives: from the adoption of too-frequently repeated catchphrases and jingles in everyday speech to the wider questions of social values and priorities. That an advertisement could be embraced in this manner shows that advertising is far from a disposable, ephemeral cultural form and can have very real influence upon the wider world. The success of the particular advertisement also speaks to more recent shifts in advertising from historically dominant media forms, such as broadcast television, to the online world of shareable and social media. The story of 'The 250km Wave' could not be told outside the context of new online networks and the associated changes in advertising. At the same time, we should also keep in mind how and why this video was produced: to promote a train service in order to make profits for a company. What does it mean when a private company becomes implicated in public grieving as part of a larger system, the explicit purpose of which is to make money? Finally, we might also want to consider the context of the ad itself: while thousands turned out to joyfully welcome the train and take part in the filming of the ad, thousands also stayed away. The train construction not only cut through existing communities and meant many had to now live in the shadow of the ten-metre-high bridges of the new infrastructure, but also led to concerns that those towns not serviced by stations would suffer economic decline (McMorran, 2013). Thus, while the ad shows us a happy, smiling world (which absolutely contributed to its post-earthquake success), it does so by simplifying and leaving out more controversial elements. All these aspects speak to the vital and complicated role of advertising in our society: its immense creativity, its implication in wider social discussions and debates, its potential to uplift and entertain, its close connection to the profit motive and its particular way of presenting the world. Those issues and more will be the subject of our study in this book.

Why study advertising?

The first question that confronts a student of advertising is as simple as it is important: why study advertising? In comparison to many of the other topics that you may address at university, advertising might appear to be a subject which most of us already know as much about as we might want to. Indeed, many of you might think that you are already experts in advertising whether you wish to be or not. Even compared to other topics in Media and Cultural Studies, let alone subjects like Chemistry or Medieval Literature, advertising is almost certainly a subject with which you are already quite familiar: maybe even more familiar than you'd like to be! Indeed, advertising may even be a media form that you're accustomed to going some lengths to avoid – through the use of technology such as browser web blockers or through cultivated habits of stubborn avoidance – rather than engaging with in detail. Advertisements, after all, are frequently framed as the bottom of the media hierarchy: brash in their claims, demanding in their tone, unsophisticated in their execution. Understood in this manner, it is fairly obvious why we'd want to steer clear of advertising whenever possible and, conversely, somewhat unclear as to why on earth we would want to pay it the attention that is necessary for detailed study (let alone read a whole book on the subject!) Nonetheless, despite such objections, in this textbook we will be committing ourselves to making sense of what might appear to be the dirty business of advertising. Having picked up this book (or signed up for a class in which you are asked to purchase this book) hopefully you already have some idea as to why – despite its negative profile – you might want to study advertising.

This book is an investigation of what advertising is, what it does and what it means. We'll be particularly concerned with what makes advertising different from other ways of using media and the historical, technical, technological, economic, political, social and cultural roles that it plays as a result. We'll be thinking about why it is that so many people hate advertising and why a few people seem to really love it: what it's meant to do and what it actually does. Along the way, we'll consider whether advertising might be best understood as a form of art or business or just manipulation and how those different ways of making sense of advertising fit with wider beliefs about the world, media, individuals, communities and communication. Moreover, we'll be doing all this in the wholehearted commitment to the idea that advertising is not only possessed of hidden depths of meaning and significance, but also has a lot to teach us about the society we live in: in particular, the media-saturated, money-driven consumer society of the rich countries of the twenty-first century. Consequently, while some of our more dismissive and negative beliefs around advertising are sometimes absolutely justified, we will also consider how they can also be limited and limiting; in almost all instances they can prevent us from properly understanding advertising as a cultural, social, political and economic practice. Therefore, in order to address possible objections and the limitations that can arise from them, in this introductory chapter I will present five key reasons why I think we might want to study advertising in terms of its ubiquity, oddness, economic importance, aesthetic possibilities and political potential. Following the presentation of these different reasons – and hopefully having made a convincing case! – I will then run through some of the particular features that will shape our engagement with advertising and society in this book.

Reason one: Advertising is everywhere

At the most straightforward level, the first reason why we might want to study advertising is relatively simple: it's everywhere. We encounter advertising on our televisions, plastered across the side of buildings, blaring out of radios, embedded in our social media, stuck between the pages of magazines and newspapers, preceding movies, stuffed into every potentially empty space in sports games, popping up and scrolling across webpages, festooning the side of highways, sprawled across the outsides of public transport (and often on the inside as well), emblazoned across our clothing, wrapped around our food and sometimes even dragged across the sky. Advertising is the medium that gets where other media don't. Even as consumers take advantage of new, easier and more efficient ways of avoiding advertisements through the use of technologies such as TiVo devices or AdBlock software, advertising manages to remain a persistent part of our everyday existence as advertisers turn to new techniques like viral marketing and colonise social media like Facebook and Instagram. Despite the massive technological and cultural changes in our media over the last century, advertising remains the wallpaper of our lives: the dull background hum of our media culture that teases, teaches, insults, provokes, informs, entertains and annoys in equal measure.

What this means, then, is that even if advertising weren't an interesting cultural form in its own right (which it is!), we'd be almost compelled to study it as a result of the sheer ubiquity of the stuff. Because it's everywhere, advertising has the power to worm its way into the fabric of our everyday lives: its power arises part from the sheer scale of its presence: the repetition, not just of individual ads or campaigns, but of advertising itself which crashes against our brains with the persistent force of waves upon a beach. It would be difficult for something that is so ever-present not to exert some influence upon our beliefs and values (Leiss et al., 2005, pp. 3–4; Wharton, 2015, p. 1). Anything that there is so much of deserves further scrutiny simply by virtue of its ubiquity, its constant presence and the power that it wields as a result of that. Consequently, given this power and influence, advertising is a subject that seems of the utmost importance to understand in order to make sense of how it intervenes in our lives and shapes our beliefs and behaviours. One of the main focuses of this book will be unpacking how advertising might work to shape the way we understand the world, not just on the level of individual purchasing decisions, but on the level of social and cultural beliefs and values.

Reason two: Advertising is weird

One of the major repercussions of the constant presence of advertising is that we all seem to have developed a blind spot regarding how absolutely bizarre it is. We don't appreciate this often enough. This is true at the level of individual advertisements – surreal tapestries of talking animals, cartoon jack-hammers pounding diagrams of distressed human heads, quick-cut montages of ludicrously jubilant young people chewing gum or slugging back sugar water – but also at the level of wider practice. Advertising is a massive system of global production, distribution and consumption based around the counter-intuitive idea that with the right combination of design and market research, hundreds of thousands of people can be convinced to part with their money to purchase goods that they possibly don't even want. Even more unlikely, advertising is produced by corporations at great expense and then distributed for free: hundreds of thousands of stories in miniature and spectacular images, prepared using countless interviews with focus groups and studies of demographics, so carefully studied as to put Hollywood to shame. And finally, despite all this effort, the dirty, half-kept secret of advertising is that nobody is actually sure if it works. As the early advertiser John Wanamaker is sometimes reported to have said, 'half the money I spend on advertising is wasted; the trouble is I don't know which half' (Keyes, 2006, p. 2).

This fairly odd state of affairs is the result of a highly contingent set of historical, economic and social circumstances, which is to say: things didn't have to be this way. If anyone were to create a society from scratch, it is highly unlikely that they would come up with the idea of advertising, nor assign such a prominent role to it. Advertising didn't have to be a central ever-present aspect of our mediated existence, advertising didn't have to underwrite a large section of our entertainment media and advertising didn't have to be an essential and unquestionable part of providing or even selling goods and services. It's very important to remember this over the course of this book: advertising isn't a fundamental part of human existence, but it has come to function as one in the rich Western countries of the twenty-first century. The way in which advertising works in our society isn't the only way advertising can or has worked, and we should never be satisfied with something just because that's the way it is, but instead should always wonder why it's this way instead of any other. Therefore, in this book we'll be looking at not only the history of advertising, in order to get a sense of how things came to be this way, but also tracing how advertising continues to reproduce the conditions of its own justification and legitimation in our current moment.

Reason three: Advertising is where the money is

The third reason advertising is fascinating is because of the money. There's no denying that advertising is a big business: the global advertising industry employs hundreds of thousands of people around the world and does about

$500 billion worth of business a year (Economist 2014). However, in economic terms, advertising is even more important than such a dollar value might suggest. This is because advertising doesn't just work as an economic entity in its own right: it also functions as an essential part of our capitalist economy. The economics of advertising are therefore always about more than just the money that changes hands with the production and distribution of advertising messages; they are also about the role that advertising plays in keeping the rest of the economy humming along (Hardy, 2015, p. 65). Without advertising (or at least the half that works...), there would be a chance that our economy would begin to slowly grind to a halt.

This is because advertising is more than just the means by which we learn about different products and services; it is also a constant reminder that as good consumer-citizens of the twenty-first century we should keep on buying things. Shampoo. Fast food. Cars. Prescription medication. Advertising is at the heart of what we refer to as consumer society: a way of living organised around the purchasing and accumulation of things, where it seems unquestionably obvious that the best way to obtain the things that sustain and bring meaning to our lives is to acquire them through the exchange of currency. Joseph Turow and Matthew McAllister describe consumer culture as the symbols and messages that surround people about products and services that they buy and use (that is, consume). Consumer culture also involves how people make meaning from these messages: how we understand ourselves and our lives through consumer messages (2009, p. 4). Much has been written about the consumer society: some have suggested that the ascension of consumerism has robbed our lives of purpose, beauty and authenticity, while others have argued that consumer culture provides new means for us to express and articulate ourselves in the world with a new-found sense of freedom. We will consider the arguments in support of both of these positions in this book, and the consequences of both for assessing the cultural, social and political roles of advertising in the wider context of consumer society.

In addition, the economic importance of advertising means that it is a rich site through which to examine and debate the role of capitalism in our society more broadly: what does it mean to live in a society where economic growth is understood as the central guiding value of government, rationality is understood in terms of profit motive and money is often the final determining mark of value? How does advertising both rely on such capitalist ideas and contribute to their reinforcement? And how might we understand these ideas in relation to media and culture – not least advertising – which has been historically denounced as a source of false information regarding the capacity of capitalism to meet social desires (Williams, 2005, pp. 184–186), as an aesthetic of alienating glamour that substitutes consumption for democracy (Berger,

1974, p. 149) or even as 'a pure representation of social power' (Horkheimer and Adorno, 1972, p. 163). We'll be exploring some of these ideas in the second part of the book through an engagement with Marxist and post-Marxist approaches to advertising, consumerism and capitalism as a means to consider how advertising produces particular forms of engagement, understandings and impressions of the economic relations that structure our lives. This involves much more than simply denouncing advertising as something 'bad' or manipulative, but instead trying to untangle its central role in our capitalist economy and consumerist society.

Reason four: Advertising is beautiful, inspiring and entertaining

The fourth reason I think we should study advertising is because of its aesthetic aspects: its ability to move us, thrill us, entertain us and inspire us. In a way, this fourth reason is almost the opposite of reason three, because it encourages us to consider advertising as more than just a sales pitch and instead appreciate it as a form of art. While much of the advertising we encounter is relatively straightforward in its appeal, and unsophisticated in its construction and presentation, advertising can also be stunningly inventive in its formal presentation and in its ability to create emotionally resonant narrative or visually striking imagery (McStay, 2011, pp. 1–3). I imagine almost all readers will be able to recall at least one example of an advertisement that they found unexpectedly moving, captivating or at least entertaining (if you have trouble thinking of any examples then I encourage you to seek out Sony's visually spectacular 2005 'Bouncy Ball' ad for Bravia televisions, or John Lewis' surprisingly emotional 2014 Christmas ad, 'Monty's Christmas'!) In fact, even those apparently simple advertisements – ads for big box furniture stores where a voice-over shouts about bargains, or an item of junk mail detailing the specials for the week at the local supermarket – are highly complex combinations of sound and colour that are specially designed to foster particular responses. We would be doing advertising a great disservice if we were to think about it only in terms of its brute purpose and thereby overlook the ways in which it reaches out to us through stories, songs, images and experiences.

In fact, at least one commentator has gone so far as to declare advertising to be not just artistic, but an actual form of art. The early media theorist Marshall McLuhan, who was famed for making over-the-top proclamations, declared that 'Advertising is the greatest art form of the twentieth century' (Gettins, 2005, p. 117). While we don't want to get bogged down in the potential details of McLuhan's claim – after all, what makes one art form 'greater' than another? – we will explore what it would mean to take seriously his central claim that advertising is a form of art. One way we can approach this claim is to think about how the forms of advertising might be interpreted in terms of art: this doesn't mean that advertising should be hung in a gallery necessarily, but how the use of aspects such as colour and movement might transform everyday spaces and lead us to think about the world in new and different ways. When we try to think about the similarities between art and advertising this can complicate our ideas about the status and role of art, and potentially present advertising in a more positive light than that in which it usually appears. Approaching advertising as art can also lead us to think about the people who make advertisements as more than just faceless drones, but as passionate, creative people with different politics and who want to tell stories and create meaningful impressions and interventions in the world. Thinking about advertising in relation to art opens up new ways of explaining the appeal of advertisements and forces us to acknowledge its wider cultural role.

Reason five: Advertising is political

My final and most important reason for studying advertising is that it is tied up in questions of politics. By this, I don't mean the role of advertising in the service of party politics and electioneering, or the manner in which political campaigns are increasingly run as if they were advertising campaigns for competing brands of toothpaste. These aspects of political advertising are certainly fascinating, but are relatively narrow in their application. Instead, what I'm referring to here is the wider point that advertising, like all forms of media, produces and reproduces certain ways of understanding the world. In his 1917 novel, *South Wind*, Norman Douglas famously suggests that 'You can tell the ideals of a nation by its advertisements' (1917, p. 55). There is little to suggest that much has changed since then, except that we now have many more advertisements, so there is arguably much more raw material from which we can read those national ideas. Advertisements present us with an easily accessible and always updating archive of a society's desires, fears, wants and anxieties as well as a range of stock characters and short repeated narratives. In the process of selling us running shoes and tea bags, advertising thus presents us with insights into what makes a society tick. So long as we pay enough attention and know where to look, we can find in advertising a wealth of material about the construction and dissemination of our values, ideas and ideals in our societies (Wernick, 1991, pp. 24–25). Such concepts are inherently political because they play a fundamental role in teaching us about the roles and functions available to us, the ways we can express ourselves and solve our problems, and therefore provide a way of making sense of how power and resources are distributed in our society. Advertising arises at the conflux of the most crudely economic demands and the loftiest cultural aspirations of our media landscape: it is simultaneously one of the most debased and one of the most creative cultural forms. As a consequence, advertising expresses some of the thorniest and most interesting dilemmas surrounding economics and politics in our society and is one of the most productive sites at which to consider some of the defining tensions of contemporary cultural production. Provided we have the right tools for the job, advertising can tell us much about how the world works.

What this book is about

These, then, are my five reasons why we would want to study advertising in detail and why I think you should take the time to read a book on the subject. Hopefully, some, if not all, of these reasons align with your own interests in advertising. In this book I'll be exploring, expanding and complicating these different approaches as well as ideally providing opportunities for you to contemplate your own interests in advertising. In order to accomplish these ends, this book is structured according to three sections that provide opportunities to pursue contrasting perspectives towards advertising. The first section will set you up with the fundamentals you'll need to study advertising; the second section will focus upon advertising as an economic form tied up with capitalism and consumerism that trains us to seek pleasure and purpose in purchases; and the third section will present a counter-argument for understanding advertising as a complicated, creative form that can serve a variety of social and cultural purposes. By the end of this book you will therefore be familiar with the two central competing models for analysing the social, cultural and political work of advertising and be able to assess the various claims of those two approaches and how they challenge and complicate one another in challenging and productive ways.

The foundations of studying advertising

The first section comprises this introduction and chapters on the formal analysis and history of advertising. The purpose of this first section is to provide you with the basic methods and knowledge needed to make sense of advertising. In Chapter 2, I will guide you through a quick history of advertising through a focus upon four key historical moments: the development of advertising in the context of the industrial revolution; the professionalisation of the industry at the turn of the twentieth century; the reinvention of advertising as a creative practice in the 1950s; and the rise of digital advertising in the twenty-first century. A familiarity with both the changing style of advertising and the different ways that the practice of advertising has been understood will enable you to place its current forms in context. Chapter 3 complements this historical account by providing a range of approaches to analysing advertisements in terms of semiotic and ideological methods, as well as making sense of how the different media and codes and conventions of the industry can contribute to the final form of advertisements. The intention of this chapter is to provide you with a basic toolkit for explaining the key features of individual examples and the fundamental concepts for talking about the construction and communications of meaning in ads. The reason we begin with this material is so that you have the ability to ground the larger theories of the later chapters in specific examples and therefore will have the means to evaluate how those arguments apply to your own advertising environment. You'll be able to practice and develop the skills introduced in this chapter throughout your studies of advertising.

Advertising and capitalism

The second section of the book will advance an argument that advertising can be best accounted for in relation to the economic context of capitalism. The three chapters in this section address key aspects of Marxist and post-Marxist approaches to advertising that have traditionally been the dominant means for making sense of advertising in Media and Cultural Studies. Chapter 4 begins by introducing the key concepts of 'capitalism' and 'ideology'. After an explanation of why capitalism is absolutely central to any attempt to understand advertising, we will address how the notion of ideology connects the economic idea of capitalism with a wider analysis of society and culture. This connection will be illustrated through the analysis of several examples that illustrate how advertising works as a way to think through our relationship to capitalism and how capitalism is usually presented as a natural and desirable way of life. Chapter 5 develops this mode of analysis further through a sustained engagement with the idea of the 'commodity'. In the context of Marxist approaches to capitalism and advertising, the term 'commodity' refers to a particular understanding of goods that have been separated from their conditions of production. We will consider how advertising functions to inject new meanings into products that are frequently far and beyond any qualities that the objects themselves possess: for example, Coca-Cola ads usually suggest that drinking Coke will lead to happiness. We will then consider how the transformation of goods into commodities sets up the conditions in which the meanings attached to products play a more influential role in purchase decisions than the actual physical qualities of the product involved. Finally, in Chapter 6, we will think about how advertising audiences are construed in this economic model. This will involve an examination of how audiences for advertising are effectively bought and sold by media producers and how the economic logic of the mass audiences might lead to conservative and conformist media content. Complicating that model, we will also look at the historical segmentation of audiences, as advertisers aspire to reach ever more precise demographic groups for their products to the extent that contemporary advertising is increasingly targeted at individuals using advanced online monitoring technologies. Overall, the Marxist approaches to advertising that inform the chapters in this section contribute to a bleak picture of advertising as a powerful cultural form that uses its ability to persuade the population to produce a profit at the expense of social and cultural awareness.

Art, agency and other complications

In contrast, the third section of this book will take up approaches to advertising informed by cultural industries and cultural studies traditions in order to challenge and complicate those conclusions we draw from the Marxist model alone. The introduction of these alternate perspectives is not meant to be a dismissal of those critical Marxist methods, but rather should be understood as part of a dialectical model: this means that rather than attempt to resolve the contradictions between these competing interpretations, such that one is right and one is wrong, we need to try to hold both in our heads simultaneously. The conflict between the two models speaks to the fact that not just in theory, but also in its actual existence and practice, advertising is a complicated and even internally contradictory practice. In the first chapter of this section, Chapter 7, we will examine the production of advertising from the perspective of those who actually produce it: rather than the faceless monolith that emerges out of Marxist accounts, we will consider the inner complexity, organisational structure and self-perception of the agencies and agents that make advertising. Chapter 8 will expand on this approach to advertising by considering the social status and critical perspective of the advertisements themselves. This will involve an interrogation of the idea of 'creativity' in the context of advertising and the possibilities and limitations of that concept. Building on that discussion, we will investigate the relationship between advertising and art, ask what it is that separates the two categories and explore what it might mean if we were to classify advertising as a form of art with the ability to offer meaningful and critical comment on the world. Chapter 9 closes off this section by taking into account the goals and gratifications that the advertising audience seeks and obtains from advertisements. Looking at the ways that audiences not only interpret advertising, but also use it as a resource for their own ends and even help produce it, this chapter leads us towards a more nuanced understanding of the audience as active participants, rather than na.ve dupes. The brief final chapter of the book will then offer an overview of the different arguments and positions staked out in the previous chapter, with a particular emphasis on how the prior material can be considered 'political' and what that means for the study of advertising in a wider social context.

What this book is not about

That then is a quick summary of what this book is about and the different topics that will be touched upon in more detail in the later chapters. However, given the potential for misunderstanding that often arises in the study of advertising, it is also important to clearly state what this book is not about so as to ensure we're all on the same page. First, if it were not already clear from the chapter summaries, this is not a book about how to make ads, at least not in any direct way. While some of the material addressed in this book might very well assist you in the production of advertising, such an outcome is very far from the primary goal of this book, which is really about understanding the role of advertising in wider social and cultural contexts. Moreover, while this book is certainly interested in taking into account how those who make advertising understand what they are doing, this does not mean that we will be beholden to industry-driven perspectives on advertising. For example, in the context of Marketing Studies there are often divisions between mass media advertising and other forms of promotion, such as branding and publicity. Rather than adhering to such distinctions as they are produced and reproduced in industry-led accounts, we will instead be following a more everyday definition of advertising. John Sinclair sums up this position well when he argues that 'when we talk about advertising in everyday life ... we don't bother drawing a line between advertising and other forms of promotion, nor do we distinguish between, say, TVCs [television commercials] and sponsored search results on the internet – it's all just advertising' (Sinclair, 2012, p. 3). As such we will be casting our net more widely than might be common practice in the context of a Marketing or Advertising Studies programme in order to make sense of advertising in the wider context of our media environment and consumer culture.

However, and this is the final point of clarification, this is also not a book about advertising as a generic media form, or a way to approach wider issues in Media and Cultural Studies. Instead, this is a book that aims to address what is most specific to advertising as a form of media and those topics that are most salient to advertising rather than other forms of cultural production. Accordingly, advertising won't be treated as the excuse or the substrate for other analyses: this means that we won't be looking at wider issues – such as the representation of gender and race, celebrity culture, music, globalisation or humour – as they emerge in advertising. While these are valid and important topics, we'll be focusing on what is particular to advertising: the concerns and questions that are central to advertising or arise with respect to advertising in a particularly pointed way compared to other media forms: these include the imperative to sell, the relation between media and economics, ideas of manipulation and persuasion and the intersection between art and commerce. Advertising is the reason we're here, not a way into other debates and discussion, and so our focus will always be on what is particular to advertising as a medium and cultural form.

CHAPTER 2

The history of advertising: Contexts, transformations and continuity

There is a lot that seems absolutely and unprecedentedly *new* about advertising in the first decades of the twenty-first century: new digital technologies allow the production of new forms of advertising; new online platforms create new spaces in which to advertise; new forms of data-gathering create the conditions for unprecedented monitoring and targeting of consumers. With the rapid and continuing development of new frontiers in advertising, especially in relation to digital and online media, it might therefore appear that advertising now is all about the new: that there has been an absolute break with advertising's past and, as a result, its history can no longer tell us anything about its future. Some have even suggested that in the advertising industry history 'is almost a dirty word' (Hegarty, 2011, p. 7). This is certainly the sort of claim that is repeated surprisingly frequently in both industry and academic literature, where the brave new world of online advertising is suggested to have changed the game so dramatically that there is little to be learnt from an investigation of what came before. One of the ironies of such claims is that when we do take a closer look at the history of advertising, we see that such declarations – that advertising has changed so dramatically as to make earlier forms of knowledge irrelevant – are one of the recurring features of advertising over the past two centuries. Indeed, constant change, or at the very least the belief that they are constantly changing, might be considered one of the consistent defining features of the institutions, practices and forms of advertising. It is a further irony, then, that if we do want to understand why advertising is so enthralled with the idea of change then we need to have a sense of the forces and priorities that shaped its shifting nature over time, and the consequent ways in which advertising has understood, presented and conducted itself.

In order to address these issues, in this chapter we will be investigating the history of advertising with a particular eye to the changes and consistencies that characterise its development as a media form from its early ramshackle days as an occupation of ill-repute to its current existence as a high-tech cornerstone of the global economy. We will think not only about what has changed, but also about what has not changed: the connections that can be drawn between the debates and direction of advertising across the twentieth century and the manifestation of advertising today. In doing so, we will gain an appreciation for how, despite the current fixation on digital reinvention, advertising remains a product of decades-old forces, including aspirations for legitimacy and respectability and conflicts between the science and the art of advertising. Unfortunately, we don't have the space in this single chapter to provide you with a complete overview of the history of advertising. Instead, we will be focusing on key moments and themes in the history of advertising that have been chosen in order to provide you with background knowledge that will help you make the most of your study of advertising. A grasp of this material will provide essential background to the following discussions of advertising in terms of concepts such as capitalism, audiences and creativity, and thus functions as an important launching pad for making sense of how advertising works today. If you are interested in reading more, there are a number of book-length studies of advertising history, including Mark Tungate's *Adland* from an industry perspective (2013), Jackson Lears' *Fables of Abundance* from a cultural history perspective (1994) and William Leiss et al.'s *Social Communication in Advertising* (2005), which offers an overview of a number of different historical approaches. I draw upon all three of these books and more in this chapter's account, and they provide a great deal of additional detail regarding the periods and themes we will explore.

Four moments in advertising history

Our journey through the history of advertising will be defined by four key moments that are roughly fifty years apart. We begin with the origins of advertising during the industrial revolution and the formation of mass society in the nineteenth century. Our investigation of this moment provides a context for advertising's ties to a number of other social, economic and technological transformations taking place at that time. By examining the conditions in which advertising began we can therefore appreciate how advertising is always part and product of its wider environment, with particular relation to ideas of consumerism and the consumer society. The second key moment is the turn of the twentieth century, when tensions came to the fore regarding the regulation and responsibilities of advertising. In the face of pressure from officials who sought to regulate the wild claims and outright lies that were exemplified in advertising for 'patent medicines', many in the industry sought to reinvent themselves as respectable businessmen. It is out of the conflicting forces of this time that the first full-service advertising agencies emerged as part of a concerted attempt to professionalise and legitimate advertising as a responsible practice.

Our third moment takes place in the mid-twentieth century following the massive expansion of American consumer society after World War Two. In this environment, advertising appeared, on the one hand, as a potential menace that could harness the power of new developments in social science and psychology to steer the minds of the masses. On the other hand, the Creative Revolution promised a rejuvenation of the power of advertising to entertain and enliven everyday life. Finally, our fourth moment takes us almost up to the present day by considering the changes in advertising since the beginning of the twenty-first century. We will consider the new forms of advertising that have arisen in digital and online spaces, and explore how these new developments both break from but also draw upon long-standing tendencies in advertising. This is not a comprehensive history of advertising, and the focus on these four moments means that other aspects will be neglected, but hopefully you will come away with a sense of some of the key themes and recurring debates in advertising and how they inform our current moment.

The first moment: Origins, industrialisation and development

Our journey through the history of advertising will begin with a question that is surprisingly difficult to answer: when did advertising begin? Some histories of advertising – especially those operating from an industry perspective – suggest that the first examples of advertising can be found as far back as the early Roman Empire (Wharton, 2015, pp. 26–33) or even that pre-historic cave paintings could be considered a form of advertising (Tungate, 2013, p. 7). Such an account acts to naturalise advertising: to present it as a universal and timeless aspect of the human condition which we as a species have carried out since pretty soon after walking on two legs. Yet it is unlikely that we would recognise such examples as what we would today consider advertising, because while they (might) constitute an attempt to communicate regarding goods and services, they bear very little in common to the mass-produced, mass-distributed, mass-mediated messages that saturate our contemporary culture.

The first advertising?

As communications historian Vincent Norris argues, the idea of advertising doesn't really even make sense in societies where economic relations were based around gift-giving, feudal redistribution and self-sufficiency, and there was therefore no 'need or opportunity to advertise' (1980, p. 49). Therefore, while some merchants in such contexts may have put out signs letting passers-by know what wares they had for sale, such displays have as much in common with the contemporary multi-billion dollar promotion industry as medieval balladry does to contemporary popular music: sure, they both involve singing, but the differences in purpose, scale, form, function and practice are so immense as they make them effectively different activities. When we imagine Roman store signs or other promotional images of earlier periods as the equivalent of contemporary advertising we are fundamentally misunderstanding the economic conditions of those moments and the role of advertising. Instead, as Raymond Williams argues, in order to grasp the history of advertising in a useful manner, it is important that we attend to the specific institutions and practices that form the basis of contemporary advertising and the way they relate to surrounding economic and social developments (2005, p. 190).

Industrialisation and mass society

What is at stake here, then, with the question of when advertising begins is the even larger question of what exactly advertising *is*. When we mark the first moment of 'actual' advertising, we are making a statement about what constitutes the key features that make advertising what it is. Consequently, in contrast to this 'long view', we'll be marking the advent of advertising from the early nineteenth century, in a period when the process of industrialisation – 'the movement within a culture or economic system toward an increased emphasis on large-scale/mechanized industry rather than agricultural/small-scale commercial activity' (Veldstra and Walters, 2004, p. 315) – was dramatically changing the European and North American societies where advertising began. Industrialisation ushered in many dramatic changes to the ways in which people lived, but the most significant in terms of our current discussion are:

- **Urbanisation**: The growth of large manufacturing plants and factories following the Industrial Revolution led to the increased possibility of employment in urban centres, which resulted in large-scale migration of people from rural areas to the growing cities across Europe. Thousands, indeed millions, flocked to the cities, thereby breaking historical bonds of locality and community.
- **Rationalisation**: In the new spaces of the city and the factory, a new organisation of space and time began to emerge with an emphasis on

efficiency and separation. Old ways of life disappeared in favour of new regimes that separated places of work from places of living and leisure. Time also became subject to the logic of the factory clock and calendar, which replaced the older systems of sun and seasons.

- **Mass production** and **mass distribution**: New developments in machine technology, notably the development of steam power and the assembly line, allowed for the mass-manufacturing of consumer goods. An increased range of goods meant an increasingly competitive marketplace, in which producers had to find ways to distinguish their products. At the same time, mass distribution allowed manufacturers to expand beyond their traditional home markets with advertising providing a way to communicate to new consumers across national contexts.
- **Mass media**: Perhaps most importantly for us, industrialisation (including mass production and distribution) produced the enabling conditions for the first mass media. While newspapers had existed since the seventeenth century, the Industrial Revolution enabled cheaper and larger print runs, transforming newspapers into a true mass medium. Defined by a centralised model and providing a venue for rapid, standardised communication, newspapers (joined by broadcast radio at the turn of the century, and television in the 1950s) offered a way to reach a growing and increasingly literate audience, who also had increasing leisure time and disposable income.

It is in the context of these four cultural shifts that the practice of advertising begins to cohere in the context of the new consumer society of Europe and the US in the late eighteenth and early nineteenth centuries (Lears, 1994, pp. 88–89; McFall, 2004, p. 111). Consumer society marked a profound transformation of prior social arrangements: as Susan Strasser argues, in this new world people would now be less defined by their job and what they produced, and instead would be more defined by what they bought (1989, p. 28). Separated from traditional systems of understanding the world, such as community status and religion, the new consuming classes turned to the world of goods to provide meaning and order in their lives. No longer was identity defined by one's place and time of birth, but instead could now be created anew in the anonymous space of the city through the purchase of goods. One of the key ways in which this was achieved was through consumption as brands and commodities became a way to map out and understand the world. This new social arrangement marked the radical and wholesale entry of capitalism into everyday life carried on the currents of the new mass media, which provided both medium and motivation for the practice of advertising (we will consider the concept of capitalism in more depth in Chapter 4).

The beginning of consumer society

In this new consumer society, goods and services that were once produced by oneself or one's family were now increasingly acquired through the exchange of currency. This was due in large part to an increasing 'division of labour' in the new rational order: where rather than engage in all the different tasks required to furnish a household, workers would instead specialise in one particular job in exchange for a wage, which could then be exchanged for goods and services. In the economic environment, consumers were faced with totally new consumer goods and new variations and types of familiar products which previously would have been self-produced, such as soap. In the absence of the guarantee that came from knowing the producer of goods or a long-term relationship with the merchant, advertising offered an alternate way of understanding and interpreting new products. Packaging provided a means to not only protect goods through mass distribution, but also to serve as marks of familiarity and quality to help distinguish goods in a changing retail environment. Branded packaging thus offered the promise of reliable, standardised, identifiable and memorable products in an age of proliferation and anonymity, and shoppers were thereby reconfigured as an audience for the spectacle of sale. Michael Schudson makes the important point that at this early stage the focus of advertising was on identification over identity (1986, pp. 69–70): not on providing a sense of what values and ideas the product stood for, but simply establishing that the product existed and making it visible. This was achieved through long-term repetition of ads: sometimes over several decades without change.

Beyond the promotion of individual goods, nineteenth-century advertising also served the wider role of presenting the new consumerist way of life in an attractive way. While the new industrialised production methods promised to usher in an era of plenty, an increase in goods was useless without a matching increase in consumption. One of the central tasks of advertising was thus to not only help sell particular products, but also to present consumption as a whole as a desirable and meaningful way of procuring the basics of life. In some cases, this was achieved through explicit instructions on how one might use the product and how it might thereby improve one's life (Leiss et al., 2005, pp. 205–207). In other cases, advertising drew on earlier iconographies and mythologies that presented industrial-produced goods as a continuation of early folk traditions and practices: drawing on a long history of imagery that presented the agricultural US as a land of bountiful harvests and general fecundity (Lears, 1994, p. 18). Through the evocation of this older tradition of carnivalesque excess, early advertisements functioned to establish connections between the new world of consumer societies and older ways of life which were quickly being lost. Through such advertising, not only were consumers being sold goods, they were also being sold the very idea of consumption: the idea that they could purchase their way to a better life.

At the same time, an equivalent campaign was also taking place addressing those who paid for advertising, as producers were also taught about the virtues of this new social institution. Ralph Hower suggests that the main promotional goal of the early advertising agencies wasn't to sell goods, but 'to promote the general use of advertising' (quoted in Schudson, 1986, p. 74) as an essential communication between producers and potential consumers. Those manufacturers that heeded this message did very well: by the early twentieth century, brand recognition built through advertising would prove a strong barrier to competition by preventing easy access to market (Norris, 1980, p. 53). However, these early agencies were quite distinct from their modern form: complicating any easy equation of advertising with creativity, the first advertising agencies didn't even produce the ads themselves. Instead, they bought space in newspapers in bulk and sold it piece by piece for profit: they were in the business of buying and selling media space, not creating promotional content (Tungate, 2013, p. 14). Agents would buy media space in bulk, primarily in print publications, then divide it into smaller packages which they would sell on to manufacturers while charging a commission (Leiss et al., 2005, p. 125). While advertising was becoming ever more tightly bound up with the wider social and economic changes of the new industrialised consumer society, it would not be till the final decades of the century that advertisers would begin to deal in advertising content as well as media space, and thereby begin to resemble the more familiar industry and media form of the twentieth and twenty-first centuries.

The second moment: Professionalisation, consolidation and redemption

Practices and forms much more similar to the modern practice of advertising would begin to emerge in the final decades of the nineteenth century amidst growing concerns regarding advertising's social role. As the industry matured and expanded, this period saw both the consolidation of the first advertising agencies and mounting fears, within and outside of the industry, regarding the power of advertising to influence consumers and the industry's lack of organisation, accountability or professionalism. Concerned above all with a struggle for social legitimacy, the late nineteenth and early twentieth centuries were a period marked by conflicts in the advertising industry regarding the establishment of acceptable practices, regulations and codes of ethics.

The problem of patent medicine

Such matters were of special concern in the case of the large percentage of advertisements that turned to false claims in order to sell their products. In particular this was true of advertisements for 'patent medicines': a class of products that promised to cure any and all manner of ill-defined ailments (Lears, 1994, p. 43), including lumbago, tooth ache, 'brain trouble', malaria and a lack of vim: often all at once! In practice, the apparently therapeutic properties of these 'medicines' were the result of generous quantities of alcohol, opium and even cocaine. The soft drink, Coca-Cola, began life as just such a product and was marketed as a remedy for fatigue and headaches: a feat it originally achieved through a dose of cocaine (which was later replaced by a hefty dose of caffeine following government regulation) (Pendergrast, 2000, pp. 8–10, 103–104). Patent medicine advertising formed the 'backbone' of most agencies' business in the late nineteenth century and constituted up to a quarter of all advertising produced in America at the time (Schudson, 1986, pp. 161–162). With the successful use of overblown rhetoric and vague claims towards pseudo-scientific research, the promotion of patent medicine demonstrated the power of advertising to move products that offered little to no actual benefits. To critics of the industry, this practice was indicative of how advertising was little more than fanciful deception and manipulation: a continuation of the older practices of travelling peddlers who combined entertainment and trickery in order to hawk their wares (Lears, 1994, p. 65). The excesses and outright lies of patent medicine advertising were thus generative of a lack of trust or respect and contributed to the persistent public perception that advertising was 'barely an honest trade, let alone a profession' (Tungate, 2013, p. 30).

This reputation for trickery and untrustworthiness did not sit well with the increasingly powerful and influential advertising agencies of the early nineteenth century. Not only were those who worked in the industry looking for greater personal prestige and social status but the notoriety of the profession also threatened to hinder agencies' abilities to secure contracts with national firms (Lears, 1994, p. 154). Consequently, in contrast to the chaotic and often outright deceptive practices of patent medicine advertising, some of the key players in the industry began to push for greater professionalism and solemnity in their practice in order to separate themselves from 'carnival barkers, snake-oil salesmen, and such celebrated promoters of ballyhoo and humbug as P.T. Barnum' (Marchand, 1985, p. 8). Part of this process involved taking control of the production of the advertisements themselves, which led to the emergence of 'full service' agencies that would provide art and copy for advertising as well as buying and selling media space. By taking control over the content of their advertising, the industry could ensure that it was not 'implicated in the sins of its clients' (Lears, 1994, p. 201). In this new style of advertising, realism and rationality would dominate: prose would be simple, claims would be accurate and imagery would be tasteful and relevant.

The search for respectability

The N.W. Ayer and Son agency was illustrative of this new approach, where agencies would provide strictly factual copy for national corporations (Lears, 1994, p. 94), but they were far from alone in such an endeavour. The turn of the twentieth century was the era of figures like John E. Powers, who advocated 'plain speech' and declared that 'fine writing is offensive' (Tungate, 2013, p. 11), or John E. Kennedy, who pioneered the highly influential concept of 'reason why' advertising (O'Reilly and Tennant, 2009, p. xviii). Such commitments spawned phenomena such as the industry-sponsored 'truth-in-advertising' movement that ostensibly sought to police standards and stamp out misinformation (and which also served as a way for the larger Anglo-Saxon agencies to stamp out minor players and other 'undesirables') (Lears, 1994, p. 204). At the heart of such approaches was a dedication to 'factual advertising' that eschewed the glitz and fanciful images of an earlier era in favour of realistic claims and calm, rational communication in order to inform the public as to the consumer choices available to them. The other key part of this shift was a transition from understanding advertising as a form of art to understanding it as a form of science through the greater integration of statistical and psychological approaches. N.W. Ayer and Sons again led the way in this regard with systematic research into demographics and brand preferences (Lears, 1994, p. 211). The development of advertising trade journals provided an outlet for the developing discipline of market research, which sought to apply the latest scientific breakthroughs to the study of consumer behaviour (Leiss et al., 2005, p. 136). Through the marriage of reputable business and sober science, advertising thus sought to exorcise the ghost of patent medicine and redefine itself as a legitimate profession that contributed to society in a rational, progressive manner.

The positive effects of this self-redemptive campaign were readily apparent by the 1920s, by which time advertising had established itself at the forefront of the new modern era, particularly in the American context. Contributions to the American 'Committee on Public Information' during World War One had demonstrated advertising's ability to play an active and positive role in public life (Marchand, 1985, p. 8), while its promotional role was increasingly understood as a means of 'educating the people in the uses of prosperity' (Lears, 1994, p. 225). Only two decades on from the ignominious days of patent medicine conmen, advertisers had established themselves as a responsible and indispensable part of the new corporate elite: 'the American advertising man of the 1920s was the most modern of men' (Marchand, 1985, p. 1). No longer the work of conmen and scoundrels, advertising was instead increasingly hailed as a 'moral and educative force', and advertisers were the model of 'business statesmanship' (Marchand, 1985, p. 8). The possible high point of this praise was President Calvin Coolidge's 1926 address to the newly formed American Association of Advertising Agencies, in which he celebrated their contributions to the 'ennoblement' of the commercial world (Marchand, 1985, pp. 8–9). This association with the new sense of progressive modernity was only strengthened by advertising's close ties with the new medium of radio: despite initial concerns about both the possible negative consequences of commercial sponsorship as a funding mechanism and the intrusion of advertising into the private home, advertising soon become a central part of the structure of the American radio industry (Merskin, 2003, pp. 767–768). Nor was this modernity restricted to America: in the aftermath of the war, American modernity and consumer culture were exported directly to the industrialised states of Western Europe (Sasson, 2006, p. 937; Tomka, 2013, p. 251): with it came the techniques and organisations of American advertising. As with many aspects of popular and mass culture, the entry of American models into Europe following World War One, and later World War Two, would prove highly influential for the rest of the twentieth century and beyond.

By the end of the 1920s, the role of agencies, connections to media and business practices that define the modern advertising industry were established (Pope, 1983, pp. 253–256). The idea of a sober, respectable and professional industry dedicated to a scientific and rational process that coalesced during this period would constitute the dominant model of advertising up until the late 1950s. This does not mean, however, that the practice and forms of advertising were absolutely static in this period. For example, although there remained a commitment to advertising as a form of rational communication, the increasing integration of consumer research meant that there was an increasing focus on 'appeals' and the use of symbols that could evoke emotional responses: the turn to research also led to a focus on market segmentation and the identification of particular consumer groups (Leiss et al., 2005, pp. 150–152). Nonetheless, despite these shifts in focus the outward form of advertisements remained largely static: especially with regards to print advertising. Sut Jhally refers to this period as the 'iconology' phase of advertising, where advertisements focused on the way in which products could intercede in the world in order to grant consumers status, health and authority (1990, pp. 201–202). During this time, the formal arrangement of advertising also became increasingly formulaic, with the combination of illustrative images, usually of people engaging with the product, and explanatory prose at the bottom or sides of the image. While shifting production technology led to an increasing integration of photography over illustration from the 1930s onwards, and colour became increasingly standard in the 1940s, this overall formula shifted little. Consequently, compared to the advertising of today, the advertisements produced in the first half of the twentieth century seem remarkably consistent and standardised: the product of a stable, self-satisfied and ostensibly 'scientific' industry that was yet to undergo the dramatic changes and challenges of the late 1950s.

The third moment: Manipulation, creativity and globalisation

Amidst the booming consumer culture of the late 1950s, advertising's nineteenth-century reputation for chicanery and roguishness must have seemed a world away. In its place, the industry was now widely perceived as 'monotonous, repetitive and dull': the natural home of the conformist and sycophantic 'organisation man' of the period (Frank, 1997, pp. 35–36). Advertising had acquired the sort of reputation that we would these days often associate with accounting: a safe, lucrative and reputable, but ultimately profoundly boring, profession that involved the careful execution of unchanging formulas. The soul-crushing dullness of the mid-century advertising world reached its apogee in Sloan Wilson's 1955 novel, *The Man in the Grey Flannel Suit* (and its 1956 film adaptation), which detailed the inauthenticity and conformity of the public relations industry in particular and corporate America more generally. However, this conception of advertising as a buttoned-down bureaucratic practice would be dramatically challenged by the end of the decade in ways that would transform the practice and profile of the industry.

The fear of advertising

The radical shifts that reverberated through the advertising industry in the middle of the last century can be summarised through two examples that represent incredibly different interventions into the practice of advertising: the first is Vance Packard's book-length exposé *The Hidden Persuaders*, and the second is Doyle Dane Bernbach's 'Think Small' advertisement for Volkswagen. While in their way both texts reflect exhaustion with the scientific model that had dominated advertising since the 1910s, they present very different responses to that situation. On the one hand, Packard's book speaks to an increasing public fear regarding the power of scientific advertising that gave rise to new counter-culture critiques of consumer culture, and which would manifest in their most paranoid form in ideas of subliminal advertising. On the other hand, the 'Think Small' campaign would offer a vision of a new self-styled 'creative' advertising that would dispense with the formulas of the past decades in search of new, more authentic forms. Both would prove definitive for the next stage of advertising's development.

Vance Packard's *The Hidden Persuaders*, originally published in 1957, has been called one of the most influential critiques of advertising ever published (Leiss et al., 2005, p. 9; Miller, 2007, p. 10). Mark Crispin Miller credits it with the complete reorientation of the public's concept of advertising from a stodgy annoyance to a frighteningly powerful machine for the wholescale manipulation of the public (2007, pp. 10–12). In the book, Packard denounces advertising as the application of cutting-edge social science in the service of corporations. At the heart of Packard's criticisms of advertising was the notion of 'motivation research': practices that involved using the latest developments in psychoanalytic research and social anthropology in order to develop a better sense of the fears, values, doubts and desires of the consuming public (2007, p. 47). Armed with such knowledge, advertisers could appeal to the subconscious and irrational drives of consumers and thereby lead them to purchase goods for which they had no rational need or desire; Packard refers to this system as 'depth manipulation' (2007, p. 170). Although such techniques may not seem particularly controversial or shocking today – Packard's chapter on 'Marketing Eight Hidden Needs', including emotional security and a sense of power, might not be out of place in a modern marketing textbook – at the time, they outraged and horrified the public and stirred substantial debate (Miller argues that our jaded response to such claims should be read as an indication of how much we've internalised the consumer framework that Packard denounces [2007, p. 25]). In such a manner, *The Hidden Persuaders* helped provide form and substance for previously nebulous concerns about the power of corporate communication in an increasingly media-saturated society.

Thus, while Packard didn't simply create popular scepticism and fear towards advertising out of thin air, his work would act as a rallying point for subsequent denunciations of advertising as a form of undemocratic manipulation. Perhaps the most influential and controversial critique of advertising to emerge in the period was the idea of subliminal advertising. Packard had suggested that advertisers were embracing psychological research in order to steer consumer behaviour, but the idea of subliminal advertising took this even further (Leiss et al., 2005, p. 7). Developed most fully in the work of Wilson Bryan Key (1973), the subliminal theory suggested that images or words secretly implanted in advertising, below the level of conscious perception, could exert powerful control over audience behaviour. Methods for inserting such subliminal messaging include subtle photo manipulation, quick-fire editing and audio back-masking. As with Packard's revelations regarding 'motivation research' in *Hidden Persuaders*, the notion of subliminal advertising struck a strong chord with the public regarding the general unease about the growing presence and power of advertising, albeit but with one important difference: unlike 'motivation research', subliminal advertising had no real basis in fact (Leiss et al., 2005, p. 7). No one has ever found any evidence to support subliminal advertising. Nonetheless, the widespread embrace of the notion and its persistent prominence in discussions of advertising and media power speak to the growing popular scepticism of advertising from the 1950s onwards and the identification of advertising with the dark side of the new consumer society.

'Think Small' and the creative revolution

In contrast, the other prominent example we'll be looking at speaks to a very different, but equally significant, transformation in advertising: the rise of the 'Creative Revolution'. Launched in 1959, the 'Think Small' campaign did more than just provide a much-needed rebranding for Volkswagen – regarded, at the time, as Nazi cars – it also signalled a reinvention of advertising and advertisements (Cracknell, 2011, p. 84). Eschewing the formal, quasi-scientific rules developed over the previous five decades, the 'Think Small' campaign emphasised simplicity and authenticity with a wry sense of humour. While it may be difficult to appreciate now from the vantage of half a century on, this was a radical campaign at the time. From its self-effacing copy to its minimalist, black-and-white design, and even its san-serif font and use of a full stop with its slogan, this campaign defied contemporary advertising conventions and did so in a manner that seemed to pull away the curtain from the systems and rules that had come to define advertising, revealing them as contrived and ineffectual. It is difficult to overstate the importance of these advertisements, which are among the most widely reproduced and most celebrated ever: the VW campaign is 'one of the most analysed, discussed, and admired campaigns in the industry's history, studied in introductory marketing classes and included in advertising retrospectives of all kinds' (Frank, 1997, p. 60). In its own way, 'Think Small' is the Mona Lisa of advertising.

The impact of 'Think Small' goes far beyond the critical and commercial success of the campaign itself, however. The campaign was not simply a groundbreaking series of advertisements: it 'epitomise[d] the Creative Revolution, and that revolution changed the face of advertising' (Cracknell, 2011, p. 100). The Creative Revolution is the name given to a period of rapid transformation in the advertising industry that emerged largely in New York in the late 1950s and 1960s, in which the quasi-scientific truths that had previously dominated the industry were dispensed with in favour of a new focus on artistry and individuality. In the wake of the 'Think Small' campaign, advertising was seemingly reborn as art directors and copywriters were elevated in stature, research was dispensed with, transgression was encouraged and rules were suddenly made to be broken. No longer would advertisements be produced by committee and the application of set formulae: they would instead emerge from the eccentric genius of unshackled creative individuals: people like Bill Bernbach of Doyle, Dane and Bernbach (DDB).

If 'Think Small' is the emblematic advertisement of the Creative Revolution, then Bernbach is the emblematic individual for this new ways of doing things: the man who 'invented the creative revolution' (Fox, 1997, p. 240). A founder of DDB, Bernbach is the figure most often identified with the Creative Revolution's straight-talking and anti-conventional approach to advertising, and with the concomitant reorganisation of agency structures along anti-hierarchical lines (Frank, 1997, pp. 56–60). Most importantly, Bernbach's restructuring meant that no longer would art directors and copywriters work in isolation: encouraged to collaborate they would increasingly come to challenge the power of not only research and accounts departments but also clients (Pray, 2009). Following the success of DDB, it seemed as if a whole new world had opened up, and DDB was quickly joined by a number of other creative agencies, such as Papert, Koenig and Lois and Young, and new creative celebrities, such as David Ogilvy, Jerry Della Femina, George Lois, Phyllis Robinson and Mary Wells.

The diversity of this group, which includes women and working-class creatives, is indicative of the new voices the Creative Revolution brought to the industry. The established agencies had traditionally enforced a largely unspoken, but widely known, hiring policy that excluded 'ethnic' groups, such as those of Italian, Greek and Jewish descent, in favour of 'Anglo-Saxons' (Femina, 2010, p. 4). However, Bernbach's triumph was indicative of a new generation of Jewish copywriters, who would work alongside a new generation of Italian and Greek art directors, like George Lois (Cracknell, 2011, p. 80). As historical prejudices began to break down, the advertising industry would increasingly welcome those who had historically been considered outsiders and encourage them to express their personalities (Fox, 1997, p. 218). The Creative Revolution was therefore much more than a celebration of the creative contributions of a few geniuses: it was also a larger shift in the way advertising was created and perceived (Leiss et al., 2005, p. 317). Advertising was no longer respectable; advertising was exciting, rebellious and fun: all the better to sell products to new generations of counter-cultural and sceptical consumers who had internalised the warnings of *The Hidden Persuaders*.

Thus, just as the commitment to staid rationality shaped advertising in the first half of the century, the new style and new way of thinking about advertising borne of the Creative Revolution – in conjunction with increased public scepticism and concern – would dominate the second half. Even as research departments regained some of the prestige they had lost in the Creative Revolution at the end of the 1960s (Frank, 1997, pp. 225–226), the displacement of power towards creative departments and away from research would continue to guide the wider profile of the advertising industry. Thus, as we will see when we examine the organisational structures of agencies in Chapter 7, the relevance of research continues to be questioned in contemporary agencies, while (as we'll see) creative departments are almost always defined by a sense of self-importance. Moreover, even though the Creative Revolution had begun primarily in print, its emphasis on visuals over words would prove well-suited to the increasingly dominant medium of television. The rise of television created the conditions for ever greater emphasis on affective appeals and aesthetic play that emerged in the Creative Revolution, which can be seen in the emphasis on 'emotional selling points' that shaped advertising in the 1980s (McFall, 2004, p. 178), and the hip, cynical appeals to 'generation X' in the 1990s (Leiss et al., 2005, pp. 481–484). However, the obsolescence of the quasi-rational style that once dominated advertising is probably best demonstrated by low status and mockery heaped upon its vestigial remains in the age of television: the almost universal ridicule of infomercials is indicative of the transformative power of the Creative Revolution and the subliminal scare.

The fourth moment: Digital advertising, algorithms and dataveillance

While the industry continued to worship at the altar of creativity, at the dawn of the twenty-first century the feisty underdogs of the Creative Revolution had grown into the globalised behemoths of the corporate world. As we will examine in more detail in Chapter 7, where we discuss the role and organisation of agencies, the 1980s and 1990s saw a string of complicated corporate manoeuvres that lead to both the 'unbundling' within agencies, whereby different divisions were spun off into separate businesses, and a series of mergers between agencies to form new global 'mega-agencies' (Sinclair, 2012, p. 42). However, these shifts, while allowing for the advent of truly global ad campaigns, did little to change either the form or social function of advertising: instead, the transformations of this moment would be driven by the shifting technology of the wider mediascape. As the dominance of television had helped cement the shifts of the Creative Revolution, the increasing importance of digital and online technology would lead to the emergence of new advertising paradigms in the 2000s. The fourth, final and current moment of our history is one defined by the rise of these new forms of advertising.

The first online advertising

Once upon a time, online advertising was addressed in the last chapter of advertising books: presented in terms of 'new media', it served as a gesture towards the future of the field. Every year, however, this approach becomes less tenable, as what was once referred to as 'new media' becomes increasingly everyday, ordinary and even old and outdated. It has been over a decade since Google became the default search engine of the English-speaking world in the early 2000s, and ad-based social media and streaming services such as Facebook and Spotify have since become commonplace. The first digital advertising actually appeared in the 1990s, when early webpages replicated existing advertising models and were subject to immense clutter in the form of banner ads and pop-up advertising. Terry Flew has argued that 'misplaced confidence in the income-earning potential of banner advertising was one of a number of critical factors that saw many internet start-ups fail when the market flow of technology stocks collapsed in the so-called dotcom bust of 2000-01' (quoted in McStay, 2009, p. 147). Such early digital advertising attempted to replicate the strategies of outdoor and print advertising in online spaces but manifestly failed to secure an income stream necessary to fund the infrastructure of the growing web. The problems of these first websites demonstrated the potential difficulty of integrating old advertising methods into the new platforms. Users were resistant to the apparent invasion of this new territory by advertising, and therefore, in the wake of this collapse, digital advertisers sought out new methods – some of which were more subtle and integrated into the structure of the web, and others which were the exact opposite.

Algorithmic advertising

You may have heard the assertion that the internet is a space of ultimate freedom in our society where neither governments nor corporations can control the flow of information and individuals can do, say and be what they want in a manner free of interference: such 'cyber-utopianism' was common in the early days of digital media. However, what such an attitude overlooks is that the internet is defined, in many important ways, by the persistence of older models of corporate sponsorship, especially advertising. Though we are not accustomed to thinking of it in this fashion, much of the content on the internet is effectively advertising in itself, with a great deal of websites acting as combinations of virtual billboards and storefronts. The remainder of the content that is not directly involved with promoting goods is 'free' in the same way that broadcast television and radio are free: content is provided to audiences in exchange for their exposure to messages about different products. Content providers and producers receive monetary compensation for their work to the extent that they are able to sell space and audiences to those who wish to sell products. Hence, while the particular ways in which those advertising messages are presented may have changed, the basic economic logic has remained remarkably consistent even as new techniques alter the way advertisers, content providers and consumers understand and approach advertising.

Therefore, as the online economy rebuilt following the dotcom bust, advertising became a key aspect of attempts to monetise the web and provide income streams for online endeavours. Probably the most successful advertising development in this new context was also the most radical, as Google managed to integrate advertising into the basic navigational tools of the web: search functionality. While we might not be accustomed to thinking of internet search engines as a form of advertising, Christina Spurgeon argues that they are the 'single most important development for informational advertising since the time of the first paid newspaper advertisement' (2008, p. 25). Google's search advertising works through their AdWords service, whereby advertisers bid in real-time auctions in order to have their information displayed alongside particular search terms. The more in-demand the search term, the more an advertiser pays to have their product information and web address displayed alongside the search result: thus 'mortgage' will cost more than 'lemur'. While the main results themselves cannot be directly bought, companies pay for ads above and besides search results based upon the terms searched for. Such keyword auctioning is the largest segment of online advertising and in large part finances the growth and management of search engines. Forbes estimates that in 2015, 67 per cent of Google's multi-billion dollar income was obtained through search advertising (Trefis Team, 2015).

Social media and viral advertising

The other major shift ushered in through online spaces is the ever-increasing integration of advertising content into the flows and spaces of everyday life via social media platforms. Whereas traditionally advertisements have been packaged with media content distributed by centralised producers, such as TV shows and magazines, online advertising frequently seeks to break down that connection between advertising and content. This overwhelmingly takes place in terms of 'social media': online platforms, such as Facebook, Twitter, Instagram and Yelp, whose content is generated through user interaction, production and communication. In the context of social media, advertising doesn't adhere to particular media content, but instead is either inserted into the flow of user interaction by paying corporate advertisers or is shared by users among themselves. In the first instance, given that advertising is tied to the digital 'space', rather than any particular content, it works in a way more similar to outdoor advertising than broadcast advertising: it is incorporated into everyday spaces with the intention that users will notice it in the background as they go about other tasks. Unlike advertising on broadcast platforms, such as television, audiences cannot simply switch to another channel to avoid advertising, because users are usually tied to specific platforms in order to carry out particular tasks, such as writing and reading blogs, discussing issues on forums or sending emails (Fuchs, 2011, p. 143). However, unlike outdoor advertising, such social media advertising is not simply additional to the environment but is an integral part of funding and maintaining the platform. Such advertising also differs from outdoor versions because it shifts depending upon the user: different users will encounter different advertisements (and even different versions of the same advertisements) when accessing the same platform. This personalisation is achieved through the use of 'cookies' and online data-gathering, usually through the social media platforms themselves, and we will consider the implication of such practices in more detail in Chapter 6.

The other main way in which social media users encounter advertising is through the sharing practices of other users. Often discussed in terms of 'virality', online advertisers seek to create content that users will decide to share with others by their own volition: when an advertisement goes 'viral', it means that it has reached a stage where it is being widely shared by consumers, usually through social media networks, without the company having to pay for distribution. There are multiple benefits to viral advertising for a company: not only do they save on distribution costs but advertising encountered in this way is often thought to be more 'credible' because it comes from peers rather than corporations (McStay, 2009, pp. 57–58). Moreover, by intruding into the online conversations and exchanges that make up life in our current digital world, advertising has the potential to become an integral part of everyday practices, rather than an interruption. While this promotional technique opens up the possibility that advertisers will lose some control over the context and meaning of their messages (an issue we will examine more in Chapter 9), the potential benefits would seem from the corporate view to outweigh the risks. As a consequence, 'virality' currently functions as something of a holy grail in advertising, with marketers trying to work through existing networks either by identifying the formal and content features that characterise widely shared content or recruiting well-connected individuals to help subtly endorse their products. To aid this end, most corporations have now opened multiple social media accounts in order to interact with their customers as if they were peers. No longer do corporations simply purchase media space from other corporations in order to advertise their goods and services: in the age of digital advertising and social media, they attempt to tap into social media networks and encourage consumers to do their advertising for them.

The changing nature of advertising

As discussed at the beginning of this chapter, advocates of these new forms of digital advertising often argue that they constitute a clean break from the past, but as I've also suggested we should be careful when dealing with claims of a clean break. Discussing the rise of virality, Andrew McStay argues that whereas prior models of advertising were based on interruption and repetition, digital advertising will increasingly be based on permission and engagement (2009, pp. 1–3). A large part of this shift can also be seen in the collapsing distinction between advertising and entertainment with the production of advertising that consumers actively want to watch and share. Key examples of this new form of 'branded entertainment' include 'The Hire' (2001–2), a series of short films starring Clive Owen, directed by a series of famous directors, including Ang Lee, John Woo and Guy Ritchie and produced by BMW (Spurgeon, 2008, pp. 40–41), and Burger King's Subservient Chicken campaign from 2004 (McStay, 2009, p. 189). However, we should be careful of overstating the extent of this break. Pre-digital advertising was not simply about repetition and interruption: such a reductive account does a huge disservice to the creators of 'Think Small' and its ancestors. While such advertising did certainly interrupt other media texts, much of it was made to grab and sustain attention in order to better sell the product and to encourage further discussion in that pre-online forum known as the offline world. Consequently, the concept of ads as entertainment, or the idea that advertisers want to encourage people to discuss advertising, well preceded the rise of digital advertising, and advertising as entertainment is nothing new in this regard.

When compared to social media advertising, which often takes the basic form of TV commercials, the disruptive role of search advertising certainly appears to be a clearer break with the past. In particular, Christina Spurgeon argues that search advertising marks a shift away from 'creative' techniques and back towards informational modes of advertising (2008, pp. 25–26). Certainly, the successful execution of search advertising is less about captivating visuals or persuasive rhetoric, and more about the construction and implementation of the computational algorithms that underlie these processes. However, again, it pays to consider claims for a radical break in their historical context. As Liz McFall has argued with respect to historical informational advertising (2004, pp. 185–187), there is a need to be wary of drawing too sharp a distinction between informational and persuasive advertising. Often ads that present themselves in terms of information are simply composed of more subtle, but nonetheless deeply rhetorical, elements. This can certainly apply in the case of search advertising, which uses a form of short-hand advertising similar to that historically used in newspaper classified advertising: it is certainly not restricted to rational claims about products, but instead makes use of the communicative resources available in order to tell micro-stories about products. While they may be presented in an apparently neutral manner, even search results take place in a cultural context that provides particular interpretive cues. Thus, while certainly there is a need to acknowledge that the skills required to produce such forms of advertising are radically different from those used in other media, this does not mean that the social and cultural work performed by such advertising is significantly different to earlier forms.

In this chapter we've run through a quick account of some of the key moments in advertising over the past two centuries. While such a brief account is always necessarily incomplete, hopefully you now have a better sense of the changing social role and media forms that advertising has taken. Such a background will provide you with the knowledge you need to better assess claims about the nature of advertising and to understand how its current form has developed as the result of a specific history of events. From its origins in the industrial consumer society of the nineteenth century to the algorithm-generated content of the twenty-first, advertising has experienced a series of upheavals, but has also remained orientated around some key debates regarding the respectability and trustworthiness of the profession, its relative indebtedness to corporate or creative demands and the question of whether advertising is at its core an art, science or con. We have seen how advertising passed from a barely regulated con game to a highly professionalised system of rules to a creative calling and how these different conceptions changed the advertisements produced, but also how these changes were always motivated by and grew out from prior historical forces and tensions. As we explore different aspects of advertising in the rest of this book, keep these transformations and consistencies in mind as a way to understand the importance of concepts like capitalism, fetishism, creativity and agency for making sense of advertising and where and how these ideas emerge, dominate and subside in its different manifestations. By understanding the history of advertising, you will be better positioned to make sense of the way it works in the present.

CHAPTER 3

Analysing advertisements: Form, semiotics and ideology

Advertisements are complex things: there are many ways to make sense of them and to understand how they communicate particular meanings and ideas about the world we live in. Consequently, while the idea of 'analysing advertisements' might make you think that there exists some sort of secret code – which when applied reveals the hidden and true meanings of advertisements – in practice the interpretation and analysis of advertisements is much more complicated, sophisticated and ultimately rewarding than the straightforward application of a predetermined code. This means that there is never one simple answer to the question 'what does an ad mean?' although there will certainly be more important and relevant answers depending on the particular context in which the advertisement appears and the conceptual model being used. In this chapter we will consider several interrelated interpretative strategies for making sense of advertisements, including semiotics and ideology critique, as well as addressing the role of different media and the codes and conventions of advertising. This isn't intended to be the final word in analysing advertisements, which, after all, is one of the main purposes of the textbook as a whole; rather this chapter will provide you with some of the basic tools that we will develop over the rest of the book. I hope you will return to this chapter as you progress through the book as a basis for your analyses of advertisements and hone your analytic and critical skills in light of the different discussions and concepts we will be addressing.

One of the main reasons that there is no one single way of analysing advertising is because advertising is not a single thing. Unlike other media, advertising is not defined by a particular set of technological or formal features, but rather by a common purpose: to sell products. As a result, unlike television, film, popular music or video games, advertising is not restricted to a single medium. Indeed, it can take the form of all those media and many more. There are entire TV shows that have been seen as ads for products, like the 1980s *Transformers*, *G.I. Joe* and *My Little Pony* cartoons, and popular songs, such as Paul Anka's 1975 'Times of Your Life' (for Kodak) and The Carpenters' 1970 'We've Only Just Begun' (for Crocker National Bank) that began their life as advertising jingles. Some companies have even produced video games as advertising promotions: for example, the Weetos 'Moustache fight' and Chewits Carnival in the UK, or games for cable TV channels National Geographic and History Channel in the USA (unfortunately, such games can be very short-lived, and so probably aren't still active by the time you read this book!). Consequently and unfortunately, no single chapter could ever account for all the different aspects of advertising that you might have to take into account to produce a useful analysis of any given example. Instead, the focus here is on introducing you to some of the broadest analytic tools we have available – semiotics and ideological analysis – while also priming you to always try to account for the specificity of different advertising media. If you are a student of media or cultural studies, this will mean that the study of advertising will give you the chance to apply analytic skills and strategies you will have learnt in other courses; if you are coming from a discipline such as marketing or public relations, you might want to think about how your experience in designing ads and campaigns could also be used to 'reverse engineer' them; and if you are from another discipline, don't worry; the purpose of this chapter is to make sure you have the basic toolset you'll need to begin to deconstruct and make sense of advertisements.

Advertising contexts, codes and conventions

Given the many different forms advertising can take, one of the first things we always have to consider is the particular context of a given advertisement and how that might affect its construction and operation. Aspects such as the cultural context, the particular medium in question and the surrounding media content can have a strong bearing on what meanings are produced, presented and prioritised in a given advertisement. On the broadest level, for example, we might consider the national and cultural contexts of an ad which carry with them different systems of values and communicative norms. It is far beyond the scope and desire of this book to provide a snapshot of all the different cultural contexts of advertising you might encounter – which are, after all, almost always incredibly internally diverse and in a state of constant change – so it will have to suffice to say that in our globalised world, where we can access ads from all over the world through the internet, it is always best to be cautious when analysing texts from unfamiliar cultures and countries. Different contexts bring with them not only different histories of advertising and consumer culture but also different ideas regarding advertising staples, like humour, family life, relationships and eating and drinking, and different ideas about gender, race and sexuality. Simply because something confuses or offends you does not mean that is the only or indeed the predominant way in which audiences will interpret that advertisement. Therefore, try to make sure that you have at least some awareness of where an ad is coming from before you offer judgement!

The importance of medium

On slightly firmer ground, we also need to consider how the specific medium (or media) of an advertisement might shape it. For our purposes, the medium of an advertisement refers to the communication channel through which the ad is distributed. There are different codes and conventions that apply to different media depending upon the institutional and technological limitations and possibilities they present. In the current media environment, predominant advertising media include televisual, poster (i.e. outdoors) and the various forms of online and digital advertising: a category that includes several new and emergent forms of advertising, such as in-game advertising, 'advergames' and mobile advertising (and search advertising, which does not lend itself very well to formal analysis). At the same time, print and radio advertising are certainly still present, though decreasingly important in many markets due to the declining economics of mass publishing and traditional broadcast radio, and film advertising persists as a relatively minor form, usually screened prior to feature films. In the context of film, product placement and sponsorship would seem to be becoming increasingly normalised as accepted practice: they are slightly different from traditional advertising though, and thus, while they certainly can be understood in the context of many of the concepts discussed elsewhere in this book, they are also not particularly conducive to formal analysis in isolation. Advertising in these different media has different formal codes and conventions according to the limitations and possibilities afforded by the institutional and technological characteristics of the different media. As such, when analysing an ad, it is important to always bear in mind how these different formal features can influence our engagement with advertising. In order to see how similar messages manifest in different ways across media, we'll now work through some different examples from an integrated multimedia advertising campaign. An integrated campaign is one which uses several different media platforms in order to deliver a central advertising message. For example, Toyota's 2014 'Elevate' campaign for the Corolla includes television, digital, print and outdoor advertising, all addressing a central theme. Although ideally from the advertiser's point of view audiences will encounter multiple versions of the campaign as part of larger whole, it is also possible to consider each aspect individually and in turn.

Analysing static advertisements

We'll begin thinking about the medium specificity of advertising with the relatively simple example of a static advertisement, such as are found in both print and outdoor media, as well as with many digital ads. A static ad refers to an ad which is composed of a single unmoving image, which often includes some text (and less often a great deal of text). In most instances, the image will dominate a static advertisement and serve as the main site of meaning and communication in the ad. Text is often included in order to provide additional information about the product advertised, but can also function to emphasise the ad's commitment to clear and rational communication. Depending on the specific medium, different forms of static advertising may be emphasised. For example, billboard advertisements need to be relatively simple in order to catch the attention and be quickly understood by passing motorists and pedestrians. Consequently, billboard ads tend to employ clear images with immediately apparent meanings and short slogans. In contrast, print ads are potentially much more complex as they can be studied closely and can contain much more detailed information through text. Print ads also target a much more specific audience than billboards, premised upon the readership of the print source (i.e. newspapers, sports magazine, business magazines, tabloids, health magazines, etc.). They are therefore more likely to assume detailed knowledge or even include details that would be offensive or confusing to a general audience. A similar logic applies with static digital ads, which rely upon web browser-tracking technology in order to target ads not just to particular interest groups, but increasingly to particular individuals. Digital ads also have greater potential to integrate animation and even sound, but more frequently simply replicate the characteristics of print and outdoors advertising.

We can see these characteristics in the central static advertisement of Toyota's 'Elevate' campaign (examples of this image can be found online, on sites such as http://toyotanews.pressroom.toyota.com/releases/2014+toyota+corolla+integrated+marketing+campaign.htm). Even when the ad is separated from its original context, we can be fairly certain that this is a print ad (or print-equivalent digital ad from a context such as a tablet-magazine): not only does the shape of the ad match that of a page, but the image also incorporates several lines of small type in the lower left corner that would be difficult to read from a distance (although this ad would also fit well in a smaller outdoor context like a bus shelter or poster). The ad features an image of the car being advertised, a number of brightly dressed figures, a campaign logo at the top and additional information and brand logo at the bottom. We can separate this ad into three main visual sections that correspond to the vertical height of the image: this is a common technique in both the production and analysis of visual images known as the law of thirds, whereby a picture is vertically divided into three sections. The law of thirds is a long-standing convention in Western art history, to the point where it seems natural and obvious to our eyes to organise a picture in this way. In this instance, the central third is the most important. Not only does it feature the car, which occupies the centre of the overall image, but because of the bold, multicolour clothes of the various figures it is also the most colourful, which helps to draw the eye. This ad is also an example of a balanced composition, where the main subject occupies the centre of the frame and is surrounded by symmetrical imagery. This focus upon the car is further emphasised by the body position of the figures, who appear to be almost blown backwards by the car: if we follow the lines of their bodies, they lead us from the edge of the image to the car at the centre. In this way, we can see that everything points us towards the centre and establishes the car as the most important part of the image.

The colourful nature of the middle third is echoed in the top third by the multi-coloured confetti swirling above the scene, which is otherwise occupied by the rather banal campaign slogan: 'the all-new 2014 Corolla'. The dullness of the phrase itself is counterpoised, however, by the placement and typography of the words. In contrast to the middle section, the top section is asymmetrically weighted towards the left of the image, which unbalances the composition and thereby creates a sense of energy and motion. This sense of energy is emphasised by the slope of the letters, which follow a diagonal line that, again, disrupts the implicit horizontal lines that divide the image into thirds. Finally, we need to also consider the typography, which refers to the shape and style of the lettering. Most obviously, the slogan in presented in capitalised letters, which in other contexts might evoke yelling, but which in this context seems to suggest excitement and boldness. Without going into too much detail, we can also think about how the font itself might communicate meaning: with its clean lines and standard repeating shapes, this font seems very modern and no-nonsense (compared to, say, a gothic style or handwritten font). Taken all together, we can see how the presentation of the slogan helps to present the product as exciting, energetic and modern. Such an analysis demonstrates how in static ads we need to pay attention not just to the content of words in ads but also their presentation. It's not just what is written that is important but how it's written.

This is in contrast to the use of type in the bottom third of the image. In contrast to the colour above, the words here are presented against the grey of the road image: this would seem to be the last place the eye travels, and following conventional English reading patterns we move from left to right. In the bottom left corner, we find additional information that provides a website, more specific details and further promotional copy: 'designed with a style as unique as your own' (a somewhat ironic claim given the uniformity of the figures in the ad). Finally, in the bottom right corner we have the Toyota brand logo and company slogan, which helps confirm that this is, after all, a car ad. This last piece of information helps lock down the image in the context of corporate communication, here linked unmistakeably to the transnational Toyota Corporation. We can then take all these aspects together – the central image of the car and the celebrating crowd, the slogan, the supporting text and the company logo – to get a sense of how this ad works through the medium of a static image. While this process of moving slowly through each aspect of the ad might seem a slow way to unpack its meanings, we've only really begun to scratch the surface of this relatively simple ad: we haven't even begun to consider the background, the composition of the crowd, the way in which the scene is cropped or the colours manipulated, all of which are important to the construction of meaning in this format. Given the apparent simplicity of static advertisements, it's therefore important to always bear in mind that pretty much nothing in an advertising image is accidental: every aspect will have been scrutinised by a team of people, and therefore we need to be particularly careful when offering an analysis. While not every aspect is equally important, every aspect of the ad is almost definitely there for a reason.

Analysing video advertisements

The process of medium-based analysis becomes arguably even more complicated when we move from a static to a moving image, like television commercials or online videos. In addition to the aspects noted above, when considering advertising video we have to take into account the ability of moving images to display a narrative or progression over time as well as the incorporation of sound. However, our task is simplified by the fact that, in practice, these video-specific characteristics tend to take precedence over composition, copy and typography. This can be seen in the centrepiece of the 'Elevate' campaign: a 60-second television commercial called 'Style never goes out of style'. As moving images, television commercials have the ability to present short narratives and usually have greater budgets than other advertising genres. In fact, television advertisements usually have higher production costs per second than feature films and television programmes, making them potentially the most expensive visual media with the highest production values! (Logue Newth, 2013, p. 34). Part of the reason for this high budget is that television commercials usually also have to compete with not only a series of other advertisements as part of an ad break but also with actual television programmes. TV commercials are therefore part of what is often referred to as television's 'flow': a concept that seeks to capture how television acts less like a series of discrete texts and more like an endless blurring stream of images and narratives (Williams, 2004, pp. 91–92). Such a situation is not desirable for television advertisers, whose central goal is to stand out from the surrounding flow in order to make their product or service particularly memorable. As a result, when analysing a television commercial we should try to take these different factors particular to television into account: how does the ad take advantage (or not) of the potential for narrative and high-end audio and visuals in order to stand out from the surrounding flow, not to mention the potential for the audience to fast-forward ads using digital recording technology?

The televisual medium's emphasis upon narrative and high-impact audio and visuals is immediately evident in the case of Toyota's 'Style never goes out of style' commercial. The basic premise of the advertisement revolves around the passage of time through distinct stylistic eras dramatised through short musical segments: a 1960s black-and-white pastiche of *American Bandstand* with 'mod' dancers; a 1970s Disco *Soul Train* tribute; a 1980s break-dancing, skate-boarding extravaganza in a graffiti-filled garage; a 1990s dark grunge-inspired mosh pit; and an extended final sequence, where multi-cultural crowds of brightly dressed dancers pour out into city streets.

Each section represents a different decade of Corolla production and is scored with representative music from soul singer Edwin Starr, disco funk band Chic, Herbie Hancock during his hip-hop phase, grunge rockers Soundgarden and electronic dance musicians, Shy Kidx. Moreover, in addition to the inclusion of decade-appropriate models of Corolla cars, each section also features period-appropriate costumes and dancing, as well as formal features, such as black and white filming in the 1960s, special effects in the 1980s and quick-cutting in the 1990s. The overall effect is to create a sense of historical passage in terms of different fashions: an evocation of retro aesthetics that acts to emphasise both the historical consistency of the car and its development over time in the context of shifting regimes of style. The inescapable sense of progression inherent in the ad is testament to the ability of television ads to tell stories in time; an aspect that is essential to this particular ad's ability to communicate its message, as is television's integration of both visual and audio elements. We can therefore see how this ad illustrates key aspects of the television medium through its presentation of a narrative developing in time and the integration of a series of highly distinctive visual and audio spectacles.

Of course, this is only one example of the possibilities of narrative in television advertising, which can consist of small self-contained stories, short factual discussions or elements that would be deemed avant-garde or experimental in the context of a longer work. As much as 'Style never goes out of style' operates as a short variant on a musical or music video, advertising examples can also draw on styles inspired by fictional film or documentary. Similarly, while the visual and audio elements of this particular ad complement each other to reinforce a central message about popular cultural trends and the product advertised, advertisements can just as frequently feature character dialogue, unrelated musical soundtracks or, very frequently, narration. However, while there are certainly a number of ways in which they can manifest, these different options all arise out of the set of formal characteristics with which we have been analysing this Corolla ad, which points towards some of the primary concerns we should have when working in this medium: narrative progression, integration of sound and visuals, tendency towards spectacle. Nor is television the only advertising medium which shares these traits. For all the discussion of their newness as an advertising medium, digital videos share an almost identical set of formal characteristics, albeit with the potential for greater length and more obscure, offensive or outlandish content in the freedom of offline spaces. Hence, for all the potential difference in distribution channels, in terms of analysis digital videos are not that different from television videos: both take advantage of the formal characteristics of video in crowded and competitive media environments.

Analysing digital advertising

However, while digital videos often follow the formal precedents of television commercials, this is not true of all digital advertising, much of which takes up the new possibilities opened up by digital technologies. Digital advertising is not a coherent category like print or television advertising, because digital media is not one thing or clear category of things. Hence, rather than being defined by a clear sense of institutional or formal features, digital advertising refers to a very broad collection of different advertisements which exist in the new computational and online spaces opened up since the mid-1990s. As previously mentioned, many of these digital ads aren't particular new in a formal sense, and instead static display ads and online videos often simply replicate the format characteristics of earlier forms. One group of digital ads that is both increasingly important and departs from previous advertising forms involves the integration of advertising and video games. Moreover, while not all digital ads are necessary games, considering advertising games does allow us to focus on one of the key defining features of new forms of digital advertising: interactivity.

For our purposes, interactivity refers to the ability of an audience to interact with an ad in ways that transform the ad's appearance and subsequent engagement with the audience. Often this takes the form of a feedback loop, where audience interaction produces changes in the ad, which then encourage additional interaction. The incorporation of interactivity allows for new forms of advertising. For example, during the initial launch of the 'Elevate' campaign, advertising for Corolla was integrated into Electronic Arts' free-to-play app 'Tetris Blitz'. One of the many variants on the classic 1980s puzzle game Tetris, where players have to arrange different shaped blocks into lines, 'Tetris Blitz' is distinguished by its short two-minute playtime, use of 'power-ups' that help players achieve a higher score and incorporation of advertising. As a contemporary update of a classic game, 'Tetris Blitz' aligns with the more directly conveyed message of the television commercial regarding the changing nature of style; however, in order to appreciate the full message of this ad, we need to consider how it integrates digital interactivity.

In the context of the game, the Toyota Corolla does not appear simply as an image, but rather was incorporated into the game as a 'power-up'. When activated the Corolla power-up clears several lines of the playing field while also presenting a player with an image of the car, the text 'The all-new Corolla' and car engine sound effects (Hodapp, 2013; Orland, 2013). What we need to consider when analysing a digital ad like this is how it integrates into the wider digital context and what this interactivity means as regards the ad's message. It is difficult to draw any particular meaning from the specific nature of the Corolla power-up, which would seem to have little bearing on the messages of the wider 'Elevate' campaign. However, as noted in one report on the ad, the 'power-up' 'can be quite lucrative for your point total' (Orland, 2013).

Following the logic of the particular gaming environment, it becomes clear that the ad is here being aligned with a positive outcome which the player is already working towards, regardless of the ad. Therefore, we could suggest that the message here is that Toyota Corolla 'gets you where you want to go'. More broadly, Corolla is also here associated with a positive outcome and thus potentially appears as a desired aspect of the game and the target of desired interactions (at least, for those who do not dismiss the advertising content as intrusive). This meaning of the ad thus arises from its place within the internal logic of the game and is therefore indicative of how the meaning of digital advertising arises out of the logic of its particular context.

A more complicated example can be found with Toyota's 'Raise the Road' mobile game, which doesn't just integrate the brand into existing digital content, but builds a whole new interactive experience around the product. Unfortunately, like many advergames, 'Raise the Road' is no longer available for download, but nonetheless can still serve as another example of how we can analyse digital advertising. In 'Raise the Road' players steered a virtual Corolla down a basic track against a count-down clock. In order to successfully complete the track, players had to collect tokens to add more time to the clock. The tokens corresponded to different features of the Corolla, and collection of the tokens caused promotional material to appear on-screen explaining the benefits of those features. Thus, the game not only 'simulated' the Corolla driving experience, but also compelled players to seek out in-game promotional material about the car in order to successfully complete the game. Such a mechanism means that, although some skill is required to complete the game, more important to successful completion of the game's challenge is the willingness to submit oneself to additional advertising within the context of a game that is already in itself a form of advertising. In addition, players could also customise the colour of their car and unlock music that tied into the larger campaign. This example thus demonstrates how, in a digital context, it is the interactive logic itself that carries meaning as regards the product, and in order to understand how such an ad works, we need to consider it through the interactive gaming logics of challenge, reward and customisation. 'Raise the Road' takes almost all aspects of the gaming experience – player avatar, reward system, in-game assistance – and turns them into a vehicle for advertising messages in a manner that takes advantage of the distinctive aspects of digital media.

In this section, we have considered how we might begin to analyse advertisements in three different media forms, and the different formal aspects that distinguish them. This is by no means an exhaustive list, but should give you some sense of how to begin to think about and take into account the specific features of the different media and how they might be used for advertising purposes. Hence, while it's impossible to provide you with a checklist that can take into account all the different media forms that circulate in our contemporary media environment, and the different ways in which they can be used to sell products, you should hopefully now have some sense of how to begin to take context and medium specificity into account in your analyses. In order to advance this analysis further, we'll now turn our consideration to semiotics: an analytic method that complements medium specificity, by focusing on broad cultural processes by which meaning is produced and communicated across a range of cultural forms.

Semiotic analysis of advertising

Semiotics is the study of how meaning is produced and reproduced within a society. It is also one of the foundational methods of Media Studies by which we can approach and understand not just advertising but also all manner of media texts. Semiotics provides us with powerful conceptual tools for analysing advertisements as well as helping us gain some distance from our everyday practices of communication of meaning, so that we can look at them with new eyes and understand them in new ways. In his guide to the semiotic analysis of advertisements, Jonathan Bignell suggests that this process involves '"unnatural" tasks' (1997, p. 34), such as abstracting the ad from its environment, and then breaking it down into constituent parts (or signs), working out what they mean and how they're organised, and then trying to determine potential ambiguities or alternative readings. In this section, we'll run through a sample semiotic analysis while explaining key terms in order to give you a sense of how to proceed with these 'unnatural tasks'.

The central concept of semiotics is the 'sign'. The sign is the name we give to the most basic discrete unit of meaning. Anything that indicates or expresses meaning can be considered a sign: a word, a colour, a sound and a particular set of lines and shapes in a picture are all different types of signs. Think of signs like atoms, or Lego blocks; they are individual units of meaning from which larger assemblages of meaning are composed. We refer to these assemblages of signs as texts. From the perspective of semiotics, everything and anything means something (or at least has the potential to mean something) and we can refer to almost everything as a text – advertisements, but also films, TV shows, books, magazines, songs, video games, fashion, flower arrangements, fun fairs, etc. – in order to indicate that we are primarily interested in the different ways in which those objects communicate meanings and messages. Advertising texts are particularly conducive to semiotic analysis, because even before we begin our analysis, we usually have a good sense of their likely message: as the famous semiotician Roland Barthes suggests 'in advertising the signification of the image is undoubtedly intentional' (1978, p. 33). What Barthes means by this is that, unlike art or visual imagery more generally, the meaning or purpose of an advertisement is rarely in doubt: the goal is to sell a product. Therefore, we can begin with the assumption that the signs that make up an advertising text have been included in order to help sell the product and proceed from there.

The semiotic tradition

The origin of the semiotic approach to communication and culture is usually traced back to the work of the nineteenth-century Swiss linguist Ferdinand de Saussure (2007). De Saussure was working out new ways to understand the power and flexibility of language as a social construction through which meaning is organised. He argued that if we understood language as a structure then it becomes possible to account for both its flexibility (language can be used to communicate an almost infinite range of meanings) and consistency (the meaning of linguistic statements are surprisingly stable over time and space).

At the heart of de Saussure's model is the idea that a sign is composed of two parts, which in modern semiotic terms are referred to as the signifier and the signified. The signifier is the sensory, physical aspect of the sign. Common examples of signifiers are the sounds (or sound waves) we hear, or the lines, shapes and colours we see. The signified is the abstract, conceptual meaning of the sign. For example, this particular arrangement of lines on a page (i.e. letters) - CAT - has a certain furry, whiskered, mice-chasing meaning attached to it. Importantly, in the context of semiotics, the connection between any combination of signifier and signified is regarded as arbitrary: that is without any reason or logic behind why a given word means what it does. The connection between a given signifier and signified (such as a word and its meaning) is not true now and forever, but rather the result of long-standing historical, social and cultural conventions.

However, just because the meaning of a sign isn't true and correct now and forever, this doesn't mean that meaning is completely up-for-grabs or individually determined either. We can't just make up our own words for things: that's the recipe for social chaos and the end of communication. This is because meaning is produced and reproduced within a culture through the form of conventions. We are all experts in a number of culturally specific codes that operate in a way similar to languages, but encompass a near infinite range of sounds, smells, colours and pictures. We make use of these codes every day when we encounter and interpret the media.

De Saussure refers to these systems that regulate the consistency of language as *langue*, which is language conceived as a giant system of grammar and vocabulary: in effect, language reduced to a set of rules. Conversely, the flexibility of language arises out of *parole*, which literally translates as 'speaking' and refers to the way in which the grammar and vocabulary of language can be manipulated, combined and re-combined to give form to almost any statement or idea. This emphasis on underlying rules as the source of meaning is the reason why semiotics is often referred to as a 'Structuralist' method. Critics of Structuralist models, like semiotics, have argued that they underestimate the dynamism and complexity of meaning and overlook the power of audiences to reinterpret and recreate texts. Taking this into account, we should therefore be aware that our analysis is never final and total and is instead always located within a particular cultural, social and above all political context.

Denotative signs

Following Bignell, the first thing we need to do, then, when conducting a semiotic analysis is break down our chosen text into its constituent signs (1997, pp. 30–32). How we do this will depend upon the medium in question. With a static image, it is often possible to address every sign in the text, starting with the most prominent and working our way down. However, with digital or video ads, we will want to restrict our interest only to those emphasised in terms of the narrative and/or visual presentation: otherwise we would quickly be overwhelmed by signs at 24 frames a second and above. In order to illustrate how this analysis might proceed, we'll work through an example: an ad for Volkswagen that originally appeared in print and outdoor media in Australia in 2012 (see http://adsoftheworld.com/media/print/volkswagen_park_assist_technology_portaloohearse). This is a relatively simple ad, especially when we start narrowing our attention down to the key signs, so it is a good place to begin thinking about the basics of semiotic analysis. The first thing we might note is that in contrast to the Corolla ad considered above, the centre of the image is conspicuously empty. What we can see is a portable toilet, or portaloo, to the left of the image, and a hearse (recognisable as such by the coffin and flowers) to the right. If we wanted to go into more detail, we could break down the hearse into its constituent signs – car, coffin, flowers – but for our purposes we will treat them all together as a coherent sign (knowing what details to include and exclude is an important part of semiotic analysis, but something you'll have to learn through conducting and discussing your own analyses: there's always some debate as to which signs are most important to the overall text). Beyond the portaloo and hearse we also have the background, including a park (fence, field, trees), a tall building, some clouds and, importantly, a road with road markings (note how the road–footpath divide corresponds to the law of thirds!). For completeness sake, we should also note that below the image the ad also includes a line of text and the VW logo and slogan.

Now that we have our constituent signs, we have to think about what they mean. In semiotics we distinguish between two different kinds of meaning. The first is denotation or the denotative meaning of the sign. This is often understood to refer to the obvious or literal meaning of the sign and is opposed to connotation or the connotative meaning of the sign, which refers to the symbolic, seemingly secondary, more metaphorical meanings that accrue to a sign and which the reader will (sometimes unconsciously) recognise. Connotations are more lightly held and more obviously socially conditioned than denotative meanings and are therefore more often subject to explicit debate and discussion. For example, in this picture the denotative meaning is 'flower'.

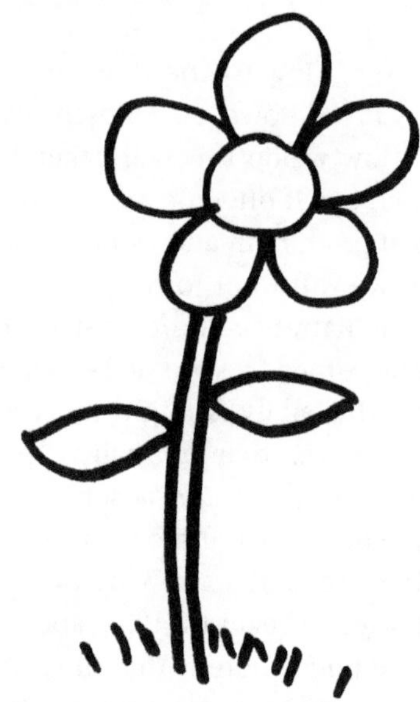

This is the literal and obvious meaning of the picture. Moreover, even though my picture doesn't really look anything like most actual flowers, we can nonetheless recognise that meaning almost automatically. In addition to this literal meaning, there are also a host of connotative meanings, such as romance, love or nature, which attach to flowers as cultural signs. Moreover, the simple nature of the drawing might be taken to connote childishness or childhood, which illustrates how meaning is not simply a matter of *what* is represented but also *how* it is represented.

Let's now consider the VW ad in those terms. As the main body of an image is a photo, the process of denotation is quite straightforward. In fact, in the case of photos, the bigger problem is remembering that it isn't an actual portaloo in the ad, but an image of a portaloo: or, in our case, a *sign* of a portaloo. The difference between a portaloo and the sign of a portaloo is that 'since the visual discourse [of television and photography] translates a three-dimensional world into two-dimensional planes, it cannot, of course, *be* the reference or concept it signifies. The dog in the film can bark but he cannot bite!' (Hall, 1996, p. 95). The same is true of our portaloo, which can signify but cannot stink. This distinction between signs and reality is clearer in terms of drawings or more abstract illustrations, which do not so accurately replicate the appearance of the real thing, but we need to always bear in mind that this is also true of photographic images, which, as Stuart Hall notes, are always two-dimensional replications of three-dimensional things. Given the preponderance of film, photography and photographic-quality digital effects in advertising, we often talk about ads as if they contained the things they signify, but for the purposes of analysis we need to keep those two different levels clear in our mind. This is especially important when we move on to considering the connotations of the signs.

Connotative meanings

As noted above, connotations are the symbolic, metaphorical meanings that are socially ascribed to signs. Thus, while on a denotative level the image of a portaloo simply signifies a portaloo, on a connotative level the sign gives rise to a whole host of additional meanings. For a start, we can consider the fact that the portaloo is a toilet: a social and cultural site that overflows (no pun intended) with all manner of meanings surrounding hygiene, disgust and privacy. Toilets signify the physical actions of defecation and urination, which are largely regarded as impolite, almost taboo, subjects in many aspects of Western culture. The sign of a toilet therefore carries a host of connotative meanings related to uncleanliness, pollution, and even shame. Even without showing the inside of the toilet or the actions associated with it, the image of a toilet can conjure up a number of such meanings, which are only emphasised by the toilet's status as a portaloo. Portaloos are historically associated with events and places that lack conventional toilet systems, such as music festivals or building sites, and therefore carry even more of a stigma than regular toilets. Regardless of our personal experiences with portaloos, such meanings circulate in film, television and other popular cultural texts that include portaloos. Importantly, then, these connotative meanings are never just individual, but instead operate on a cultural and social level. This means that, while the image of the portaloo might evoke particular memories and feelings for you, these don't really matter (sorry!) in terms of your analysis. Instead, we want to be trying to offer a more general, social account of how these signs speak to widely shared meanings. Semiotic connotations operate on a social rather than individual level.

Having considered the portaloo in some depth, we should now turn our attention to the other aspects of the advertisement. The second prominent sign I noted earlier is the hearse, which is an assemblage of other signs such as the car, coffin and flowers. As with the portaloo, the connotations attached to the hearse are quite socially distinct and powerful. As the portaloo is associated with defection and urination, the hearse is associated with death, which then conjures up a whole host of associated meaning. In the specific context of the hearse, we also have a sign for the funeral process as a whole and the associated rituals of mourning and bereavement. The hearse is therefore a powerful sign attached to connotations of mortality and grief. Not, at first glance, the sort of things one would want to evoke when selling a car. We therefore have the meanings of the two most prominent signs, but in order to make sense of this image it is clear that we will have to extend our analysis out further. As noted earlier, the other signs are the park scene and the road. The backdrop of the park plays a subtle but crucial role in the construction of meaning. The pleasant park landscape can be read to connote ideas of normality and everydayness, while the blue sky with white clouds connotes ideas of pleasant weather and perhaps even a generalised sense of 'happiness'. This scene of pleasant normality therefore goes some way towards counteracting the potentially upsetting meanings of the portaloo and coffin by situating them in a pointedly non-threatening environment. Think about how the different meanings could be evoked if the portaloo and the hearse were against the background of a strip mall or an abandoned building site.

The other key sign for pulling everything together is the road in the foreground or more specifically the road markings. These relatively simple t-shaped road markings are good examples of the power of signs. Even when encountered in reality, such lines do not really denote anything in particular: it is only at the level of connotation that they begin to have a purpose, as they refer indirectly to the size and shape of a car, and through social convention we know that they refer to a place where one can park a car. Taking this fairly discrete set of signs into account thus helps situate and explain the particular role the other signs are playing in the advertising text: we are not simply presented with a portaloo and a hearse; we are presented with a portaloo and a hearse on either side of a parking space. This adds another layer of meaning to the signs, which no longer just represent waste and death but also now represent obstacles, and in particular potential obstacles to anyone who would seek to park their car in the parking space presented. Taking the image as a whole, then, we have a representation of aspects of life often considered taboo, which transforms the parking space from a simple empty gap to an anxious and potentially horrifying experience if the hypothetical driver were to make a mistake while attempting to park in this space. This meaning is not carried by any of the signs on its own, but only arises when we take the signs together at the level of the text.

Anchorage and meaning

However, even with this level of meaning it is still not clear how this might convince us to buy a Volkswagen car. Taking just the image, we would seem to have a message about the anxieties of driving, rather than advocating for the pleasures in order to convince us to part with our cash (a much more common practice in car adverts). In order to resolve this final ambiguity, we now have to turn to what the semiotic theorist Roland Barthes refers to as 'anchorage': a term that refers to use of captions or slogans in order to lock down, or anchor, one possible meaning out of the many offered by the images (1978, 38–41). As we can see in this example, visual texts like photographs can usually be interpreted in a number of ways, and the purpose of anchorage is to emphasise one particular possible meaning above all others. In this instance the anchorage is the final signs of the text, which we've so far overlooked: the words and logo at the bottom of the ad. Words are signs just as much as pictures. Like pictures, words denote certain things: the letters h-e-a-r-s-e denote hearse as much as, if not more than, the picture we've discussed so far. In fact I've been relying on the semiotic capacity of words to make my argument: that, after all, is how writing works!

Returning to our particular example, the words at the bottom of this ad are 'park assist technology from Volkswagen'. Taken in conjunction with the meanings of the image discussed so far, these words offer us one of the final clues. The sentence suggests that the ad pertains to something called 'Park Assist Technology': at this stage, a small amount of prior knowledge is required in order to understand that when activated the technology in question will automatically park the car for the driver. Armed with his additional information, we can thus return to the image in order to offer a reading more in keeping with its status as an advertisement: the parking scenario on display is unappealing, but the product being advertised will help the driver successfully address the situation. Just in case we needed any further confirmation, we can also turn to the VW logo and slogan in the bottom right corner which anchors the initial assumption that this is indeed an advertisement: the presence of a brand operating to confirm the particular genre of this text. Having taken all the different signs into account, we can thus be fairly certain that we not only have correctly ascertained the meaning of the ad but also reverse engineered it in order to work out how exactly that meaning is being produced and communicated: buy a Volkswagen car because the in-built technology will help you overcome potentially horrific driving situations (and perhaps, implicitly, also help you deal with life's challenges more broadly!). The ad expresses and indeed emphasises the possible anxieties of the parallel parking process in order to highlight the solution offered by the product.

What we've seen through this process of analysis is how semiotics involves (metaphorically) breaking down the object of study into its various signs, considering what they mean by themselves and then how their interaction and relation gives rise to new, more complex meanings. In applying semiotics to advertising, the purpose isn't simply to work out what an advertisement means – I assume you're already good at that as a consumer-inhabitant of a rich, media-saturated country in the twenty-first century – but rather to think about *how* an advertisement means. Semiotics involves slowing down what we already do automatically in order to render it unfamiliar and thereby allow us to think more carefully about how advertisements construct meaning. The biggest mistake most students make when carrying out semiotic analysis is to jump straight to the final meaning, when the rewarding but difficult part of the process is determining the steps along the way. We've worked through the different steps of a semiotic analysis, and in doing so I've introduced a number of conceptual terms – sign, text, denotation, connotation, anchorage – which should help guide your analysis while also making you slow down and consider what each aspect means and how it applies to your object of analysis. We've really only scratched the service of semiotics though, and considered aspects which are directly relevant to the analysis of advertising. If you're interested in developing your analytic skills more there is a wealth of resources in print and online dedicated to more in-depth semiotics processes, concepts and analyses – some of which are listed at the end of this chapter – that you might to want to check out.

Mythology and ideology

An important and central aspect of semiotic analysis is that the meanings of a sign – both its denotation and connotation – are not natural. For example, there is no eternal and natural connection between the letters t-r-e-e and the form of plant life those letters bring to mind. This can be easily seen if we note that different languages have different words for 'tree', and it makes no sense to say that one language is more correct than another. This is an example of the arbitrary nature of denotation, which raises a number of thorny questions in Media and Cultural studies about how meaning is formed and communicated. However, for our purposes, we'll be focusing almost exclusively on connotative meanings, which have more immediate relations to wider social, economic and political questions. Think again about the portaloo, the hearse and their particular connotative meanings, such as shame, waste, taboo and death. A semiotic perspective suggests that these meanings are also arbitrary, in the sense that they are not natural, universal and eternal, but rather come to have particular connotative meanings as a result of historical, social and political forces: the meaning of a sign isn't simply given, it's produced, and often produced in such a way that reflects and reinforces particular arrangements of society and social power. Roland Barthes, who we already mentioned in relation to the concept of 'anchorage', refers to this aspect of signs as mythology (1972, pp. 109–117).

Mythology is a complicated idea, but at its heart it is concerned with the idea that signs are never natural and neutral, but rather always attain their connotations in relation to particular histories and culture. This definition of mythology is not the same as the probably more familiar definition of mythology as a fable that helps explain the world – such as the legend of Theseus and the Minotaur or the story of how Māui fished up the North Island of Aotearoa – but does share with those definitions the idea that stories can have real consequences for how we understand and engage with the world. Barthes was particularly interested in the ways in which these meanings reflect the social and cultural arrangement of power, and communicate unspoken understandings about the way the world works. We can see this in more detail if we return to portaloo and the hearse. In our initial analysis, it was suggested that the portaloo signified waste and shame, and the hearse signified death and grief. What was not discussed, though, was how or why they came to signify in that manner: in order to answer those questions we have to turn to mythology and consider how the meanings of the portaloo and hearse signs are part of larger social structures. What does it mean, then, that these signs carry those meanings?

Mythological analysis

One possible answer might be that both are tied to larger social and cultural issues of our understanding of ourselves as bodies. In their own way, both the portaloo and the hearse speak to our existence as embodied biological creatures who are made of flesh and bone. The portaloo is connected to our embodied existence because, as biological creatures, we need to eat and drink to stay alive: a process that leads inevitably to bodily waste. In Western society, we don't tend to be particularly comfortable discussing that waste. As a result we build large infrastructure systems including toilets, sewers and treatment plants to keep that waste out of sight and out of mind and develop complementary cultural structures that keep acknowledgement of waste at bay through a system of privacy and euphemism. The meaning of the portaloo is part of those larger systems: a toilet would not be an object of anxiety, as presented in the ad, if it were not part of that larger cultural, social and infrastructural system designed to hide the inescapable biological fact that we produce waste. The meaning of the hearse is related to an even more indisputable biological fact – death – that is even less acknowledged and more suppressed in Western society than waste. As with waste, our society often goes a long way to avoid talking about death, and we have physical and cultural systems in place that keep awareness and discussion of death out of everyday lives. Consequently, the reason that the hearse connotes anxiety and grief needs to be understood as part of a larger cultural fear of death. Both the portaloo and the hearse connote anxiety as part of a larger social aversion to the ramifications of the biological nature of our bodies.

To see both human waste and human death as they are presented in the Volkswagen ad, as sources of anxiety, is to see them in terms of a particular mythology that denies or at least minimises awareness of the biological embodiedness of human beings. The anxiety which the VW ad invokes, indeed which is central to its message, is thus part of a larger mythology about how we understand our existence as human beings, which parts of our lives we embrace and which parts we hide from and produce fear and worry. This is not to say that this was the purpose of the ad: to reinforce this particular mythology of human existence or somehow confront us with those biological aspects of our bodies we repress. The relevant mythology is incidental, rather than intentional, but is nonetheless incredibly important to the meaning of this ad. What's more, the ad's invocation of these meanings around bodies does more than just draw on those mythological structures in order to create meaning; in doing so, it also enacts and thus reproduces that mythology as part of a larger social-cultural process of communication. We can therefore see how the concept of mythology is particularly relevant to the analysis of advertising because it draws our attention to how meanings can be communicated in unconscious and indirect ways. In this way, mythology is quite similar to another important concept: ideology.

Ideological analysis

An ideology is a set of beliefs, values, ideas and feelings that shape how we understand, approach and engage with the world around us: it is the shared assumptions about what is correct, logical and desirable that inform not just our decisions but also the things we take for granted or do without thinking. Ideology is always at work: it informs every action and idea in a society, but is of particular relevance to the study of media. This is because media are one of the main ways in which ideologies are communicated and thereby reproduced. Every media text – from news broadcast to action film to advertising – can be interpreted in terms of ideology, which isn't just about what the text is trying to say in a direct and upfront way, but also about what the text is not saying: what are the things that are assumed, what is explained and what is not. Like mythology, ideology relates to how meanings, values and ideas can be communicated in indirect and unconscious ways. Every media text makes assumptions about what is correct, logical and desirable. This is inevitable – no one media text could represent everything. As a result of the partial nature of representation, media texts, such as advertising, will always imply a particular vision of the world. Certain things will seem more normal than others, certain things more acceptable and certain things more reasonable. In this way, the media come to inform our actions and choices, but not in a simple way where we simply mimic what we see on the TV. Rather, ideology suggests that the media form an important part of a larger social process, whereby constantly repeated ideas, values and beliefs come to seem normal and obvious. Ultimately, ideology is a much more subtle and powerful way of considering the influence of advertising than any simple model of direct media effects.

Writing in 1978, advertising scholar Judith Williamson asserted that 'advertisements are one of the most important cultural factors moulding and reflecting our life today' (1978, p. 11). Williamson's statement is indicative of an ideological understanding of advertising as a media form that shapes how we understand and engage with our world. While much has changed since the late 1970s, and several aspects of Williamson's analysis seem less than convincing today, her broader point regarding the ideology of advertising still seems broadly applicable. If anything, the expansion of branding practices and mediated spaces means that advertising is even more ever-present and constant than it was four decades ago, and therefore we will close out our introduction to analysing advertising by considering how we can analyse advertising in terms of ideology. We'll return to the concept of ideology in more detail in Chapter 4, so for now we'll just be focusing on how it can help complete our initial analytic toolkit. For our purposes, ideology differs from mythology because whereas mythology is concerned with the social and cultural basis of semiotic meaning, we'll be looking at ideology in terms of how an advertisement assumes and communicates particular ideas about the world. This distinction oversimplifies the complicated and often overlapping relation between the concepts of mythology and ideology, but will work for our purposes.

When we analyse an ad in terms of ideology, we are interested in unpacking how our chosen ad presents the world. We can consider this in many different ways, including what problems or obstacles are presented in the ad, what the ad presents as desirable or ideal or what culturally specific knowledge the ad relies upon. One of the key ideological sites at which ads operate, and which you might already be familiar with, is the construction of different aspects of personal identity such as gender and race. When considering an ad in these terms, we might think about the race and gender of the actors that have been cast in the ad, the representations of the appearances and bodies of the different characters and what sort of roles and functions are played by different characters: for example, if the ad takes place in a domestic setting, who is responsible for domestic chores? If the ad takes in a work setting, who is the boss? This sort of analysis has become relatively common in recent years to the extent that it often takes place outside the university and now can be found relatively frequently online. We need to be careful, though, when conducting this kind of analysis that we pay close attention to the specifics of the ad and don't try to force it into an outdated paradigm. Remember that advertisers aren't idiots, and are very aware of the criticisms levelled at their work as well as the need to address those criticisms if they are to reach particular (highly educated and lucrative) consumer markets. You also might want to think about how the ad is portraying potential customers for the product in question: are there assumptions being made about who would buy this product? Remember, though, that there isn't a simple equivalence between the people portrayed in the ad and the target market: an ad populated entirely by bikini-clad women is just as likely to be targeting teenage men as bikini-clad women.

Moreover, as suggested above there are other areas of potentially productive ideological analysis beyond the representation of identity that can be investigated. For example, many ads work by presenting a particular problem – boredom, poor health, lack of social status – that can be solved by the product in question. Frequently, however, these problems will be more implicit than explicit, and so we need to think about the promised pleasures of the product in order to unpack the ideological assumptions at work. On the one hand, it is therefore productive to ask questions like 'what does this advertisement present as a problem?' and 'how is that problem to be addressed in the context of the ad?', while, on the other hand, we also need to be think about the ways in which the ad presents pleasure, enjoyment and fulfilment, what aspects are present in the ad that make the product desirable and, conversely, what aspects are absent. By focusing on how the ad presents the problems and solutions of our lives we can get at larger questions about how it presents the hopes, dreams, desires and fears of society at large. Moreover, this isn't simply a question of what is presented as desirable, but how the object of desire is characterised. For example, Coca-Cola ads are often themed around the promise of 'happiness', but by itself the idea of 'happiness' isn't particularly meaningful or useful in making sense of the ad. It is only when we consider the specifics of how Coca-Cola is advertised, including a frequent use of beach imagery, young people, athletic activities and partying, that we get a more productive sense of the ideological texture of Coca-Cola's particular presentation of happiness, which is tied into a celebration of youth, physicality and leisure.

Conducting an ideological analysis

As with our other modes of analysis discussed so far, the actual practice of ideological analysis will make more sense in terms of an extended analysis.

For this final example, I'll be drawing on a 2014 television commercial for the Kia Sportage from New Zealand. Compared to the previous advertisements we've addressed, this is a relatively obscure example (at the time of publication, the video can be found at www.youtube.com/watch?v=Bt9uDCiYWE0). However, this ad is useful for our purposes in large part because it is relatively banal and generic as far as ads go: this ad brings together several of the key themes of ideological analysis in a package that is not particularly memorable or different, and therefore can be considered broadly emblematic of automobile ads in general. The 30-second commercial opens with a short 5-second sequence in which a woman, working in a warmly lit office, glances up at a stylish minimalist clock.

The clock then match-cuts to a car's speedometer. The next 20 seconds of the ad involve interspersed footage from a variety of angles and lengths of the woman swimming in the open sea and a car driving along empty roads in rural and rugged natural landscapes. During one shot of the car driving, the word 'freedom' hovers next to the car, with a short dictionary-style definition below it: 'noun: the power or right to act, speak, or think as one wants'. The ad then closes with another short 5-second sequence, set back in the office, in which a drop of water falls onto a notepad from the woman's hair. The ad is scored with a guitar heavy, indie folk-rockish track. We therefore have an implied narrative, whereby a woman escapes her workplace, drives to an isolated beach, swims and then returns to work. While this story certainly draws on a number of specifically New Zealand ideas and themes – there are very few parts of the UK or USA where one could drive to an isolated beach and back during a work day – the general ideological message of the ad is broadly applicable in other national contexts.

Gender and ideology We can start our analysis by considering the representation of the central female character. From what we can see, she is a white woman, probably in her mid-30s, with long hair that is neatly cut and falls past her shoulders. At the beginning of the ad, she is dressed in a white blazer and wearing quite a lot of 'naturalistic' make-up, including lipstick. We are provided with a number of markers regarding her professional status: the ad opens in an open-plan office where she works on a laptop at an uncluttered desk. We see little of her in the driving shots, which are very brief, and dominated by her long hair, which moves around her face in the wind. In the swimming shots, she is wearing a one-piece swimsuit and, as is clear in some close-ups, is still somehow wearing make-up. Contrary to a historical tendency in advertising imagery, the depiction of the woman swimming is not particularly sexualised: we have a shot of her diving under a wave; several shots of her head and shoulders above water as she swims or floats, smiling; a long birds-eye shot of her floating; and several under-water shots of her diving and swimming, one of which is silhouetted against an above-water light source.

With a focus on the woman's smile and swimming abilities, the overall effect of these swimming shots is to create an impression of joy in the experience of nature. The ad ends with the woman back at her desk, wearing a formal white sleeveless top, her hair wet and swept to one side. As a drop falls from her hair to a notepad, she smiles to herself.

Focusing on the ideologies of gender identity, we might be tempted at first to read this as a relatively progressive representation: the woman is presented as an empowered individual with a desirable job and the ability to 'escape' (courtesy of Kia Sportage) when she wishes to. In a point that is hardly remarkable in real life, but curiously rare in advertising, she drives a car by herself: something usually reserved for male drivers in ads. Moreover, as mentioned earlier, despite the ad's extended swimming sequences, the woman remains notably unsexualised, with little to no voyeuristic focus on her body. In this sense, this particular ad is certainly representative of a broader trend of gender representation in advertising, where women are no longer restricted to domestic situations and are instead presented as powerful and self-assured figures capable of self-determination. However, we should also be aware that the ad continues to conform to aspects historically criticised by feminist representation scholars: the woman is white, as if by default; she is conventionally attractive and remains made-up even while swimming; and the ongoing emphasis on her smile in the ad ties into a long history of female representation as unthreatening and friendly, in contrast to masculine swagger and toughness. Consequently, as with almost all representations of particular identity, this ad is neither wholly progressive nor reactionary. It is also important to note that it makes little sense to draw wider claims regarding identity representation from one advertising example. Arguments about representational trends only make sense when premised in close readings of multiple examples in order to establish evidence of larger patterns.

Freedom as ideology Nor does an account of identity representation in this advertisement exhaust its ideological content. As discussed above, we can also consider the ideology of the ad in terms of its presentation of problems and solutions. The central problem represented in this ad is not particularly stark, but it is quite clear: the central character wishes to escape from her workplace. Unlike many ads, however, her workplace is not presented as particularly oppressive or uncomfortable. It is suffused with a warm light; the furnishings appear modern and trendy. There is no sign of annoying colleagues or an unreasonable boss. It thus seems reasonable to infer that the desire to escape is here presented as an internal drive towards freedom, rather than an attempt to avoid external pressures. This particular ad, therefore, seems to be more about a promised improvement to the world, rather than the solution of a problem. The ad makes no secret of the nature of this 'improvement': the digital caption, 'freedom', floats alongside the driving car near the end of the ad and acts as a form of anchorage. In this way, the appeal of the advertised car is unambiguously presented in terms of an appeal to freedom.

The precise nature of the freedom on offer is partly clarified by the accompanying definition – 'the power or right to act, speak, or think as one wants' – but is really given specificity by the ad's visuals, which illustrate how it is the character wishes to act: she wishes to swim. Furthermore, this swimming is not in a pool or a lake, but in the sea: we never see the beach, but only the waves and swell of the open ocean, the expanse of which is emphasised through several long shots where the human figure is dwarfed by the environment. This is a wild nature – which could be described as sublime if the term did not seem so ridiculous in the context of a sports utility vehicle ad – but one in which the unnamed woman is completely at ease. The freedom on offer can therefore be understood as an emotional, experiential freedom from everyday life, as opposed to a more directly political freedom.

This reading is supported by the corresponding footage of the car driving along empty roads alongside rugged hilly farmland, which drops away into the distance, or thick native forest. There is a long tradition in car advertising of depicting cars in the context of natural environments as they zoom through mountain passes and along unspoilt coastlands. This is despite the fact that most driving takes place in suburban and urban settings, where drivers have to share the road with hundreds, if not thousands, of others, and start and stop according to traffic lights and pedestrian crossings.

Contrary to this reality, car ads tend to represent the act of driving in terms that emphasis the car's promise of freedom and mobility: as a conduit from everyday life to the promised freedom of the wild spaces that still exist beyond the city. In fact, even when car ads represent driving in the city, driving remains a practice of freedom as cars race down empty motorways and even through downtown streets with never a red light in sight. To return to our particular Kia Sportage ad, we can see how the driving images reinforce the idea of the powerful individual who is comfortable in wild nature. As with the swimming scenes, the driving scenes evoke a character who seems confidently joyful in this potentially threatening environment: an idea which, in turn, can be read as a particular iteration of a long-standing trope in car advertising of cars alone in the wilderness (which isn't even to mention the damage that car-associated pollution does to those natural spaces).

We thus have identified two major ideological sites in this ad: the first points towards contemporary constructions of femininity, the second towards the conception of the car as a site of freedom and escape. Bringing these two together, we can see how the two complement one another as the empowered, professional woman becomes an agent capable of enacting freedom. She does this literally in the ad by escaping from her work in order to swim in the sea, but also more figuratively through her confident engagement with the wider world in terms of both driving and swimming. The woman's central place in the ad as a figure able to experience this freedom further reinforces her distance from historical sexist depictions of women in advertising as homemakers or sex symbols. Thus, in a sense, her role as the traditional protagonist of a car ad who seeks and acquires freedom through driving aligns with the less explicit freedom as a confident female character who is able to realise her own desires. The woman's ability to escape her work environment complements her ability to escape the most obvious of traditional advertising stereotypes, while she still nonetheless retains several more subtle aspects of conservative femininity in advertising. We might therefore suggest that the overall ideology of the ad can be understood in terms of a qualified freedom or freedom-up-to-a-point. The female character can leave her work when she wishes, but still corresponds to traditional markers of feminine beauty in terms of appearance and cheerful disposition: the car is framed in terms of a freedom that ironically will likely not be realised in its actual day-to-day use.

An ideological analysis thus seeks to consider how various aspects of an advertisement can work in an implicit manner to communicate particular concepts and ideas about the world in terms of categories such as gender, nature and politics. To conduct an ideological (or mythological) analysis is to consider how the ad might speak, directly or indirectly, to larger issues than simply selling a product. However, when conducting an ideological analysis, it is always important to remember that when we are offering an ideological reading, we are always offering a form of argument. This means that there is always the possibility that others might offer counter-arguments. For example, you may disagree with my reading of the Kia Sportage ad. For instance, you may think that I have not appreciated the extent to which the ad sexualises the central character when she swims, or overstated the apparent comfortableness of the office setting. Alternatively, you may think I have overlooked a crucial detail of the ad. Or you may even suggest that I have read too much into the ad, which is simply about the pleasures of car ownership. Such objections are not infrequent in the context of ideological analysis, which is the reason we need to always be careful and considered when offering ideological readings.

Careful reading

To this end, in closing I want to emphasise that there are several aspects of the argument that we need to consider when analysing advertisements. This applies not just in the case of ideological analysis, but also the other forms of analysis considered in this chapter. For starters, it is not enough simply to 'feel' that a given aspect of an ad means something: the analyst is always required to offer reasoning and evidence for a particular interpretation. As such, an ideological reading should never be taken as a true statement in itself, but rather as a proposition that is open to discussion and needs to be based on the gathering and arrangement of suitable evidence from the text. For example, I have not simply stated that the Kia ad is about 'freedom', but gathered evidence from different aspects of the ad – anchorage, filming techniques, narrative, characterisation – in order to support this claim. Given that an ideological analysis is an argument, it is important that you do the same in your own analyses. You need to make a case for why the elements you have focused on are the most important and offer reasoning behind your interpretation. This will necessarily involve a degree of reflexivity, which means an awareness of your own prejudices and concerns and how they might shape your readings. Try to consider counter-arguments and counter-evidence. If you can't account for them, maybe you need to change your argument, or at least acknowledge the complexities of your position.

At the other end of the scale, it's also incredibly important to avoid speculation and over-reading. What I mean by this is that sometimes a potted plant is just a potted plant. If you see an apple in the background of an ad, it doesn't necessarily refer to Snow White and the Seven Dwarves or Johnny Appleseed. The colour red doesn't always mean stop, blood or a matador taunting a bull. Meanings are always produced in context, so make sure you have a good sense of why particular aspects are important and the meanings are clear. Advertisements are not created out of the ether, nor do advertisers have carte blanche, and so some choices can be the result of budget constraints or personal preferences. At the same time, most aspects of an ad will have been intentionally included, so it's a careful balancing act between giving all aspects their due and not overstating the potential depth of meanings. This is a very difficult thing to do, and the only way to get better is to conduct your own analyses and discuss them with others. Consider why you think an ad means what it does, and how you can communicate it in a convincing and well-supported manner.

From media to semiotics to ideology

In this chapter, we've considered several different ways of analysing an advertisement focusing on different aspects like medium specificity, semiotics and ideology. These different approaches are not meant to be mutually exclusive; instead they overlap and speak to different but complementary aspects of advertising analysis. An ideological analysis can be enhanced by an awareness of the specific features of a medium, and a semiotic analysis can work alongside medium-specific, ideological or mythological analysis. As mentioned at the beginning of the chapter, these methods of analysis are by no means exhaustive: there are many other ways to analyse advertisements, and we've addressed only a few methods that are largely focused on qualitative analysis of the production and communication of meaning. One of the main reasons for this selection is that these meanings complement the approach to advertising that we take on elsewhere in the book. Other major methods of advertising analysis involve quantitative methods, where relevant features are defined and counted across large collections of advertisements, or methods informed by psychology or marketing.

As hinted at in the final discussions associated with ideology analysis, the best way to improve your analytic skills is with practice. It helps to both conduct analyses and discuss them with other students, or to consider the analyses of others: thinking about the possible gaps or limitations of the work of others can help you identify similar aspects in your own work. Nor do you always need to engage in formal, long-form analysis: we are surrounded by ads in our daily lives, and the more we think about what and how those ads convey meaning, the more actively aware we can be with respect to our advertising environment. Analysing advertisements doesn't just have to be a formal exercise for classroom purposes; it's also a way to start thinking about the role of advertising in your life and to become a more critical consumer of advertising messages. Analysis is one of the first and most important steps in coming to terms with the social and cultural role of advertising and I hope that you'll return to this chapter throughout your study of advertising as you practice and develop your ability to unpack, deconstruct and explain the inner workings of advertising texts.

CHAPTER 4

Advertising, capitalism and ideology

We cannot really understand advertising without understanding capitalism. Not only is this because advertising would not exist without capitalism, but also because advertising is one of the major sites at which we, as a society, engage with, interpret and most often celebrate capitalism. In other words, advertising and contemporary capitalism are essential for one another – they are locked together in a tight embrace and can only exist in relation to one another. Consequently, in this chapter we'll be ensuring that you have a solid grasp of capitalism as an economic, political and cultural form in order to set up further discussion regarding the relationship between advertising and society. While this might seem like a bit of a detour at first, it is actually essential that you have a working knowledge of some of the basics of capitalism in order to understand how and why advertising operates the way it does. Following this quick introduction to capitalism, we'll then turn our attention to the concept of ideology. We touched on ideology as it relates to the analysis of advertising in Chapter 3; here, we'll think about what ideology might mean in particular relation to capitalism. This engagement with ideology will then lead us back to advertising, and in the second half of this chapter we will engage with three different models for making sense of advertising in the context of capitalist ideology that draw on the work of Louis Althusser, Raymond Williams and Michael Schudson. These different models will be illustrated through an analysis of credit card advertisements. By the end of this chapter, you will therefore have a sense of what capitalism is, how it relates to society and politics in general, and advertising in particular, and be familiar with a range of theoretical and critical approaches for understanding advertising in terms of capitalism and ideology. To begin with, though, we're going to have to sort out what capitalism is.

What is capitalism?

For many readers, 'capitalism' might be one of those terms you've heard in passing, but never given much thought to. If you were to look up 'capitalism' in a dictionary, you would probably find reference to concepts such as private ownership, the free market and the pursuit of profit. Almost undoubtedly, you would also find reference to capitalism as an economic system, because that is what capitalism is at its heart: a particular set of principles for organising the economic arrangement of a society. However, capitalism is also much more than just the abstract economic arrangement of our society. In practice, capitalism shapes our everyday lives, including the ways we eat, sleep, work, relax, express ourselves, understand ourselves and our world, and engage with our friends, families and community. In many major respects, capitalism is the reason most of us get out of bed in the morning and it's almost certainly the reason we're tired at the end of the day. It's no overstatement to declare that we live in the age of capitalism.

Yet, despite the importance and ubiquity of capitalism, it is not often a frequent topic of conversation. There are very few front-page headlines or news-media feature stories about capitalism. It is not a word that we often hear on the lips of mainstream politicians. With some important exceptions, there have been very few movies, TV shows, popular songs, comics, novels or video games about capitalism. It is not a subject that is discussed in most schools. Indeed, based on its visibility, if we were to assess its relative importance in contemporary Western countries, most would probably place it after democracy, and possibly even after Christianity, as a formative idea. This social invisibility of capitalism has become particularly pronounced since the collapse of the USSR in the late 1980s and China's embrace of capitalist economics in all but name during the 2000s: two important historical moments which marked the end of communism, which was the main alternative to capitalism for most of the twentieth century. With the end of communism came the end of conversations about capitalism, which went from being one of two options to the only game in town (there was a brief flurry of explicit naming, discussion and even tentative questioning of capitalism following the global financial crisis of 2007; however, the common decision reached following such questioning was that capitalism was the only answer after all). The seeming obviousness of capitalism and the profit motive is a central example of ideology – because it shows how a situation that is historically and culturally contingent can come to seem unquestionable and inescapable – but before we begin considering capitalism in these terms, it will be useful if we first establish more precisely what is meant by capitalism.

Three definitions of capitalism

One of the earliest and certainly one of the most influential attempts to offer a systematic account of capitalism can be found in the writings of Max Weber.

Often celebrated as one of the founders of modern social science, Weber was born in 1840 in what was then Prussia, and lived to see the end of World War One. His writings cover a range of subjects, including political theory, the social role of science and extensive work on the social role of religion, and he was one of the first scholars to offer a detailed analysis of capitalism, which he defined as a system where 'property is an object of trade and is utilized by individuals for profit-making enterprise in a market economy' (Weber quoted in Swedberg and Agevall, 2005, p. 25). In the posthumously published *General Economic History* Weber would further expand on this definition, offering six characteristics of modern capitalism:

1. Private ownership of property
2. Free trade in markets
3. Rational accounting practices
4. Predictable and consistent legal systems
5. Free (non-slave) labour
6. A formal system for partial ownership of business and property

Taking all these characteristics together, Weber argued that modern capitalism was an economic system where needs could be met through the process of trade with a mind to the calculation of income or, more particularly, profit realised through the exchange of property (1961, pp. 207–209).

Although he was writing almost a century ago, Weber's definition continues to be useful today, and it is interesting to note which aspects of his definition continue to be employed in more recent definitions of capitalism. While aspects such as rational accounting, non-slave labour and a formal system of partial ownership are now largely taken for granted, other elements of Weber's definition are front and centre in more recent definitions of capitalism. For example, the Nobel Prize–winning economist Milton Friedman describes capitalism as 'the organisation of the bulk of economic activity through private enterprise operating in a free market' (1982, p. 4). As with Weber, private in this sense refers not to that which is secret or personal, but rather activity and goods that do not belong to government: this is 'private' as in 'private property', meaning that it is owned by individuals, not by the community. 'Enterprise' is a little trickier to unpack; technically, enterprise refers to any purposeful project. However, Friedman is almost certainly thinking about a particular form of enterprise, that which we would refer to as a business, company or corporation. This particular reading is confirmed when we consider the last element of Friedman's definition: the free market. A market is a physical place – or more frequently these days, a metaphorical space – where buyers and sellers exchange goods and services. A *free* market is a system for the exchange of goods and services that is unhindered by outside influences or internal imbalances. Friedman's evocation of the free market helps nail down what he means by 'private enterprise', which is here framed in terms of taking part in this market (rather than, say, planting community flower beds or hacking internet servers). Taken all together, we thus have Friedman's definition of capitalism: a system where non-government entities (i.e. companies) freely exchange goods and services.

A third, final and more recent again definition of capitalism can be found in James Fulcher's 2004 book *Capitalism: A Very Short Introduction*, where he states that 'capitalism is essentially the investment of money in the expectation of making a profit' (2003, p. 2). At first glance, this might seem a departure from the definitions offered by Weber and Friedman. Fulcher does not mention markets or private ownership, let alone legal or accounting systems. However, in his attention to profit, Fulcher encapsulates much of the wider system of markets and ownership. Moreover, Fulcher does so in terms of a concept that brings us back to the most fundamental concept of capitalism: capital. Although the exact definition of the term is debated in contemporary economics, for our purposes it's enough to think of capital as any manmade object or asset that has a price and can be used to produce other objects or assets. Capital is any input that goes into the production of goods and services that is not a natural resource (i.e. minerals, water, geographic space) or the labour of the workers producing the goods and services. Consequently, capital is more of a way of looking at things than an actual set of objects: when someone thinks they can make money out of something, it becomes capital. Capital can take the form of factories, social networks, intellectual property or cold, hard cash; the determining factor is whether or not that thing or idea is being used to turn a profit. Tying in nicely with Fulcher's definition, capitalism can therefore be seen as a system of thought that is primarily concerned with seeing the world in terms of the generation of profit. By re-centring the notion of profit, this definition of capitalism also helps to fill in the gaps left by Weber and Friedman's broader definitions by providing the reason that private enterprise engages in the free market in the first place. They do so in order to make money: in order to make a profit. If we take the three definitions together, we come up with a multi-layered approach to understanding capitalism: at the top, we have Weber's six characteristics of modern capitalism that speak to the sort of society capitalism needs to thrive; one layer down we have Friedman's central capitalist concerns of private property and the market; and at the bottom we have the ultimate motivating force of capitalism – the thing that makes the capitalist world go round: profit.

What is political economy?

Although we now have a clearer sense of how we might define capitalism, there's still a chance that you're not clear on how it relates to advertising. Sure, advertising might seem to be an important part of how companies increase demand for products, and thereby increase profits, but that's not a strong argument for why we need to know about capitalism in order to understand that function. Rather, the importance of capitalism arises from the fact that, while capitalism might be an economic system, it is not *just* an economic system. As suggested earlier, capitalism can be considered to influence much more than just the profit-directed actions of corporations. Such an assertion is an example of a political economic approach: a school of thought that argues that economics influences not just the buying and selling of goods but also wider and seemingly unrelated aspects of our society. Political economy is one of the central methodologies in Media Studies, whereby scholars seek to understand the textual forms, social influence and political role of the media through the study of the economics of the media industries.

While in practice there are several different understandings of political economy in circulation (for example, in economics, political economy is often taken to refer to the relation between the government and economics or even the ability of economic methods to explain everything, including politics [Gilpin, 2001, p. 29]), for our purposes we will be drawing on the broadest and oldest definition of political economics: the study of how economic relations inform and are informed by other aspects of society and culture. For political economists, economic conditions are crucial factors that contribute to the larger social, cultural and political conditions of a society. This means that their understanding of economic arrangements forms the basis of their wider accounts of society. This approach to political economics involves thinking of society as a 'totality' – a mode of analysis that doesn't break down the world into different units like economics, culture, religion, sports and science but instead considers how all these aspects interrelate as part of a larger whole (Best, 2010, pp. 44–45). For example, while an idea like 'profit' might make absolute sense when we look at the world through the lens of economics, it becomes far more difficult to understand and justify what exactly profit is when we integrate economics into the rest of the world and try to make sense of it as an ethical, social or political category. Looking at the world from the perspective of the totality (or at least trying to look at it in this way) helps us to appreciate the complexities and consequences of ideas that can remain hidden when we stay within the boundaries of one discipline or area of study. Understanding political economics is therefore an important aspect of interpreting advertising in terms of totality, which is to say in terms of wider social functions and influences.

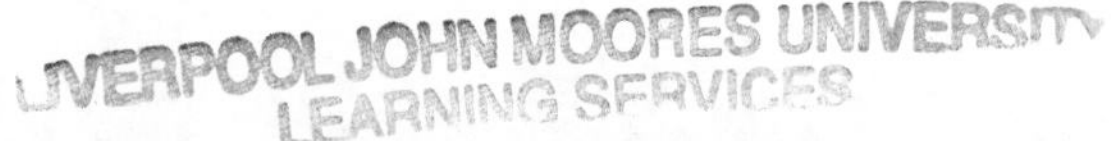

Marxism and capitalism

The mode of analysis informed by totality finds its origins in the work of Karl Marx: a nineteenth-century German philosopher, social scientist and economist whose work had an unmatched influence on the societies and politics of the twentieth century. Most of this influence came courtesy of Marxism, a body of thought that grew out of Marx's work and for a time was ostensibly the guiding philosophy of two major communist world powers: China and the Union of Soviet Socialist Republics. As a consequence, 25 years ago everybody knew what Marxism was, or at least assumed they knew: it was understood as a political programme defined by its opposition to capitalism and feared by many as a nefarious global conspiracy dedicated to the destruction of truth, freedom and the American way. However, with the fall of the Berlin Wall and the collapse of the USSR in 1991, Marxism quickly vanished from the world scene with China and North Korea these days remaining communist in name only (the former is increasingly capitalist, while North Korea is effectively a theological monarchy). What, though, does this have to do with advertising? Well, to start, Marxism is a bit more complicated than its fading impressions in the popular memory might suggest: not only are the representations of Marxism that circulated in the Western media (and which continue to circulate largely through parody and reference humour) significantly different from the content of actual Marxist thought, but much Marxist thought is also significantly different than the original work of Marx himself. Importantly, Marx was one of the first thinkers to consider the social and political implications of modern economics, and therefore his work is a useful place to continue thinking about the relation between capitalism and society more generally.

The key way in which Marx sought to understand capitalism in terms of totality was through the characterisation of capitalism as a 'mode of production'. In Marxist terms, a mode of production is a particular way of organising the people, technology and resources of society in order to produce the necessities of life (Marx and Engels, 1993, p. 50). Other modes of production besides capitalism include feudalism and communism, which both involve different ways of producing and distributing goods (Marx and Engels, 1987, pp. 22–23). For example, in feudalism the majority of people are peasants who exist in a semi-slave-like existence where they lack freedom of movement, work their master's land and submit regular tax to their lord: such production takes place in the context of a complex system of semi-religious obligations and ancestral alliances and is assisted by relatively developed farming techniques and basic machinery like windmills, and guild structures. In contrast, the capitalist mode of production is defined by advanced manufacturing technologies and very few people work as part of their service for a lord and master: rather, most people work because they are paid to do so. Contrary to how he is sometimes represented, Marx saw many benefits to capitalism and regarded it as a marked improvement on feudalism: capitalism stripped away mystification and superstition, created the conditions for global culture and unlocked human productivity in a manner that 'accomplished wonders far surpassing Egyptian pyramids, Roman aqueducts, and Gothic cathedrals; it has conducted expeditions that put in the shade all former Exoduses of nations and crusades' (Marx and Engels, 1987, p. 25). For Marx, capitalism was part of the progress of human civilisation that saved millions from ignorance and created the conditions that could do away with poverty and want. However, Marx did not see capitalism in only positive terms.

The recognition of both positive and negative aspects is part of what is referred to as Marx's dialectical view of capitalism. A dialectical view is one that seeks to understand the world not in terms of stable categories, but rather in terms of contradictions and struggles. For Marx, capitalism was a state of contradiction because it not only liberated the masses from the whims of their feudal masters and achieved wondrous breakthroughs in education and productivity but also, at the same time, instituted new forms of dominance and exploitation. At the centre of this contradiction was the idea of the 'means of production': a constituent part of the mode of production that refers to the particular technologies and resources that go into production, such as factories or computer networks. In particular, Marx was interested in who owned the means of production, which in a capitalist economy are held in private hands. Marx labelled this group who owned the factories, or who more generally owned 'capital', the bourgeoisie, or the 'capitalist class'. If you own a factory, or a business more generally, then you make a profit when your business produces goods and services people want to purchase. But in order to produce those goods and services, you need more than just a business: you need people to work in the business. These workers constitute what Marx referred to as the proletariat, or the 'working class': they are those who make a living through their labour, or in other terms by selling their ability to work. Those who do not own the means of production (the proletariat) work for those who do own them (the bourgeoisie). This distinction between the bourgeoisie and proletariat is referred to as the 'relations of production': the different relationships between the people and groups involved in the economy. Taken together the means of production (the tools, factories and infrastructure of production) and the relations of production (employment relationships) constitute the mode of production (i.e. capitalism).

For Marx, this split constituted a form of domination and exploitation, because the proletariat are compelled to work for the bourgeoisie, who in turn pocket part of the value of their labour generated without having done any work themselves. The proletariat is thus forced to live in a relatively short-term manner determined by their wages, while the bourgeoisie can accumulate wealth through investment and extraction of surplus value from the labour of the proletariat. In practice this means that one group lives off the money they receive by selling their labour, while the other group lives off the profits they make by selling the products of that labour. From a Marxist perspective, this means that the capitalist class are making money not by virtue of their own work, but simply because they own the company. This is a great arrangement for those who own the factory or company: less great for those who work at the factory or company. One counter-argument to this is that capitalists are not simply extracting profit from the work of others, but are taking on a great deal of risk and that their payment is compensation for that risk. One look at the Forbes global rich list, however, confirms that there is a lot more money to be made in ownership and investment than in working for a wage: the top of the list is dominated by those who own large stakes in global businesses like Microsoft, Zara, L'Oréal, Facebook and Walmart. Bill Gates may be an exceptional programmer, but he made his millions as a CEO, not as a computer programmer. However, having determined the nature of this relationship and what appears to be a fundamental inequality within the capitalist system, the next question is: why do the people who lose out in this system support its continued existence?

What is ideology?

Ideology is the cultural and contingent mistaken for the natural and inevitable: it is the set of assumptions about values, priorities, ideals, beliefs and reasonable expectations and behaviours that surround and inform our lives We first encountered ideology in the second chapter, where we considered its usefulness as an analytic category for interpreting advertisements: our goal now is to expand on that account in order to examine the particular relationship between advertising, ideology and capitalism. This means moving beyond a conception of ideology as simply a synonym for 'worldview' and instead considering how it relates to questions of power and dominance. One of the key ways in which we can do this is by examining how ideology relates to the material conditions of our lives: this means thinking of ideology not as something that floats around in the ether or simply 'happens' to be, but rather as a way of thinking tied directly to our material and economic existence.

The questions of who owns what and what they do with it are central to a Marxist approach to the world because these questions are the central facts of the lives of most people. While you might not wake up in the morning and think about capitalism, most of us do think about our job, or the future

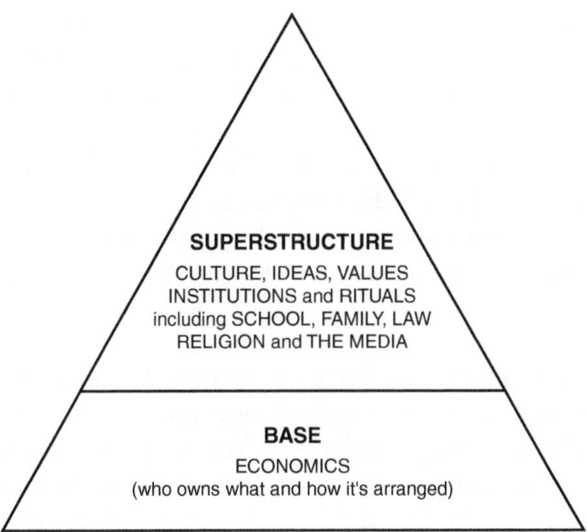

possibility of a job. This is because working at a job is the main way in which most of us obtain the money we need to purchase food, shelter and the other necessities, comforts and desires of life. Put more bluntly: we need to work or we will not be able to afford to live. We work in order to not die. In classic Marxist theory, the priority afforded to the economic aspects of life is expressed in terms of a spatial metaphor of base and superstructure – where the economic arrangement of society is understood as the base upon which the superstructure, which includes culture, ideas, values, institutions and rituals (including importantly the media), is built (Marx, 2011, p. 107). According to this model, society is understood as a building where the economic base is the foundation upon which the upper floors of the cultural superstructure are constructed. The two are therefore fundamentally interrelated and changes in one will produce or require changes in the other. From what we've covered so far, we can consider advertising part of the superstructure of society: advertising is one of the most immediately direct cultural symptoms of the underlying economic logic of capitalism. That is to say, if our economy wasn't organised according to capitalist systems, then the rituals, ideas and forms of advertising wouldn't exist. Advertising also has another important role, however, one which adds another quirk to our model and suggests more clearly how the influence between base and superstructure can work both ways: advertising is not simply a consequence of capitalism, but can also influence how we perceive our economic situation. This is what we refer to as the ideological role of advertising.

When we approach ideology in this way, then we can begin to understand how it fits in the base and superstructure model and thereby further develop an appreciation for how economic conditions can shape social and cultural conditions. It is this relation between the material conditions of existence and the ideas, beliefs and values of a given society that Marx was trying to explain when he argued that:

> Men make their own history, but they do not make it as they please; they do not make it under self-selected circumstances, but under circumstances existing already, given and transmitted from the past. The tradition of all dead generations weighs like a nightmare on the brains of the living.
>
> (Marx, 1999)

What Marx means here is that while we certainly do have a say in how our world is organised, i.e. we can make our own history, we don't start from a clean slate (we'll give Marx a pass on his gender-specific language for now: it's not really reasonable to expect nineteenth-century authors to conform to twenty-first-century language politics). Rather, we are always bound not only by our ideas, but also by economic and physical arrangement of our culture, which have, in turn, a bearing on the ways we think and understand the world. For example, the centrality of the automobile to our culture is not simply a set of ideas; it is a dense network of material structures, most prominently road networks and petrol stations that enable and encourage thinking about cars as necessary and important to our way of life. Changing our society's reliance on automobiles is therefore not as simple as waking up one morning and deciding that we don't need or want cars anymore. This is because those material structures, like roads, make it easier to operate in a car-focused way: everything is already set up to enable that particular way of living. Beliefs about how and why society exists and how it should operate don't just float around in the air; they exist in concrete, physical forms, such as the buildings, infrastructure, vehicles and objects that surround us. Even more importantly, the ownership of those material objects is in no way random: rather it both reflects and produces the economic conditions of our lives. You might dream of being rich, but that doesn't make you rich, and one of the consequences of not being rich is that many aspects of the world are closed to you. It doesn't matter what you believe or even what you argue; you're not going to get a free ticket to a concert, a fancy meal or an expensive smartphone without the money to pay for it. That is the overwhelming and inescapable economic fact of our lives that, from a Marxist perspective, determines our values, ideas and priorities, rather than vice versa.

Naturalising capitalism

We also need to be aware of how economic power (i.e. being rich and owning things) can change how ideas are produced and distributed. Again, Marx makes this point quite succinctly when he suggests that 'the ideas of the ruling class are in every epoch the ruling ideas, i.e. the class which is the ruling material force of society, is at the same time its ruling intellectual force' (Marx and Engels, 1993, p. 64). In other words – those who have economic control over the means of production and distribution will have the ability to determine what ideas are distributed and which are not. It's very important to note that this doesn't mean that a bunch of rich people in suits sit in a little room conspiring as to what makes it on TV and what doesn't; rather, it refers to how the instincts, values, tastes and worldview of the rich(er) shape media content in more indirect ways. For example, as we'll consider in more detail in a later chapter, advertisers want messages about their products to reach rich audiences with high levels of disposable income; therefore, more programming that can deliver audiences to those advertisers is produced, and, further, the programming that appeals to those groups comes to play a disproportionately prevalent and powerful role in the media. Consequently, stories, ideas and images that appeal to that particular group and reflect their life experiences and expectations become more prevalent at the expense of other worldviews. This is one example of how ideas that benefit one group over others can come to seem natural and obvious.

The idea that ideology can work to make the worldview of one group seem natural, obvious and applicable to everyone also explains how ideology can stabilise a particular arrangement of society, even under conditions of economic inequality such as exist in capitalism. As mentioned earlier, in a Marxist model the fundamental relation of capitalist economics is between those who own capital (factories, companies, infrastructure, etc.) and those who work for them. In this context, ideology works to make this inequality seem like an unavoidable and possibly even desirable state of affairs from the perspective of owners and workers alike. The ideological role of the superstructure is to tell everyone that not only is this particular arrangement, where one group works for another, a natural and obvious arrangement but that, what's more, it is a highly desirable, advantageous and potentially even ethically good arrangement. Marxist theories of ideology therefore suggest that superstructural aspects of society, like advertising, will reflect the existing economic arrangement of society and will work to legitimate and naturalise that arrangement. In terms of those who do not do well under the capitalist system, ideology therefore works to cancel out any ill-feeling by certain groups and individuals that society is organised in a way that benefits other groups over themselves. Ideology therefore explains why people will support an economic system that is not in their best interest. At the other end of the scale, ideology also does important work in convincing people who do well in the system that their success is a product of their own hard work and deserving nature, rather than any structural advantage. In terms of an ideological understanding, the stories, themes, tropes and values that are present in advertising in particular and culture more generally at a given historical moment are not therefore simply there as a result of some natural process, but instead are dominant because they reflect the interests of a particular dominant section of society. Understood in this way, ideology is more than just the values, beliefs and ideas about society that the text advocates, naturalises or takes for granted: it's also a force that almost inevitably acts to justify the current state or direction of society and therefore works in the interests of those who are the most dominant or do the best under the current arrangements.

Advertising and ideology

What, then, does advertising have to do with ideology and with capitalist ideology in particular? The relation between advertising and capitalism is a long and storied one: a once common term of phrase referred to advertising as the 'Handmaiden of Capitalism', and the founding figure of cultural studies, Raymond Williams, refers to advertising as 'the official art of modern capitalist society' (2005, p. 207). In this next section, we'll more directly consider the relationship between capitalism and advertising in more detail, and begin to address critical perspectives on advertising that build on the Marxist model we've been dealing with so far.

As has already been mentioned, advertising fits into the Marxist model of base and superstructure because it is quite clear that advertising as we know it wouldn't exist without capitalism. Capitalism is an economic system premised upon the delivery of services and sale of goods to generate a profit: to this end, contemporary capitalists make use of a number of techniques and strategies in order to maximise that profit, including mass production, global distribution and advertising. Within marketing contexts, advertising is widely regarded as necessary in order to establish and maintain consumer knowledge of products as well as to promote products by aligning them with a variety of ideas and beliefs. However, if it were not for the capitalist need to generate profits, then there would be no need to advertise in this way: the drive to increase a consumer base makes little sense as an end in itself outside of a capitalist system. Not only does this point illustrate how advertising can be understood as one of the most direct and unmediated superstructural expressions of the economic base of capitalism, it also points us towards the larger question of how advertising works as an ideological force that legitimates the capitalist system more broadly.

Furthermore, advertising is not only a direct product of capitalism; it is also one of the central sites in our media culture where we encounter different messages about capitalism. For the most part, capitalism exists as a kind of background noise in most media forms, such as TV shows, films, video games and novels (the one exception being popular music, where these is a strong tradition of music about capitalism and the music industry in particular); however, in the case of advertising, direct acknowledgment and engagement with discussions of capitalism are never far from the surface. This is probably because advertising is, after all, about convincing us to part with our hard-earned cash in exchange for goods and services. No matter how indirect and opaque the messages of contemporary advertising may be, we all know from a very young age that there is a fairly simple and ever-present motivation for advertising: to get you to spend your money. This observation – which hopefully should not come as a particular shock to any reader – points us towards one of the central ideological roles of advertising: the manner in which it teaches us how and when to consume. In a capitalist society, it is important that we all consume as much and as frequently as possible. This is what keeps the system functioning smoothly. Consider President George W. Bush's request to the American people following the events of 11 September 2001, when he asked for their 'continued participation and confidence in the American economy': a request widely interpreted as a call to 'go shopping'. Such moments are indicative of the importance of shopping as a central behaviour in a capitalist society. But how is it that we not only learn to consume but also learn to regard it as a natural, important and even desirable activity?

Advertising as ideological state apparatus

One way to approach this question is via the concept of an 'ideological state apparatus': a term that comes from the work of Louis Althusser, one of the foremost theorists of ideology. Althusser was interested in how a society maintains a similar set of institutions, rules and social norms over time and between generations, which he referred to as the 'reproduction of the relations of production' (1971, p. 127). This involved both the literal biological reproduction of people that constitute a society and the training of those people to fulfil their role within society. To this end, Althusser suggests that there exist different institutions within society that carry out the work of teaching us how to behave in different aspects of our lives: these are what he referred to as Ideological State Apparatuses or ISAs (1971, p. 143). ISAs are distinguished from the Repressive State Apparatus (or RSA), which are the parts of our society that get us to behave in certain ways through force or the threat of force or repression. The police are the main example of an RSA: they influence our behaviour not through encouraging us to see the world in certain ways, but by possessing the authority to physically remove and imprison us. In contrast, ISAs do not possess the ability to use force: they must convince, rather than compel, their subjects. ISAs include schools and education (which teach us the basic skills necessary to function as both workers and citizens), the family unit (which teaches us ethics and interpersonal relations) and the media. Advertising is particularly important in this model, because advertising can be considered a special subset of the media, in which we learn one of the most important lessons of modern capitalism: how to consume. Whereas most of the ISAs teach us the skills, beliefs and behaviours necessary to help us participate in the workplace, advertising is one of the few places where we learn how to take part in the other part of capitalism: the consumption of goods and services. This does not just mean learning the actual physical and social practices that make up consumption (although as discussed in the previous chapter, such education was a part of the earliest advertising) but also internalising a set of assumptions and beliefs about consumption. Consequently, most ads don't provide us with a set of instructions about how or where to buy the product. That knowledge is assumed. Instead, contemporary advertising is more concerned with presenting purchasing as a fun and natural activity.

While this ideological endorsement of consumerism is present in all ads – in that pretty much all advertising works to inculcate a desire to own commodities, make purchases and celebrate a life structured by consumption – it is perhaps most immediately apparent in those ads which seek to directly represent the act of purchase. For example, the moment of purchase is routinely represented in ads for credit cards, especially in the recent round of ads that demonstrate contactless and online payment technologies. Such ads are unusual because in part they do actually demonstrate how to use the technology in question, but they also do much more than that: these ads are also an excellent illustration of an ideological perspective that prioritises the subject's role as a consumer within capitalism and casts purchase as an easy, fun and necessary activity. While the particulars of this advertising changes depending on the local context and the advertising agency in charge of production, there nonetheless remain strong parallels.

Ideology in practice

Consequently, as new payment technologies were rolled out around the world during the first decades of the twenty-first century, a number of similar advertisements began to emerge in different national contexts. These ads shared an emphasis not only on the speed and efficacy of the system, but they also conveyed similar attitudes towards the act of purchase, which was routinely presented as a joyful and empowering experience and frequently equated with athletic prowess and success. A common theme across different contexts was the connection between consumption and seemingly effortless running or other high-speed pursuits. In the UK, one early notable example of this trend was an award-winning 2008 ad for Barclaycard, which presented an office worker commuting home via a gigantic waterslide that navigated through various everyday venues. With the waterslide acting as a visual metaphor for the ease and fun of life with contactless payment, the anonymous (and somewhat schlubby) worker is able to overcome the implied boredom of mundane everyday spaces. Nor is this a lone example of the everyday figure transformed through the appropriate form of payment. In the same year, Visa released a similar ad, where an initially naked man runs through a variety of landscapes, overcoming challenges, in order to arrive at his wedding on time. While the premise might sound potentially alienating or threatening, the narrative of the ad is more empowering and vaguely comic in tone, as the man is enabled by his credit card to find solutions to the threats and annoyances that block his path. Whereas the first ad promises that the credit card will transform the mundane into the joyful, this example offers a different, but parallel, promise that appropriate consumption can transform potentially dangerous experiences into adventures. Both, however, share in common a depiction of consumption as more than simply everyday purchase, but rather as a way of gaining mastery over the world around you.

More recent ads for credit cards continue this trend: in the build-up for the 2012 London Olympic Games, a UK Visa ad featured a seemingly everyday man in a race against word record sprinter Usain Bolt through the streets of London. The everyday man – who is revealed at the ad's end to be the starting official for Bolt's race – is able to keep pace with the world champion thanks to the powers afforded by his credit card. Similarly, in a 2014 Australian ad, the act of payment was represented in the context of a skate-park with various retail outlets, such as a café and a pizzeria, on the edge of a skate-bowl. Various skate-boarders, the most prominent dressed in a business suit, make payments as they fly past the various outlets, while one poor fool attempts to pay with cash, drops his money and bails on his trick (Many commentators interpreted the ad in light of a previous Australian ad for the same product in 2011, where robot-like consumers used contactless credit cards to pay for their lunch in a musically timed but machine-like food court. One customer attempts to pay with cash and the regular timing of the system breaks down. The ad was ridiculed for what was interpreted as its dystopian pro-conformity message and can be read as a failed attempt to emphasise aspects of consumption that are usually ignored in advertising, rather than celebrated). Finally, a recent series of ads in the USA have taken this trend to what may be its extreme endpoint by emphasising the empowered experience of consumption in believable, rather than fantastical, ways. Some of the ads in this series do this by featuring famous professional athletes using Visa systems to quickly make online payments while also engaged in sporting feats: surfing in Tahiti's Teahupo'o break or catching rapid-fire passes from NFL quarterbacks. The realism of these ads is further emphasised by reflexively documenting the filming techniques and technologies themselves in a manner that downplays the potential for visual trickery and thereby steps up the impression of *real* empowerment. Other ads in the series take a different tack, by focusing on more mundane and everyday shopping experiences, which nonetheless are presented in mock heroic terms. In one example, a customer orders clothes online on board an airplane following the announcement to turn off electronics, while in another wedding gifts are purchased only seconds before the beginning of the wedding ceremony. In contrast to earlier ads though, these scenarios do not appear as magical transformations of everyday life, but instead simply as relatively banal acts of purchase, albeit in time-sensitive moments that create a sense of ironic tension. However, this does not mean that they therefore present an any less ideological take on consumption. Thus, even though these last examples apparently reject the fantastical images of empowerment, they nonetheless still include many features of the other credit card ads: consumption as an easy and empowering leisure activity, with no apparent connection to the work required to make the purchase or the need for budgeting with limited funds.

Whether fantastical or realistic, presented in terms of fantastic daydreams of power and enjoyment or small stories of everyday victory, all the different forms of credit card ads considered here share a common concern with the different ways we might imagine the act of consumption. These ads don't just teach us how we might go about the act of consumption, they also teach us to adopt a particular attitude towards consumption: an attitude that regards consumption as an expression of human potential and a pathway towards self-realisation and satisfaction. There is no buyer's remorse here, no budgeting or compromise: not even any waiting in line. Instead, what these ads present us with is a vision of consumption as an entirely pleasurable and potentially transformative act. Moreover, such advertising encourages its audience to think of themselves, and their relation to capitalism, in terms of consumption, rather than production. In the act of consumption we are free and powerful: in the act of consumption, we are all equal (provided we have the required funds). However, what these ads leave out in order to present this highly attractive world is the other half of capitalism: production, or, in other words, work. In order to get the money we need to make purchases, we need to work and at work we are much less likely to feel the freedom and joy promised us in these credit card ads. In part, it is the absence of work in these ads that makes the experience of purchase and consumption appear too joyful. It's also worth noting that our purchases also rely on the production of others: while we might thrill at the sight of Kolohe Andino surfing the Teahupo'o break, we never see the people making the pizzas he orders. Chances are that their experience is less exciting and less fun (though in the ad, the pizzas are delivered by jet ski at the same time as he climbs back aboard the support boat – a highly unlikely timeframe that undercuts the realism the ad goes to lengths to create). This separation between relations of production and consumption will be considered in more detail in the next chapter.

With the observation that such ads prioritise our economic role as consumers, rather than producers, we arrive at one of the major ideological operations of this advertising: rather than try to represent the totality of capitalism, they cut out the grind of work and production in order to focus instead on the enjoyable side of consumption. This brings us back to Althusser, and his particular definition of ideology as 'the imaginary relationship of individuals to their real conditions of production' (1971, p. 162). What he means by this is that under ideology we cannot fully grasp our role within the real capitalist conditions of production. What is imaginary here is the idea that our primary point of interaction with capitalism is consumption. Instead, and in contrast to what is promised by these ads, our major interaction with capitalism isn't spending money, but earning it when we sell our labour for a wage. The fact is that most of us spend much more of our lives earning money than we do spending it, and the two halves of that equation are rarely experienced as utterly separate activities. The credit card ads investigated here don't pretend that our society is anything but capitalist; in fact, they celebrate that fact. However, they do so by emphasising certain enjoyable aspects of our lives at the expense of other, potentially less fun, aspects. Therefore, the image presented here is not so much false, as incomplete. Such advertising encourages us to make sense of our role in capitalism in terms that might not be entirely incorrect, but are certainly incomplete. This is also a productive way of understanding ideology more generally, which is not so much an act of deception as one of selection and emphasis.

This focus on consumption over production makes absolute sense if we consider advertising to be an ISA: a site at which we learn skills, beliefs and behaviours central to dominant capitalist ideology. Just as the family unit teaches us how to relate to others and engage in domestic duties, and school teaches us how to read, write and do what we're told, advertising teaches us one of the cornerstone beliefs of the capitalist economic order: that the act of purchasing and consuming is, in itself, fun and rewarding. However, we shouldn't overstate the ability of the ISA model to explain everything about advertising. After all, it would be nonsensical to suggest that all ads teach us about the pleasures and practices of consumption as directly as credit card advertising: while advertising is certainly deeply connected with the purchase of goods, it would be a stretch to try to directly interpret all advertising through the lens of the ISA model. Rather, it makes more sense to consider how advertising's role as the ISA of consumption might be interpreted in terms of the wider structure of a consumer society.

Consumer society and the magic system

A consumer society is one in which almost every action from the time we wake up to the time we go to sleep is informed by acts of purchase and consumption. Chances are that almost all readers of this book live in just such a society, where almost all aspects of our lives – from the food you eat to the clothes you wear and the things that entertain and inform you, not to mention health, education, transport and even personal security – are tied up with the exchange of money for goods and services. In a consumer society we do not so much buy in order to live, as we live in order to buy. The lifestyle inherent in a consumer society is often characterised in terms of the concept of 'consumerism': a system of belief and behaviour characterised by the assumption that all needs and wants can be met through the purchase of goods in a marketplace. Consumerism is far from a neutral term, though, and historically has been used to condemn as much as describe this state of affairs, which has been declared inferior to supposedly more authentic ways of living and interacting (Sassatelli, 2007, p. 2). Early critics of consumerism in the mid-twentieth century worried that this new way of life would lead to a destructive passion for the accumulation of material wealth and a focus on superficial appearances over authentic experiences. Part of this fear was tied into the ever-increasing visibility of advertising that threatened to flatter, threaten, pander, deceive, bamboozle and sometimes even flat out lie in order to convince consumers to part with their money. Consequently, to those observers who venerated traditional values and lifestyles, it appeared that the twin forces of advertising and consumerism were going to sweep away older forms of community and society in favour of a new world of glamour, excess and material goods.

It therefore might come as a surprise to read that Raymond Williams, one of the earliest critical commentators on advertising as a cultural form, argues that one of the main problems with our consumer society is that we're not actually materialist enough. While Williams' point might seem counterintuitive, and even downright odd, the basis for his argument provides us with a very useful insight into the connection between advertising, consumer society and capitalism more generally. Writing in the late 1950s during the first real burst of consumerism following the end of World War Two, Williams was one of first scholars to take advertising as a serious object of study and to ask questions about how and why it operates as a social and cultural force. Since the beginning of the century, he argues, advertising 'has passed the frontier of the selling of goods and services and has become involved with the teaching of social and personal values' (2005, p. 207). Williams' account, then, fits well with an ideological assessment of advertising, where its social purpose is understood in terms of more than just buying and selling particular goods and services, but instead speaks to broader considerations about what Williams refers to as the 'magic system' of advertising. Indeed, while Williams does not take up the language of ideology in his treatment of advertising, the concept of the 'magic system' does similar theoretical work while also pointing towards some of the ways in which ideology can lead us to consider the world in irrational or superstitious ways.

Materialism in advertising

At the heart of Williams' account of advertising as 'magic' is the way that it can lead us to ascribe qualities to objects which go far beyond their physical properties. Advertising, Williams argues, very rarely suggests that we should purchase objects simply because of their usefulness in accomplishing particular tasks (although one contemporary exception might be the often ridiculed category of infomercials). Instead, advertising usually suggests that correct consumption will not only obtain for us useful goods and services, but will also grant us particular powers and attributes. As a consequence, 'you do not only buy an object: you buy social respect, discrimination, health, beauty, success, power to control your environment' (2005, p. 211). This is why Williams suggests that we are not materialist enough as a society, because if we were actually focused on the material qualities of the things we buy, then we would not pay any attention to advertising. For example:

> Beer would be enough for us, without the additional promise that in drinking it we show ourselves to be manly, young in heart or neighbourly. A washing machine would be a useful machine to wash clothes, rather than an indication that we are forward-looking or an object of envy to our neighbours.
>
> (2005, p. 207)

To these examples (which still feel remarkably relevant to current advertisements despite being over 50 years old!), we might also add that a car would be enough as a means of transport, without the promise of ultimate freedom and escape, or that toilet cleaner would be sufficient because it cleaned toilets, rather than as a demonstration of one's commitment and love for one's family. It is this apparent belief in the ability of objects to grant us powers and qualities that Williams describes as 'magic': similar to the superstitious belief that a rabbit's foot or a four-leaf clover can grant good luck, advertising would seem to suggest that consuming beer can make us masculine or that home appliances can help produce happy families.

Williams' central point here, though, is not simply that ads promise us things that products cannot deliver. Such an insight would not be particularly useful or original; after all, in our consumer society we tend to know from a very young age that the 'magic' promises of advertising should not be taken literally. Rather, Williams' point is that we do not engage in consumerism simply because we wish to obtain more material goods. In fact, for Williams the problem is almost the exact opposite: in a consumer society we too quickly overlook the material nature of our purchases in favour of the ideas associated with those products by advertising. Importantly, we need to note here that Williams' use of 'materialism' is slightly different than that which we might use in everyday speech. Rather, than referring to an overwhelming desire to consume and accumulate material goods, for Williams 'materialism' refers to a focus upon the physical material existence of things. This definition of materialism takes us back to the Marxist account of economics and society earlier in this chapter. As a Marxist, Williams' point is that we should need to pay more attention to the materiality of our lives, rather than ideas that become attached to those objects. To return to an earlier metaphor, the products are like the base, and the meanings associated with products by advertising are the superstructure. So when Williams argues that consumer society is not materialist enough, he is not suggesting that we should desire more things, but rather that if we were 'properly materialist', that is only interested in material things, then 'we should find most advertising to be of insane irrelevance' (2005, p. 207).

Williams is not, though, suggesting that we therefore dismiss advertising as irrelevant, because it is clear that we do not live in a materialist society of the sort he describes. Rather, his point is that we should acknowledge that we live in a 'magic society', and that we should understand how our engagement with products takes place on a quasi-superstitious level. Advertising is what drives the magic of this system, because it is the main cultural force that attaches meaning to the goods and services beyond their material existence. In describing this ideological system as magic akin to superstition, Williams is not simply dismissing it as a trick or sham: after all, if you make the right purchases, there's a good chance people *will* treat you differently. For example, in some contexts, we'll treat a Coke drinker differently than a Pepsi drinker, or a Mercedes driver different than a Ford driver, and for Williams this shows how magic is capable of 'real if limited success' (2005, p. 212). Even though on a material level products can't grant powers and qualities, if enough people believe in their ability to do so, then some real changes may occur. Similarly, we should not think that the advertisers regard their magic as a ruse. Rather, Williams suggests that advertisers are just as swept up in the system they help perpetuate and are just as much invested in the apparent powers of this magic of advertising to attribute qualities to products: another sign of how Williams' 'magic system' can be considered a form of ideology.

Materialism in practice

A clear example of the magic system at work can be seen in MasterCard's iconic Priceless campaign, which has been running in multiple international markets across multiple media platforms for over seventeen years. Almost all readers will be familiar with the basic formula, which has not only been replicated endlessly in a number of scenarios with celebrities and fictional characters, but has also been subject to a number of high-profile parodies: the ad lists the price for a series of goods and services before concluding with a priceless outcome that money cannot buy. For example, in the first 1997 Priceless ad, a father and a son attend a baseball game (tickets: $28; hotdogs, popcorn, sodas: $18; autographed baseball: $45) and then have a 'real conversation', which is deemed priceless. We are then presented with the now familiar slogan: 'there are some things in life money can't buy, for everything else there's MasterCard'. Perhaps the deepest irony of these ads, in whichever format they emerge, is how they superficially reject the idea of buying happiness, while simultaneously reasserting the necessity of consumption for attaining the priceless moments. Even as MasterCard declares it cannot purchase those priceless moments, it nonetheless presents the idea that consumption in general, and MasterCard in particular, is a necessary part of all activities, specifically beautiful and heart-warming moments. To put this in Williams' terms: if we were properly materialist, we would be happy enough with a convenient service that allowed us to borrow money against future income (or maybe we wouldn't be happy, but would be aware of the massive debt trap upon which the credit industry is predicated!). Therefore, we wouldn't need MasterCard to evoke those moments, which by its own admission are outside its ability to provide, in order to justify our subscription to their credit service. Furthermore, the magic of the Priceless campaign is not limited to the MasterCard brand, but also speaks to consumer society more generally, as it presents the idea that consumption is not only natural and obvious but also the way to attain all those special moments in life that we would normally consider separate and distinct from consumer activities.

The MasterCard priceless campaign is therefore a perfect example of the logic of consumerism, whereby the act of consumption becomes a central part of everyday life and an essential aspect of even those moments framed as priceless and beyond the reach of consumer society. As Williams' points out though, this promise of happiness through consumption is doomed never to be fulfilled, because while the magic system can achieve some outcomes up to a point, consumerism can never fully deliver on advertising's promises (2005, p. 211). However, this failure to deliver isn't a problem: in fact it's part of the recipe for success. Consumerism relies on us purchasing material goods and services in search of immaterial outcomes like happiness, security, respect, community and fulfilment, and when our purchases fail to deliver those intangibles, we simply buy some more in an apparently never-ending cycle that is fantastic for profits, but has more troubling outcomes for society more generally. The overall consequence of this magic system of advertising is therefore to perpetuate a sense of confusion about the possibilities and problems of consumer society. In particular, the magic of advertising works to suggest that consumption is the answer to any problem we might face in our lives and therefore suggests that there is no need to fix or change the world. If a given product fails to solve your problems it simply means that you haven't yet bought enough things. Advertising tells us that any unhappiness or frustration we might feel is not the result of larger social or economic structures, but simply a consequence of not buying enough: by translating almost all human needs and wants into the language of the market, advertising thereby advocates for consumer capitalism as the ultimate solution to all life's problems.

From the magic system to the society of the spectacle

Writing a few years after Williams, but in a radically different and more unstable political context, the French philosopher Guy Debord would refer to this situation not as the magic system, but as the 'society of the spectacle'. In the context of Debord's work, the idea of a spectacle means something different from the customary meaning of a visually striking event, and instead refers to a social situation where the vast array of images and stories in the mass media, including advertising, are no longer superstructural epiphenomena, but instead take on the power to shape and steer reality (2005, p. 14–25). For Debord, the ascendancy of the spectacle was the ultimate consequence of the expansion and intrusion of capitalism into all aspects of everyday life. One of the major consequences of this transformation, as he saw it, was that the media had now come to serve a key determining function: everything that was once worked out in the physical world was now part of the spectacle.

However, the difference was that the spectacle obeyed only its own inherently capitalist rules, and therefore lacked the capacity for democratic input and participation that had previously been the case. Thus, while in the context of the magic system, we might say advertising actually has limited power to bestow qualities and features upon purchase, in terms of the spectacle this is not because the power of advertising is somehow 'true', but rather because the whole world is now *false*. As a consequence, the fact that consumption and advertising now exert actual influence cannot be separated from the absolute intrusion of consumer society into every aspect of our lives: that advertising is now the central guiding logic that determines how we lives our lives, engage with others and understand the world around us.

Selling capitalism

What both Williams' model of the magic system and Debord's idea of the society of the spectacle suggest, then, is that advertising isn't just selling particular products; it's selling a whole consumerist way of life. Think about the overall message of advertising: what kinds of situations, settings, fantasies and characters frequently occur, and which ones are largely absent? Does the world as presented through advertising look like your life or a life that appeals to you? Whose interest might this world reflect and whose interests might it ignore? Remember, though, that the question here is not particularly meaningful in the context of any single advertising text, because no one advertisement – not even one TV show, novel or film – can speak to everyone's life experience, and therefore there always has to be a choice as to what is being represented and what is not. What is important here, then, is not the fact that a choice has been made to represent one perspective rather than another, but that in the context of advertising, overwhelmingly it is the same choices being made time and time again to show the same kinds of people living the same kinds of lives with the same kinds of problems and the same kinds of solutions, all within what appears to be the natural and desirable context of capitalism.

Seen in this light, the main message of any given advertisement is never just that you should buy the product on offer, but the broader suggestion that you should simply just buy something, anything, and maybe everything. Advertising is not only one of the key sites by which capitalist society reproduces behaviour necessary for the perpetuation of capitalism; it also serves the equally important role of legitimating consumer behaviour as obvious and good. This is because advertising is more than just a constant series of different messages about products we could buy, but it also, when taken as a whole, constitutes one massive, single message: that consumerism is a natural and obvious way of arranging a society and that it provides us with everything we need. Regarded in this way, individual advertisements can be understood as variations on an overarching theme: the ideological belief that the capitalist world is meaningful, desirable and, above all, obvious. Thus, even when we question or reject the message of any single advertisement (i.e. I'd never fall for an ad like that), we remain caught up in the deeper and more important logics (i.e. I must buy something though). We therefore certainly have some agency as we move and navigate our way through the terrain of advertising, but it is only very rarely that we question our role as consumers. One of the consequences of this situation is that we often come to see ourselves as consumers over and above other possible social roles – such as citizens – or that we come to understand and interpret those other roles through the logic of consumerism and capitalism. Marxist critics of advertising have suggested that this means we increasingly come to see previously separate spheres of life, such as politics or family relations, in terms of the logic of capitalism and consumerism. For example, political activism is understood in terms of consumer categories like product boycotts and purchase decisions, and even political parties come to speak the language of branding and representation in place of debates around policy and values. Advertising isn't therefore just about the products we buy: it's also more importantly about the way we live.

Capitalist Realism in advertising

Consequently, we can see that the ideological role of advertising legitimates not just consumerism but also the larger economic structures of capitalism. One way to make sense of advertising's ideological role at this level is via Michael Schudson's concept of 'Capitalist Realism', which also helps bring our discussion of capitalist, ideology and advertising full circle by addressing how advertising both emerges out of and legitimates capitalist economics (1986, pp. 210–211). At the heart of the idea of Capitalist Realism is just how much fun everyday life under capitalism seems to be when viewed through the lens of advertising. Happy families, good friends and good times, wish-fulfilment, problems solved, pain and drudgery banished: advertising shows us what amounts to a highlight reel of our society where even if everyone isn't smiling and content at the beginning of the ad, they probably will be by the end. This rose-tinted view of the world is what Schudson refers to as 'Capitalist Realism': a term that evokes the historical referent of Socialist Realism: a historical school of art in general, and painting in particular, that was the officially mandated style of the USSR from 1934 up till the late 1980s (1986, pp. 214–215). The goal of Socialist Realism was to speak directly to the general public about the positive directions of contemporary life in the USSR: to this end, abstraction and experimentation were frowned upon and artists were not permitted to create painting, literature, sculpture, film or music that was deemed critical of the status quo. Socialist Realism is quite an odd thing to understand from the perspective of our society, because it was a style of art which artists in the USSR were compelled to adopt subject to the threat of force by the state. In other words, if you were an artist, you had to accept the Socialist Realist style or risk prison or worse.

How, then, is this government-enforced Utopian application of art in anyway similar to advertising? Well, for a start, Schudson notes that there are a number of formal and thematic similarities between advertising and Socialist Realism that can be broadly captured by the idea that both work to 'simplify and typify' (1986, p. 215). In practice, this means that both advertising and Socialist Realism are not 'realistic' in any regular sense, but instead present a generic and flattened out vision of the world that lacks much in the way of particulars or details. Consequently, both forms deal in generalities and types: in the case of Socialist Realism, the characters depicted in paintings and literature are meant to represent certain types of people, most commonly the proud and heroic labourer, rather than individuals. Compounding this concern with the general over the specific, there is also never a clear sense of distinct time or location. Thus, instead of taking place in a particular town or locale, the backdrop of Social Realism is usually an unspecified urban or rural setting. What Schudson notes, then, is that unlike most of the other media in our lives, which are primarily concerned with defined individuals, advertising also follows this emphasis on generic types rather than specific characters. Thus, in advertising, we are also usually dealing with types, such as 'housewife' or 'businessman'. These characters are designed to be examples of broader categories of people, rather than individuals: all the better to encourage widespread sympathy and identification. Moreover, much of the action of advertisements takes place in front of a generic environment, such as a children's playground or a generic cubicle-filled workplace. With such an example, there is no sense or even expectation that the ad will tell us what company's workplace is being depicted, because, like Socialist Realism, advertising is about general impressions, rather than individuals and details. This is indicative of the odd form of realism that Socialist Realism and advertising share, where they gesture towards a familiar but flat and abstract world, where it doesn't matter whether the person in a Nike ad is actually an athlete, only that they look like we imagine an athlete should. As a result, in the case of both Socialist and Capitalist Realism, the realism in question is not an accurate representation of the world as it actually exists, but rather a simplified vision of the world 'as it should be' that sits somewhere between an entirely fictional and the actually existing world (1986, pp. 214–216).

This shared tendency towards both simplification and celebration of existing society lies at the heart of the common ideological role of Socialist and Capitalist Realism and points towards the more provocative nature of Schudson's argument. Socialist Realism was widely regarded in the capitalist world as a form of propaganda that was designed to convince the people of the USSR that life was much better than it actually was. At its most brutal, Socialist Realism was considered to be the artistic manifestation of the most oppressive aspects of Stalinist rule. Therefore, while Schudson freely admits that advertising isn't government-directed and enforced in the same way that Socialist Realism was, he nonetheless suggests that it still seems to serve a similar function: making our political and economic systems seem as wonderful and desirable as possible. Thus, even though there's nobody in charge of advertising and there is no compulsion that advertising celebrate the capitalist world, it nonetheless does exactly that: in many ways advertising couldn't be a better form of propaganda for capitalism if it tried. Schudson's example of this tendency is advertising's representation of couples, who are almost always portrayed as constantly happy and intimate. Hardly anyone ever gets upset or offended; couples are always supporting and paying attention to one another, and dedicating their time to romantic gestures and gifts. This particular example can be expanded more broadly to consider how advertising manifests as a never-ending celebration of our society as it currently exists: a society where there are cars but no traffic jams, relationships but no misunderstandings, wild parties but no hangovers, love affairs but no break-ups, and purchase without regret. Hence, whereas Socialist Realism had the explicit goal of 'dignify[ing] the simplicity of human labor in the service of the state', the Capitalist Realism of advertising performs an equivalent role celebrating the 'pleasures and freedoms of consumer choice' in the context of a consumerist, capitalist economy (1986, p. 218).

Capitalist Realism in practice

To return to the example of credit cards advertising one last time, a good example of this phenomenon can be seen in American Express' 'Realise The Potential' campaign that featured in print, TV and digital media in the UK, Australia and Canada from 2009. The central TV spot for the campaign – which was dubbed and released in local accents in different markets – is clearly not realist in any conventional sense. Indeed the ad is incredibly abstract in execution, with the letters from the word 'impossible' being presented in turn and transformed into illustrations of American Express' customer service: an 'i' becomes a skyscraper to represent the corporate world, a 'p' becomes a key for an implied hotel room, an 'o' becomes a globe around which planes travel and then an alarm clock in a representation of ever-present global reach. These transformations are presented as computer-generated approximations of illustration and paper art, which further enhances the abstract nature of the representation. However, as discussed above, the question of 'realism' in terms of Socialist and Capitalist Realism is less to do with the conventions of representation: Schudson points out that just as often advertising embraces surrealist or farcical modes, a fact that is probably even truer now than it was when he was originally writing in the mid-1980s. Indeed, it is (a little confusingly) not the drive towards a realist representation that drives Capitalist Realism, but a tendency towards a flat, abstracted representation that purports to present our society and our world as they actually are. Hence, even though the 'Realise the Potential' ad is clearly not realistic in a conventional sense, it is still Capitalist Realist because it speaks to an understanding of our capitalist society as a wonderful society that is practically without flaws (and those flaws that do exist can be solved by signing up with Amex!). As the ad catalogues the different ways that American Express can enrich our lives over the chilled out soundtrack of double bass, we are therefore not just being sold a credit card, but also the final piece of a puzzle that will once and for all solve all life's problems. This example thus illustrates how Capitalist Realism is not so much a question of formal presentation as much as a question of the ideological work of advertisements. Considering ads in terms of Capitalist Realism leads us to think in what ways a particular ad, or advertising in general, is working as a form of propaganda for the capitalist society we live in.

Moreover, Schudson argues that perhaps the most powerful aspect of Capitalist Realism is the fact that although most of us would argue that we know the promises of advertising are pleasant fictions, if not outright lies, we still behave in ways that suggest we actually do believe those promises. This is well illustrated by exposés about fast food: where advertising images of burgers are compared with the real products. You've probably seen a picture like this in soft journalistic accounts or on a blog, where the perfectly formed and presented advertising image of a burger is contrasted with the inevitably crushed and shrivelled reality. The purpose of such accounts would seem to be to make us aware of the trick that is being perpetrated on consumers of fast food. Perhaps the oddest thing about such exposés, though, is that they are largely redundant: most of us, after all, are already familiar with the realities of fast food. We know that the burgers in the store will never match the ones we see in the ads. And yet many of us buy them anyway. This fact points towards perhaps the most important point about Capitalist Realism: we are under no illusion that ads present us with the real world and yet we still tend to act in ways that suggest that we do believe their claims. This situation aligns with the Slovenian philosopher Slavoj Žižek's ideological model, where the power of ideology is no longer conceived in terms of an ability to deceive people into acting against their interests, but rather becomes a cynical acceptance of the way things are. In his words, 'the formula ... is no longer the classic Marxian "they do not know it, but they are doing it"; it is "they know very well what they are doing yet they are doing it"' (2012, p. 8). Whereas there was once the hope that capitalist ideology could be revealed by analysis and thereby dispelled, now it appears even more powerful, because even when people ostensibly don't believe in the messages, they still behave as if they did. In our cynical times, even when we see through the promises of advertising, this fact doesn't change our behaviour.

What this means in terms of advertising is that we see through the hype and glamour, but continue to buy anyway. We know that a new credit card won't magically transform our lives: it won't grant us powers, fill our lives with fun and joy, or smooth our passage through the obstacles and tribulations of our society in any demonstrable way. In fact, for many people, a credit card has the potential to make their lives much harder by enabling, and maybe even encouraging, them to rack up large amounts of debt. And yet despite all this, we nonetheless take part in the process of consumerism and allow our hopes and dreams for a better world and better society to be shaped by the promises of advertising. Presented in this way, ideology becomes even more powerful. Moreover, it is not just our impressions of the world we live in, but our aspirations for what would make us truly happy and what a better society would look like, that are shaped by the ideology of advertising. Even if we don't believe in the promises of ads to deliver us happiness through consumption, we nonetheless seem to aspire to the things that advertising offers us, and overwhelmingly we do so through the methods of purchase and consumption.

From economics to ideology to advertising

We've covered a lot of ground in this chapter as we moved from an introduction to capitalism as an economic formation to a broader understanding of advertising's different roles in the context of capitalism, particularly in relation to ideology. It is important to understand what is meant by capitalism, because so much of what advertising does and, indeed, the reason for advertising's existence as a media form, is tied up with it. Understanding the connections between a cultural media form like advertising and the deeper economic structures of capitalism is an example of a political economic approach to the media. Political economy, particularly the Marxist approach we've considered here, seeks to understand society as a whole by drawing connections between different areas of our world that are often only considered separately. One way to do this is through the base and superstructure model, although this is far from the only way to think about the way in which different aspects of society connect and complicate one another. Indeed, while the base and superstructure model has helped to introduce us to the idea of political economy, it has long been the subject of debate in Media Studies, with many claiming that it grants too much power to economics or that it is too simplistic in the characterisation of the influence of economics on other parts of our lives.

Our engagement with capitalism has been particularly concerned with the idea of consumerism. One way to understand consumerism is as the interface between capitalism and everyday life: when everyday activities, systems and relationships are carried out according to the logic of capitalism – that is to say the logic of markets and profit – then consumerism is the result. It is in the context of consumerism that advertising really comes into its own as an important media form: advertising does important ideological work to teach us, persuade us and excite us about the potential of consumerism. From a traditional Marxist point of view, ideology works to obscure our real conditions of existence, and, while it doesn't necessarily straight up lie, it certainly distorts our engagement with society. In order to address the ideological work of advertising, we addressed three different models for characterising the social and cultural role of advertising. Louis Althusser's work on ideology and the ideological state apparatuses might not address advertising directly, but provides us with a clear framework for thinking about how advertising doesn't only teach us to consume but also to love doing it. Considered as an Ideological State Apparatus, advertising serves the important social role of teaching us to consume in order to keep the wheels of capitalism and consumerism in motion. Raymond Williams' account of advertising as a magic system takes this perspective further, but not only considering how advertising teaches us to consume but also how it works to reduce most of the questions and challenges in our lives to consumption. What's more, what Williams refers to as 'magic' shows us how ideology doesn't just obscure the world, but can also create: the magic of advertising can have real world consequences if we all accept it as a given! Finally, we considered advertising in terms of Michael Schudson's concept of 'Capitalist Realism', which suggests that advertising functions in a manner surprisingly similar to Soviet propaganda by hiding the negatives and accentuating the positives about our capitalist lives. What you've hopefully gained from considering these different perspectives is a sense of how advertising can fulfil a social and cultural role that is more than just pushing particular products but also intervening in larger discussions about how we understand and engage with the world. To understand advertising in terms of capitalist ideology is to think about how it relates to the wider context of our lives and can play a very important role in the legitimation and reproduction of the fundamental structures of our world.

CHAPTER 5

Advertising commodities and commodity fetishism

Without a doubt, Apple is one of the most successful brands of the early twenty-first century. Responsible for a number of innovations in personal computing and technological gadgetry over the past few decades, the company transformed itself from a secondary player in the desktop computer market to the defining brand of a new online, always-connected world with the introduction of devices such as the iPod, iPad and iPhone. However, Apple's success isn't just as about technology: the company's branding strategy also played an equally important part. From the once ubiquitous white headphones of the iPod to the ever-present default 'marimba' ringtone of the iPhone, Apple Incorporated and its various products have had such a powerful influence on so many aspects of our everyday lives – the way we communicate, listen to music, make purchases, entertain and inform ourselves – that Apple has become simply a familiar, ever-present, increasingly unremarkable part of our lives. As a consequence of such ubiquity, in early 2015 Apple become the first company in the history of the capitalist world with a market valuation in excess of $700 billion US dollars: a financial milestone reported in breathless tones by much of the world's news media. For many consumers, however, Apple's continued wealth and success probably doesn't come as much of a surprise. There is, however, one possible complication to this familiar story about Apple. After all, while many of you are no doubt acquainted with the finer points of the company's interface design, their carefully cultivated reputation for innovation and reliability, or even the late Steve Job's fondness for turtleneck sweaters, there is one aspect of iProducts that is not always as immediately obvious: where is it that these gadgets actually come from?

The short answer – as some readers may already know or suspect – is China. Although global manufacturing chains are usually difficult to unravel because they are considered commercially sensitive information, all publically available information suggests that the majority of iPhones, iPads and iPods are assembled in the People's Republic of China. In particular, Apple contracts out the manufacture of its products to a Taiwanese company, Foxconn, which in turn operates a number of factories around the world: most notably in mainland China. Moreover, in addition to Apple gadgets, Foxconn also manufactures products for a range of other American and Japan-based companies, including Amazon's Kindle, Sony's PlayStation, Microsoft's Xbox and Nintendo's Wii U. This answer, however, opens up more questions: what are iProducts made out of? Who makes them and how much do they get paid? How do iProducts make it from Asian factories to your local approved Apple retailer? If Foxconn is the company that actually makes the iProducts, then why don't we ever talk about a Foxconn phone? To some readers these questions might seem odd or even unnecessary – to dedicated Apple fans that might even seem a little blasphemous – but they are important to understanding the role of advertising in a capitalist economy and in particular the way in which advertising works to shape the meanings we attach to the different products and the ways in which we encounter them. Our goal in this chapter will be to think through the relation between manufacturing and advertising and reconnect the often overlooked threads that link together advertising with the products themselves and the method and manner of their production.

On the one hand, it might seem obvious and untroubling that we don't know, or at least don't think regularly, about where iProducts come from. After all, we're not often aware of the origin of most of the products we purchase and consume on a regular basis. From computers to cars, drinks and snacks, clothes and shoes, most of the goods we encounter seem to appear for the first time in the context of the store. Looking around my office, I'm not even sure where simple things like my notepaper or the bricks I've been using to hold up a shelf come from, let alone the components that make up my computer. Consequently, on the other hand, although it's perfectly normal in our society to not know where products come from, when we begin to focus on the mysterious nature of the objects that surround us, the result can seem disorientating. How is something simple like paper made in the twenty-first century? Where does it come from? How much does it cost to make? These questions become even more complex when applied to an object like an iProduct. Staring into the polished plastic sheen of an Apple gadget, we might see the dancing silhouettes that helped launch the iPod into popular consciousness in the early 2000s or the affable hipster Justin Long as Mac arguing with stodgy John Hodgman as PC. You might 'Think Different' or know that 'There's an app for that'. But none of these familiar images or stories tells us much about how the product is made or what it actually contains. We know a lot about the cultural meanings and values attached to iProducts, but most of us know very little about what goes on inside the gadgets.

This imbalance of knowledge, where we might know the jingle associated with a product but not where and how it was made, is one of the consequences of our industrial capitalist society: where we no longer have any knowledge of the origin or maker of most of the products we take for granted. In this vacuum, advertising takes on a central role in investing products with meaning, values and ideas. In this chapter, we'll be following the causes and consequences of advertising's role in relation to the production, distribution and sale of commodities. This examination will involve considering how advertising can work to change the meanings we associate with goods and services, the processes by which we can apparently purchase happiness, security and success in the form of material possessions and how this ties into larger questions about the influence of capitalism on society and culture. Apple will be central to our discussion because the company has not only been so successful in its cultivation of a particular corporate image, but also because it's sub-contracted manufacturing (and the controversies and problems that accompany that practice) provides an unusually clear illustration of the relations between manufacturing and advertising. However, it is important that you remember that the ideas discussed in this chapter are in no way specific to Apple, but are broadly applicable to most companies and brands we encounter. Therefore, as you read this chapter, think about how you might apply the concepts addressed to the examination and analysis of other examples, and thereby extend the discussion further.

What is a commodity?

In order to unravel the complicated relationship between advertising and physical products, we will start with what might appear to be a relatively simple concept: the commodity. In the most basic terms, a commodity is the name we give to any object being bought and sold in a market. On the surface, commodities appear to be straightforward things, but they embody a complex web of cultural, social, political and economic relations which have a direct bearing on how we can understand the social role of advertising. In neoclassical economics, a commodity refers to an item whose value does not depend on its origins or conditions of production and which is not usually considered in terms of different brands. Petrol is a frequently cited example of a commodity in this sense: consumers normally do not know or care where their petrol comes from in terms of country of origin or processing, and, while we might feel loyalty to a particular petrol brand, it's usually based on service and amenities, rather than any quality of the petrol itself. The neoclassical model is not, however, the only way to think about commodities. Returning to the Marxist models we considered in the last chapter, we can also think about commodities as part of wider webs of cultural, economic and political meaning. In terms of this approach, we not only recognise how the price of commodities can be unrelated to their origin, but we also seek to understand how and why this disconnection happens and what this means for advertising.

The commodity in capitalism

Marx places the idea of the commodity at the heart of his account of economics: the first chapter of his mammoth work *Capital* is dedicated to unpacking the complexities of commodities. At first glance, Marx suggests, a commodity appears to be rather simple, but this apparent simplicity hides a tangled web of human interaction, privilege, negotiation, oppression and competition:

> A commodity appears, at first sight, a very trivial thing, and easily understood. Its analysis shows that it is, in reality, a very queer thing, abounding in metaphysical subtleties and theological niceties. So far as it is a value in use, there is nothing mysterious about it, whether we consider it from the point of view that by its properties it is capable of satisfying human wants, or from the point that those properties are the product of human labour....But, so soon as it steps forth as a commodity, it is changed into something transcendent. It not only stands with its feet on the ground, but, in relation to all other commodities, it stands on its head, and evolves out of its wooden brain grotesque ideas.
>
> (Marx, 2001, pp. 102–103)

If this seems a little overwhelming, try thinking about Marx's argument in terms of the earlier discussion of iProducts. When we think about what an iPhone does (what Marx refers to as its 'value in use') it is relatively easy to understand: it connects us to the internet and a variety of apps (I'm told it can also be used to make phone calls). There is therefore little that is 'mysterious' about an iPhone in those terms: they exist because they do things that people want to be able to do. However, when we think about an iPhone as something to be bought and sold, what goes on inside and where it comes from, then another whole world opens up: after all, the people who make iProducts aren't making them because they personally want to own an iProduct (or at least not *just* because they want one), let alone the dozens or hundreds or thousands they make at work. Instead, they are making iProducts as part of a larger system that doesn't depend on their own want, but the wants of people thousands of kilometres away.

The factory workers who make iProducts are making them so that they will be paid money, which they can then use to buy other things, which have also been made by yet another group of people. Likewise, the advertisers who work to craft messages and images designed to help sell iProducts are also doing so not simply out of a desire to express themselves, but rather as part of a larger economic system. We are therefore no longer dealing with people making things because they want to use them, but with a massive global web of competing wants and exchange: a much more complicated system than simply making something because you want to use it. Understood in this context, an iProduct exists only insofar as there is a market for it: a commodity is something that is produced in order to be sold, rather than to be used.

Use value and exchange value

The first trick to untangling the commodity is to distinguish between what we can think of as the 'use value' and 'exchange value' of a commodity (Marx, 2001, pp. 52–121). The use value is the ability of an object to assist in the accomplishment of a task or goal as part of human life. For example, the use value of a shovel is to dig, the use value of a washing machine is to wash, the use value of make-up is to change and hopefully enhance one's appearance and the use value of a saxophone is to create music. You can be pedantic if you want and split hairs about potentially different or even multiple uses for an object (it's amazing how many household objects can be used to open a bottle of beer!), but the point remains the same: the use value refers to the ability of an object to accomplish a specific task(s). This is opposed to the exchange value of an object, which refers to its ability to be exchanged for other goods in a market: in this sense, the exchange value is similar to the 'price' of the object. An important distinction between these two values is that whereas the use value is specific to the object itself, the exchange value only arises in relation to other objects. That is to say, the price of an object can only be expressed in terms of another object, usually currency. The use value is therefore concrete and involved with the physical form and existence of the object, whereas the exchange value is abstract and consequently has no direct bearing on the object's physical existence.

Thinking in Marxist terms, we can use the concepts of use and exchange value to better define a commodity: an object becomes a commodity when its exchange value takes precedence over its use value; i.e. when its price in a market is more important than its function. This isn't a one-off process, though, and objects can change back and forth with their use or exchange value taking precedence at different moments. For example, when buying and selling something its exchange value is obviously more important that its use, but once an object is bought its use value becomes more important until the moment that we want to sell it again. The commodity is therefore one category among many by which an object can be understood, though in a capitalist society it is 'the dominant and most general' of those categories (Sassatelli, 2007, p. 146). This is because exchange value frequently takes precedence in the context of a capitalist society, where goods are produced primarily in order to generate a profit, rather than to serve a use. After all, regardless of how often they declare their desire to help improve the world, at the end of the day, Apple wouldn't make iPhones if they couldn't make money by selling them. We can therefore say that it is the ability to exchange iProducts, rather than use them, which drives their manufacture. Exchange value is also one place where advertising enters into this process, working to increase the price people are willing to pay for an object by increasing its desirability and demand. Advertising doesn't change the way we use objects, but it can change the amount of currency we're willing to exchange for them. In this way, advertising is tied to manufacturing and production, the purpose of which is not particularly concerned with use, but to maximise exchange value and thereby maximise profit. This is not to say that commodities have no use: simply that the use value is secondary to the exchange value with regards to advertising and the buying and selling of commodities more generally.

Equivalence of commodities

So far, so good – but where is it then, that the apparent mystery of the commodity arises? Certainly not in terms of use value, which Marx is at pains to argue is immediately apparent in terms of the actual physical object (even if the actual potential uses of any given object are often more complex in real situations). Use value is not a mystery: an object can be used for whatever it can be used for, end of story. It is therefore in terms of the exchange value that we need to turn for the potential complications of the commodity: in particular, the way in which exchange value is determined. How much is an iProduct worth? In the simplest terms, it's worth whatever the price is set at, but as Marx points out a price is never a quality of a single object (Marx, 2001, pp. 137–138). Rather, a price always expresses an object in terms of another object. Thus, we can understand an iPhone in terms of other objects it might be exchanged for, such as three shirts, one bike, half a washing machine, 1/100th of a new car or simply $300, which is a way of expressing its value in terms of something else: in this instance, currency. Presented in this way, we can see that a price is therefore never simply the quality of an object, but of a relation between objects.

This can be referred to as the principle of 'equivalence', because understood in terms of exchange value, any commodity can be expressed in terms of any other commodity. As a commodity, an iPhone thus enters into a circuit of exchange – where a commodity is exchanged for money which is in turn exchanged for a commodity – which is then linked to other circuits, which all together constitute a potentially worldwide system (Lefebvre, 2008, p. 97).

One of the consequences about thinking about the world in this way is that now anything can be exchanged for anything else: anything can be bought and sold! Thinking about the world in terms of commodities thus redefines anything and everything in terms of price: a state of affairs where calculations around profit, rather than function, come to increasingly define the worth and relevance of products, services and even people. This way of thinking marks a sharp break from the world considered in terms of use value, where objects are distinct: a lamp provides light, and a mug holds a liquid, and those two uses are utterly different and incomparable. Only in terms of exchange value do commodities enter into relations with one another through an exchange in a (usually virtual) marketplace, and it is in the marketplace that advertising becomes truly relevant.

Advertising and commodity fetishism

What, though, does advertising have to do with the commodity and the mystery of exchange value? The short answer is that advertising is absolutely central to the creation and communication of exchange value, but the longer and more interesting answer is that advertising is also inextricably tangled up with the condition known as 'commodity fetishism'. Originally proposed as part of Marx's concept of the commodity, the idea of the commodity fetish has served a central role in critical studies of advertising, particularly in the work of Sut Jhally, who articulates the manner in which fetishism plays a central role in contemporary advertising.

History of the fetish

The notion of commodity fetishism takes its lead from historical work in anthropology and psychoanalysis, where 'fetish' is a term that describes an inanimate object to which human qualities or powers are attributed. The traditional (and vaguely racist) example of a fetish is a voodoo doll: an item shaped like a person, which is seen to have powers to hurt, heal and control people through the manipulation of the doll. A more contemporary example is the psychoanalytic concept of a sexual fetish, where an inanimate object, such as a shoe, becomes a source of sexual satisfaction. In both instances, objects are being attributed power and abilities which, from a materialist perspective, they do not possess. The shoe is being attributed the power to grant sexual satisfaction, the doll the ability to control people. In both instances, the objects are seen to possess powers to influence the world around them: powers that actually belong to other humans and are mistakenly attributed to the objects. In the case of the shoe, the ability to achieve sexual satisfaction lies with the person themselves. In the case of the voodoo doll, the power to influence people is actually the result of the web of social influence and interaction in which the doll circulates. With both examples, attributes that are a function of human relations and social power (such as sexual fulfilment and social acceptance and status) are mistakenly believed to be housed in an object. Social relations are thereby seen to arise from an object, rather than from people. A fetish is therefore an item which has been mistakenly understood to have powers in itself, rather than as a function of the social and cultural framework in which it exists.

While such beliefs in the powers of objects to influence might seem far away from everyday behaviour, the manner in which we interact with commodities is surprisingly similar to that of the voodoo doll. Such behaviour is the origin for the notion of commodity fetishism, where a commodity is mistakenly thought to have innate importance, powers and qualities that actually arise from its social and cultural context. We can certainly see how this might apply to iProducts, which over the years have been presented as having the power to innovate, imagine, enliven and empower: to make their owner cool and stylish, to help people fit in and to distinguish themselves from others. Moreover, most, if not all, of these fetishistic beliefs – that promise that iProducts have the power to bestow attributes far beyond the real abilities of plastic, silicon and metal – have been created and distributed by advertising. In fact, we can say that there are at least two different layers of fetishism at work in the case of the commodity. The most obvious examples of fetish power relate to the direct promises of advertising regarding the ability of commodities to influence our lives, but before we consider these messages, we first need to consider an even deeper and more fundamental level of fetishistic meaning: the price or exchange value.

The secret life of commodities

As discussed above, a commodity's exchange value is determined in relation to other commodities: however, if we think about this in terms of fetishism, then we can see that there's a problem with that explanation. This is because our everyday experiences tell us that commodities can't relate to each other: they're just commodities. The stapler doesn't cut a deal with the lamp. So when we're talking about commodities relating to one another, we're actually talking about people relating to one another regarding commodities. Objects do not possess the ability to enter into relations with each other: they can only do so through the interaction of people. Without people, they just sit there. To think that objects can interact with one another on their own is to fall prey to fetish thinking: to make a mistake about the nature of the world.

However, when we think that a price is somehow a quality of an object – like its texture or colour – this is exactly the mistake we're making. This is because a price is a fetish: it is a measure of the ability of a commodity to be exchanged by people for other commodities expressed as if it were an aspect of the commodity itself (Marx, 2001, p. 120). This is a complicated, but important, idea, so I recommend that you look it over again. While we might be accustomed to seeing the price as a quality possessed by a commodity, in actual fact the exchange value isn't a quality of the object by itself, nor is it a measure of the relations between objects. The exchange value is actually a factor of the relationship between different people (Marx, 2001, p. 105). Therefore, when we regard the price as the quality of an object we are making a category mistake: we are misperceiving the true source of that value, which is not the relations between objects, but rather the relations between people. A commodity is an object that is primarily defined in terms of social relations between people.

One of the major repercussions of seeing the world in terms of commodities is that relations between people appear transformed and thereby seem as if they were relations between objects. This is the world that advertising presents to us: a series of dramas and adventures where commodities take centre stage and often act under their own power. Cars drive themselves, toilet cleaners scrub away without human intervention and household appliances come to life to help make life easier. Presented in such a way, commodities seem to possess agency – the ability to engage with and change the world – in contrast to the humans in such advertising, who only communicate and act through the strategic purchase and deployment of commodities. A mother shows love for her children through purchase of nappies; a business man demonstrates decisiveness by wearing the right deodorant; a teen demonstrates their independent spirit through the consumption of a carbonated beverage. While most of us would never take such scenes literally – we do not buy a product thinking that it will come to life and do our work for us – what is surprising is that we often interact with commodities in a way that nonetheless suggests that we have partially bought into the fetish of the commodity. This can be seen in the way we encounter commodities in advertising and in stores: goods spring up fully formed without any history attached to them and we only see products once they are finished and presented in advertising and the marketplace. When we engage with commodities in this way, we are treating them as if they were entities in their own right, rather than things made by somebody, often quite far away, and in a context we struggle to understand. When we understand commodities as something that just appear in a 30-second TV spot and on a store shelf, we are forgetting the massive global journeys that most commodities have been on. In practice, even some of the simplest goods have travelled further around the world than most people!

Where do commodities come from?

What is missing in such encounters are the people that produced those goods: that made them possible. In place of these relations we have only the price of an object, which is encountered as if it were an innate aspect of the object. In fact, the price is actually the product of a complex web of relations of production and distribution, which in a globalised economy involves large numbers of people from around the world. Although these people play a central role in the production and distribution of the commodity, and crucially it is their relation to the consumer that determines exchange value, they are absent from the commodity: present only indirectly in the form of price. This applies as much to the people who produce advertising as those who produce the goods: they are all involved in the manufacture of not only the actual commodity but also the stories and images that surround it and become part of it. In this way, the manner in which we encounter goods through shops and advertising hides the actual conditions of production because a commodity 'disguis[es] its own origins and the secret of its birth, namely that it is the product of specific human interrelations' (Lefebvre, 2008, p. 47). People are often horrified when children don't know milk comes from cows, but exactly the same thing applies here as most of us don't know where most of our goods come from. We do not think about the different aspects that contribute to production and distribution, such as the planning and designing aspects, the global network of factories, the conditions, wages and benefits of the workers, or the environmental effects of resource extraction and processing to name only a few aspects. Thus, just as the power of a voodoo doll stems from the socially obscured and misrecognised relations of power between the shaman and others, the price of the commodity stems from the obscured and misrecognised relations of production and thus objects appear as if they sprung out from nowhere.

In the case of iProducts, one of the major pieces of the puzzle we are missing is any sense of the people who produce the products and the conditions they produce them in. This takes us back to our earlier discussion of China and in particular the Chinese factories owned by Foxconn: the manufacturing contractor to which Apple outsources much of the production of iProducts. Normally absent in mainstream accounts of iProducts seen in marketing and advertising, Foxconn was thrust into the spotlight in 2012 following reports in *The New York Times* and other news outlets that brought to light poor working conditions in the factories. Alleging not only low wages, common in manufacturing in China, but also dangerous working conditions, excessive working hours (up to seven days a week), child labour and lax environmental protection standards, the story marked the beginning of a wave of investigations of the Foxconn plants at which most Apple iProducts are produced.

Perhaps the most disturbing revelation was of the rash of suicides at the Foxconn plants, in response to which the company instituted several measures, including the installation of anti-suicide nets and asking employees to sign pledges that they would not commit suicide (Economist, 2010; MSNBC, 2010). That these revelations came as such a shock is indicative of the way in which our relations to commodities are almost completely detached from their conditions of production. In the current global system of production, we no longer know very much about the people, places and ways that commodities are produced.

The reason that this is important to advertising is that, historically, it was these webs of production and distribution that imbued products with meaning. You wouldn't go to the store to buy vegetables or soap or a bike; you would buy vegetables grown down the street, soap manufactured in the next town or a bike made in the neighbouring province. These connections and locations were the source of the meanings that attach to products, but this way of thinking about commodities was largely brought to an end by the historical shifts discussed in the second chapter. One of the consequences of this situation is that the meaning that was historically assigned to objects as a function of their context and relations of production is now absent. Whereas once objects came to us full of meanings tied to who produced them, when, where and how, now they sit on store shelves as context-less objects and are difficult to distinguish from one another on those terms. This is where advertising comes in. The absence of meaning from the relations of productions creates a void which advertising fills: replacing information about the relations of production with a wealth of narratives, images, songs, characters and promises. Sut Jhally presents this process in a polemical fashion when he argues that 'the real and full meaning of production is hidden beneath the empty appearance in exchange. Only once the real meaning has been systematically emptied out of commodities does advertising then refill this void with its own symbols' (1990, p. 51). It is through this process that the cultural meaning of an iPod comes to be seen in terms of dancing silhouettes with white earbuds, rather than teams of Chinese workers in grim conditions and hairnets. Jhally thus argues that the meanings that arise out of the conditions of production are the 'real' meanings of a commodity, and while we might not need to cast the different layers of meaning in such stark terms, it is clear that those meanings that arise out of the production and material context of commodities are usually not as prevalent or prominent as those that arise out of advertising. Accordingly, we will now turn our attention to what Jhally refers to as the 'symbols' of advertising in order to consider how those symbols help build what we can think of as a second layer of fetishism.

Fair trade and organic commodities

There are some exceptions to the unknown backgrounds of most commodities: in recent decades, fair trade, free-range and organic products have made a point of informing potential consumers of their origins. The goal of fair trade is to provide better trading and working conditions to exploited groups, usually based in poor countries, through the payment of higher prices for goods and a greater focus on environmental and employment conditions. Free-range and organic products make a point of telling purchasers where they come from, how they were made and what they were made from. Both sets of commodities involve an explicit commitment to educating consumers about the conditions of production. On the one hand, such practices demonstrate the extent to which such knowledge is absent in most other examples. Fair trade and organic goods help raise awareness of where our consumables come from and the social and environmental costs sometimes associated with them, while also seeking to alleviate the most egregious examples of exploitation and damaging practices. On the other hand, we also need to be aware of how with fair trade and organic products, the conditions of production are often highlighted as a selling point. This marks something of a collapse between the conditions of consumption and the conditions of production, because the process of production becomes part of the advertising and promotion of the goods. In some instances, the rhetoric of fair trade might hide as much as it reveals, by substituting feel-good stories for structural economic change and thereby perpetuating unequal economic relations. After all, the most prominent fair trade goods continue to be luxuries and knick-knacks, rather than major goods and durables like cars, white ware and electronics.

Commodity fetishism and super powers

We can identify two different sites at which the meaning of commodities is produced: first, the meanings that arise out of actual material conditions of production and, second, the meanings that arise out of the promotion and circulation of a product in a market: that is, advertising. While the first set of meanings lead to the first level of fetishism – the price – the second set of meanings also lead to another level of possibly more familiar fetishism, to which we will now turn our attention.

Whereas the fetish of price is largely a consequence of forgetting, this second level of fetishism is much more a matter of intentional construction and presentation. If you recall, in its original context, a fetish is an inanimate object that is thought to possess particular powers and grant qualities and abilities to its possessor. We therefore might refer to any object as a fetish if it seems to promise us things that are beyond its ability to deliver: things like security, success, confidence, love, peace of mind, belonging, excitement or happiness. In short, all the things that advertising holds out to consumers as a matter of course: the promise that advertising constantly makes to transfer desirable human abilities and qualities to the consumer via the purchase of a commodity. Approached in this way, the very purpose of advertising can be understood as a cultivation of fetishistic meaning and powers by drawing connections between products and different attributes and qualities. For example, some products suggest they will make you more attractive, more fun, more funny, more frugal or more confident, whereas others offer the possibility of being able to organise and understand your life or work or home; still others make one a better mother, father or lover. While fetishism can be found to some extent in almost all advertising (with the possible exception of the most matter-of-fact infomercials), the appeal to fetishism is particularly prevalent in the advertising of those goods that lack a clear, distinct use value (such as soft drinks or cigarettes) or where the use value is difficult to differentiate between different versions of the same product (all perfumes theoretically make you smell good, all basic model cars get you from A to B). In these instances, the images and narratives created by advertising are called upon to a great extent to help define the product and provide reasons for its purchases: consequently, we see a lot more advertisements for these types of products.

Through the use of miniature narratives or striking imagery, advertisements help cultivate the impression that commodities have the potential to directly and dramatically improve your life. The reason that these promises can be considered a form of fetishism is that – I'm sorry to say – commodities are unable to exercise this sort of influence in the world. While some products may no doubt assist you in achieving particular goals and ends in your life, they are not able to bestow the life-changing properties so often implied in advertising. The fetish arises in this gap between the power of inanimate objects and the powers often implied in advertising. Thus we have the second and more direct level of fetishism, where commodities are promoted in terms that would seem to go beyond the potential of everyday material objects to actually deliver.

To help clarify what this means, we can now turn our attention to some particular examples from Apple marketing that can be understood in terms of fetishism. Apple's advertising has a long history of presenting the company's products as capable of empowering consumers in a very direct and immediate way. Empowerment, for example, was the theme of Apple's inaugural television commercial, screened during the 1984 Super Bowl, in which a single woman liberates a brain-washed dystopian society through the enthusiastic use of a sledge hammer; however, a further discussion of that famous example will have to wait until Chapter 10. For now, we'll turn our attention to a slightly more recent advertising campaign: 'Thing Different' from the late 1990s and that campaign's central television commercial 'The Crazy Ones'. The campaign is particularly notable because it has been linked by many to the resurgence of Apple at the time, as the company recovered from a long period of decline and cultural obscurity, and the 'Think Different' campaign has been directly credited with reviving the Apple brand (Siltanen, 2011, p. 7).

'The Crazy Ones' and fetishism

The centrepiece of the campaign was a one-minute television commercial called 'The Crazy Ones': the visual track of the commercial is composed of a montage of black and white film clips of famous figures from many different walks of life – including Albert Einstein, Bob Dylan, Martin Luther King Jr., Richard Branson, John Lennon, Muhammad Ali, Mahatma Ghandi, Amelia Earhart and Pablo Picasso. The footage is accompanied by a sparse piano sound track and a voiceover, in which the actor Richard Dreyfuss reads a poem written especially for the ad:

> Here's to the crazy ones. The misfits. The rebels. The troublemakers. The round pegs in the square holes. The ones who see things differently. They're not fond of rules. And they have no respect for the status quo. You can quote them, disagree with them, glorify or vilify them. About the only thing you can't do is ignore them. Because they change things. They push the human race forward. And while some may see them as the crazy ones, we see genius. Because the people who are crazy enough to think they can change the world, are the ones who do.

With its combination of inspiring, quasi-political rhetoric and eminently tasteful black-and-white imagery, the ad can be considered almost motivational in a broad sense: it constructs a narrative around a series of highly acclaimed historical figures who found success in fields of science, art, sport, music, politics and business. What's more, the ad suggests a common reason for these various forms of success: these people were all rebels, and as a result they had the power to change the world. This is also when Apple products enter into the advertisement, which ends with the tagline 'think different' and the first appearance of the (now long-gone) 'rainbow' Apple logo.

Coming, as it does, at the end of the commercial, it might seem that the Apple logo is not a big part of the text: that Apple are somehow downplaying their brand and almost giving up an opportunity to push the product. However, such an interpretation overlooks two major aspects of this subtle final placement of the brand. First, the montage format means that Apple appears as another link in the chain of people we have just been told are geniuses and visionaries (and in comparison the Apple logo is the only colourful part of the ad!): by the associative logic built up in the editing of the ad, Apple thus appears as part of the set of rebel geniuses which preceded it. Second, by appearing at the end of the ad, Apple is positioned as the final word, and perhaps as something akin to an artist's signature or a movie's credits: the brand thus takes the position of the authoring presence of the ad and its message, which is in itself also presented as a work of poetry. Through the logic of 'The Crazy Ones', Apple therefore appears as both a part of this parade of world-changers and as the guiding presence that has brought them together. As we considered in more detail in Chapter 3, this association through juxtaposition is a common means by which advertising builds connections between the brand or product on offer and the attributes of the story or images that accompany it. While few contemporary ads are so blunt as to declare that their product will actually grant qualities and abilities, almost every example will do their best to imply connections between the products and the textual aspects of the advertisement – this is where fetishism enters in.

'The Crazy Ones' draws a connection between the represented figures and Apple by way of a shared sense of 'difference'. Hard as it may be to believe now, Apple was once an obvious candidate for the 'different' company: a minor player with regard to computing behemoths like IBM. Apple's difference is thus a matter of market share. The ad reassesses that difference, however, by also presenting figures such as Einstein and Dylan as 'different' (whether many of these figures are different in any meaningful way is up for debate: most of them are white, male and come from relatively mainstream or privileged backgrounds!). Consequently, the ad not only aligns the historical figures and the Apple brand by invoking a shared notion of 'difference', but it also then does the extra work of implying that Apple products can also therefore be read as an extension of this difference. By playing on the ambiguities of the word 'difference', the ad implies a connection between a company that lacks market share and historical figures who were instrumental in bringing about social, political and cultural change. Moreover, the ad also constructs an implied connection whereby Apple products act as a bridge between consumers and these widely acclaimed historical figures, which means that through the purchase of Apple products consumers can also become part of this world-changing form of difference. What 'The Crazy One' therefore implies, but never states directly, is that Apple products through their vague affiliation with geniuses (most of whom, importantly, never would have had the chance to use an Apple product) can impart the quality of genius and the ability to change the world onto consumers.

The Apple brand thus works as a fetish that promises to situate the consumer in a line of difference-makers or at the very least articulate the individual differences of consumers in progressive ways that help inspire the world and include just a dash of celebrity as an added benefit. Importantly, the commercial is not saying directly that the purchase of an Apple product will help you change the word, but it is implying an unspecific connection between the product and the process of world-changing. It's up to the consumer to connect the rest of the dots themselves. Through the purchase of an Apple product, in this instance probably the iMac, the consumer is held out the promise of potential entry into a pantheon of creatives and heroes, the re-articulation of personal difference as a marker of genius, and, most dramatically, the possibility to change the world. Of course, it goes almost without saying that the purchase of an Apple product will not provide a consumer with such power: if it did, given the current success of Apple products, we would now inhabit a world of constant, never-ceasing change! Indeed, the commercial itself constantly flirts with that mundane fact, because the world-changers it depicts managed to make their respective marks without the benefit of a personal computer.

In this moment, 'The Crazy Ones' actually veers very close to acknowledging the complicated fact at the heart of this second form of fetishism: that it is an open secret that commodities do not actually deliver the powers that advertising often implies. Only the most deluded consumers would expect to be able to change the world simply on the basis of an Apple purchase. Consequently, as a result most of those involved do not anticipate that consumers will take the advertising's intentionally vague propositions literally. Advertisers are not working on the assumption that their audiences will be 'fooled' by their ad. However, and this is the catch, the consumer audience will nonetheless continue to purchase products – indeed pay a premium for certain brands – almost *as if* they did take those propositions literally. Even when we know that the majority of claims made by advertising are false, we still continue to buy the advertised products and many consumers can even recall the qualities and attributes associated with the related advertising. Thus, on the one hand then, when questioned directly, very few people would admit to actually believing the literal truth of advertising's promises. But, on the other hand, when making a purchase, consumers despite their disavowals will frequently act in a way that seems to indicate they do believe in the fetishistic powers of commodities, at least in part. While professing scepticism and asserting that they see through advertising, consumers nevertheless act in a way that would seem to indicate they do believe on some level. As the Marxist critics Max Horkheimer and Theodor Adorno suggested many decades ago: 'The triumph of advertising ... is that consumers feel compelled to buy and use its products even though they see through them' (1972, p. 167).

'You're more powerful than you think' and fetishism

In order to consider why this might be the case, we'll now shift our attention from 'The Crazy Ones' to a more recent example: the 2014 campaign for the iPhone 5s. Titled 'You're more powerful than you think', just the name of this campaign begins to indicate how Apple's historical appeal to personal empowerment continues into the present day. If anything, the 'You're more powerful' campaign is even more openly and directly fetishistic than 'The Crazy Ones', because it openly foregrounds the realisation of personal power in ways only suggested at in the earlier example. In contrast to the relatively basic format of the 1990s 'Think Different' campaign, 'You're more powerful' has four video commercials providing different variations on the central theme (and designed to be shared online by different target markets): 'Strength', 'Parenthood', 'Powerful' and 'Dreams'. Each ad in the series focuses on a different set of skills and attributes that are visualised through a montage representing everyday life as a series of tiny triumphs. Accordingly, in the case of 'Strength' we have images of sport and fitness training (to the sounds of the old-timey 1961 school athletic song 'Chicken Fat'); 'Parenthood' has images of child rearing and wrangling; 'Dreams' shows us people using iPhones to assist in a range of careers, including a vet, doctor, fireman, ecologist, pilot and artist; and, finally, 'Powerful' opens with artists, musicians and dancers, but then switches to include a range of different activities that can be read as a riff on the idea of 'power'. This reading of the imagery of 'powerful' is anchored by the soundtrack, which is a cover of 'Gigantic': the first single of the formative alternative rock band, The Pixies, here repurposed to sell Apple phones. Importantly and somewhat predictably, all the ads in the series feature footage of people using iPhones in order to accomplish their fitness training, parenting, career tasks or general creativity.

In all these commercials we see everyday people achieving everyday goals through the use of apps available through their iPhones. Understood at that basic level, it is difficult to really question the claims of the ad: smartphones do provide access to a range of portable, digital functions that can prove useful in a number of different circumstances. However, when we turn our attention to the campaign's central slogan – 'You're more powerful than you think' – we can see that we have now passed out of the world of use and into the world of fetishism. If you recall the initial discussion of a fetish earlier in the chapter, you will remember that a fetish is an object that is attributed power and abilities which, from a materialist perspective, they do not possess. With these examples, then, we have an almost 'textbook' case of a fetish: where the product is tied to the idea of increased power on behalf of the consumer (although you'll note that the vague working of the ads' slogan shies away from stating such a promise outright). The not-quite-direct, but not-so-subtle implication of the ad is that the purchase of an iPhone 5 will enable the consumer to unlock power that they didn't know they had beforehand. The purchase of an iPhone thus becomes a means by which to unlock hidden power inside yourself: by presenting the increased ability of smartphone users in terms of a gain in personal power, the ads present the Apple product as more than a handy gadget. Here, the iPhone 5 becomes a potent fetish for self-realisation.

What is particularly noticeable in this case is that the ad acknowledges that the powers which the commodity fetish promises to unlock are those which the consumer already possesses. Consequently, in this instance, the commodity isn't so much promising to give you new powers and abilities, but instead to help realise powers and abilities already inside of you. This brings us closer to the heart of fetishism, because as is hopefully clear by now commodities can't grant us superhuman powers and abilities. Making such promises is therefore not usually in the best interest of an advertiser because they're easy to disprove and therefore can potentially bring the practice of advertising into disrepute. However, what they can grant us – or at least appear to grant us – are the regular human abilities we already possess.

To briefly change our example, we can think of this in terms of the long-standing advertising slogan for Red Bull energy drink: 'Red Bull gives you wings'. We all know the drink does not literally give us wings. However, beneath that first rejection, we don't necessarily reject the idea that Red Bull 'gives us wings' in a more metaphorical and less supernatural sense: by making us more alert and awake. That is certainly one thing that Red Bull can do by virtue of its chemical composition, but depending on a host of other factors, Red Bull can also do other things: like many other caffeinated drinks or energy products, it can make us anxious, nauseous or uncomfortable. The ability of Red Bull to metaphorically give us wings is therefore also in some doubt and depends upon a wide range of complicating other factors. Therefore, the ability of Red Bull to make us alert and awake is also in a sense a fetish, because it promises things that are beyond the ability of the product to deliver on its own. However, 'Red Bull might make you jittery' is a less appealing slogan.

To turn our attention back to the Apple example, we can see how the 'You're more powerful' campaign encourages consumers to understand their ability to successfully engage in fitness, parenting, career or other activates through the fetishistic function of an iPhone. The basic premise of the campaign is that if you have an iPhone you will be able to accomplish all manner of things. However, the point that the ad skirts over is that people are quite capable of accomplishing such things as physical fitness, parenting and creative expression without an expensive smartphone. The fetishism at play here is therefore based on the vague and patently false sense that the consumer will be more powerful – will be a better athlete or parent or artist – following their purchase. This points us towards the other important aspect of fetishism: that the promises of the commodity fetish are not necessarily entirely false, but they are false insofar as the fetish seeks to attribute credit for positive outcomes to commodities rather than human actions and endeavours. The qualities and attributes suggested in the ad are not, after all, properties of the commodities, they are human qualities. The ability to be a good parent or to engage in athletic training are human potentials that require dedication and effort on our part. When a product implies that it can help us attain qualities and products simply through purchase, then this process is referred to as 'alienation'. This act of misrecognition involves the alienation of innately human qualities, which the consumer comes to see as separate from themselves and instead as part of the commodity. In the case of the Apple ads, such advertising encourages the consumer to attribute their sense of themselves as a powerful and capable agent to the commodity, rather than understanding them to be a part of themselves. In this way, the commodity is seen to have the ability to bestow those human qualities that the consumer thinks themselves lacking, but which the commodity can transfer to the consumer upon purchase. Understood in this manner, advertising doesn't so much create new meanings and values, but rather connects commodities with pre-existing meanings and values. We can therefore say that through alienation and fetishism, advertising abstracts human attributes and then sells them back to consumers via the purchase of commodities.

It is important to note, then, that these needs and wants that advertising plays upon are in no way false. Advertisements don't create new meanings, values and wants, but rather they tap into existing aspirations. Consequently, commodity fetishism doesn't just summon up desires out of nowhere: the reason it is so effective is because advertising promises to provide us with qualities (being fun, funny, sophisticated, ironic, rugged, proudly idiotic) and situations (belonging, success, safety) that are already things we want. Advertising therefore isn't creating false desires: it's taking advantage of ones that alright exist (and are in part a product of the anxiety-inducing, constantly competitive conditions of contemporary capitalism). What is false, however, is the idea that the simple purchase of a commodity can help us solve those needs and wants (this is not to say that commodities are completely without use or function: only that they are a relatively small part of achieving our desires). Through the process of advertising, the commodity is thus assigned a power over people which it does not actually possess in any rational or material sense. The fetish does this by promising to transfer desirable human abilities and qualities to the consumer: abilities and qualities which the consumer already possesses the power to enact by virtue of their being an active human agent. Through commodity fetishism, products are selling you yourself and your attributes back to you.

Fetishism and consumerism

What we see in the Apple 'You're more powerful' campaign, then, is a series of images of people finding success which the narrative of the ad encourages us to see as a result of those fictional consumers owning iPhones, rather than as a result of their own efforts. Consequently, through the logic of commodity fetishism, the 'power' on display is being enabled by the Apple products, rather than the consumers themselves and the desirable meanings and identities on display are attributed to commodities, rather than to aspects of those fictional consumers. In this way, consumers are being told that they can also unlock their own potential power through particular consumption practices – by which they can buy access to those qualities that (in any logical material assessment) we know they already possess. The Apple ad is therefore promising to sell consumers their own power, which the ad has led them to misattribute to the product. Like Dumbo's feather that he thought allowed him to fly (in the Disney movie of the same name), ownership of a material object is mistakenly thought to be the only way that we can gain access to powers which are ours all along. This is why the concepts of the commodity and fetishism are so important for understanding the workings of advertising, because the logic of commodity fetishism is at the heart of advertising's appeal and its ability to lead us to misperceive our own interests and abilities.

It's also well worth noting that this misperception isn't simply some form of sinister deception, but actually serves a fundamental economic function in the context of consumer capitalism. If the promises of advertising were more in keeping with what commodities could deliver, then there is a good chance that people would be happy enough with the limited improvements in their lives when they buy a new toaster, cardigan or SUV. However, satisfaction doesn't really have a place in the economic logic of consumerism, which requires consumption to be frequent and ongoing. Oddly enough, where satisfaction fails the inevitable failure of commodities to deliver on the benefits implied by advertising might actually help encourage spending. This is because the failure of the iPhone 5s to deliver mastery over all aspects of life isn't experienced in terms of the larger system of commodity fetishism. Instead, the continued inability of a given consumer to get their life in perfect Apple-advertising style order is experienced in the more limited sense of the individual product. After all, why would we ever expect a phone to solve all our problems? This return to cool-headed rationality doesn't prevent us from buying more though. If anything, it does the opposite, because where one purchase fails to transform us into a perfect human specimen, there's always the chance of the next purchase, which holds out hope: the next model of smartphone, the addition of a new car which will talk to the phone, the purchase of the right sneakers. There's always something more to purchase in our pursuit of advertising's promise of security, satisfaction and power, and if we haven't realised all our dreams yet, it's because the instant we unwrap our new product it transforms from fetish into object – from exchange value to use value – and in that moment it loses all its supernatural powers. Ironically, it is therefore because commodities can't actually help us do these things we see in advertisements that we keep going back for more.

From commodity to commodity-sign

What then is the final consequence of all this? Is the lesson of commodity fetishism simply that we should ensure that we only ever look at commodities with coldly rational eyes in order to see them for what they actually are? Do we just have to wake up? However appealing such an approach might sound when first confronted with the concept of commodity fetishism, in practice the questions posed by commodity fetishism cannot be answered on an individual level. This is because the processes of commodity production, circulation and promotion do not happen at an individual level. These are undeniably inextricably social processes, and this means that commodity fetishism cannot be challenged in any real way by individuals, but instead can only be addressed on the level of a community or a society. Advertising isn't simply about talking to us as individuals, it's about addressing large groups and communities of potential consumers, and it is for this reason that Robert Goldman and Stephen Papson refer to advertising as the industrial organisation of the assignation of meaning to goods (2006, p. 327). When we recognise, following Goldman, that advertising is an industrial process, or that it at least operates on a scale comparable to industry, then we are faced with a situation where the actions of an individual are not sufficient to bring about change. The purchasing choices of one person are not enough to influence the output of a factory, because a factory works on a larger scale, and the same is true of advertising, which similarly produces consumer fetishism on a social level.

Operating on such a wide level, the question then becomes whether commodity fetishism is actually a mistaken understanding of the commodity? Such a position is implied in the Marxist focus on use value that can be seen in the work of Jhally mentioned earlier or in Raymond Williams' denunciation of the 'magic system' in the previous chapter. However, other writers on advertising have suggested that fetishism might not be so much a mistake as a realisation of the new conditions of capitalism, in which advertising plays a central part. Jean Baudrillard refers to this new condition of capitalism as a passage from political economy to the 'political economy of the sign': a movement from commodity to 'commodity-sign', where the meaning of the commodity becomes the main reason for its production, distribution and consumption

(1981, pp. 146–147). Under such conditions, fetishism is no longer a mistake, but a realisation of the real relations of production that drive contemporary consumerism. In this new world we no longer consume products, but rather we consume meanings, which is to say 'signs'.

While, historically, capitalism has worked to generate profit through the production of 'things', Baudrillard argues that the rise of advertising had led to a profound shift in the central logic of capitalism. As a result of the meaning, ideas and particularly the fetishes of advertising, ads are no longer a distraction: they are the main event. As such, the 'sign value', or meaning, of a commodity comes to take precedence over the physical existence of that commodity. What this means in practice is that capitalism becomes about the buying and selling of meanings, such that the commodities are simply the physical container for those meanings. What's more, because it is impossible to purchase meanings in the abstract, those meanings are rooted to particular products through the work of advertising and those products are then put up for sale. The advent of the commodity-sign over the commodity thus marks a situation where advertising has become more important than the product itself. This, then, is advertising regarded not as an addition to an existing product – an addition that manipulates and distorts the consumer's relation to the product – but as the truth of the commodity: as the real motivation that the commodity exists at all. Under these conditions, capitalism becomes about the exchange of meanings rather than objects and, consequently, fetishism can be understood as the correct recognition of a shift in capitalism towards the production and exchange of meaning for profit rather than objects.

The rise of the commodity-sign marks a final twist in ways of thinking about the relation between advertising and commodities, which no longer appear as solutions to particular problems or aids for a particular function, but rather become the material aspect of the sign: the concrete object one purchases in order to gain access to the values and ideas presented in the advertising. In this chapter, we've considered the concept of the commodity and how it can help us make sense of the economic, social and political role of advertising. While the idea of the commodity as the material object of purchase is in many ways opposed to the stories, images and aspirations of advertising, in practice the two aspects of the commodity are deeply entwined, as becomes clear through a consideration of the centrality of fetishism to advertising culture.

The life cycle of the commodity

Through an examination of Apple iProducts, we've looked at how a commodity contains both use and exchange value, and how those different types of value rise to the surface at different moments of a product's life cycle. At the moment of selling, it is the exchange value that is very much in control, and therefore advertising and exchange value become closely interlinked. Whereas the use value can be understood as arising out of the material conditions of production and use – the resource extraction, the labour of workers in different international locations, the global movements of distribution systems – such meanings tend to drop away in our encounters with commodities. Instead, we engage with products as if they appeared on our shelves from out of nowhere. Apple iProducts are more likely to be understood in terms of dancing silhouettes, historical geniuses and good parenting practices, rather than in terms of the teams of Chinese labourers who assemble the products under difficult conditions.

It is the centrality of these images, stories and values, which arise out of the relations of marketing rather than the relations of production, that form the basis of commodity fetishism. We are all aware that advertising makes us promises that it cannot follow through on. Advertising draws on widespread desires for security, popularity and liberty in order to make products seem desirable. In this way commodities are transformed into fetishes: inanimate objects that promise powers and abilities the likes of which could never be delivered through a simple act of purchase. We know these promises are hollow and that an iPhone won't make us fitter or a better parent, but the ongoing success of the consumption economy suggests that despite our declarations that we don't believe advertising, we nonetheless act as if we do. The search for transformations and empowerment of the self through purchase is almost inevitably doomed to failure, and it is this failure that keeps the consumer economy ticking along, because most of us seem to keep going back for more.

To be clear, not many people, if any, are exempt from this: I'm certainly not. The belief in commodity fetish isn't an individual failing; it's a social and economic structure that lies at the heart of advertising. However, that doesn't mean that we shouldn't give up thinking how and why we consume and whether we're actually purchasing the thing or the ideas that have been constructed and communicated around it. However, at the same time, we also need to think about how the meanings of commodities can be as real as the products themselves. The symbolic or social use of a commodity in order to gain status or communicate ideas about self-identity to others, for example, is no less real than a physical use – something which we'll think about more in the next chapter. With the purported passage from the commodity to the commodity-sign, the point here is not to hold up one set of uses as correct and proper, but to note the ways in which cultural uses of commodities in particular are bound up in wider questions about society, the role of ideology and the distribution of power. Advertising does more than just provide information about products, but is instead always caught up in wider processes of communication about how and why commodities mean and how they structure our lives. However, we need to be aware that the communication around commodities produced by advertising is just one way of talking about production and consumption and far from the whole story. By learning more about commodities we can therefore learn more about not just products but also about the economic and cultural systems set up around them, and the central role of advertising in both.

CHAPTER 6

Audiences for sale: Quantification, segmentation and personalisation

When it comes to purchasing everyday consumables – like toothpaste, soap or beer – pretty much everyone has a set of preferences as to which products they prefer. The reasons for these preferences can differ: some might feel loyalty to a familiar product or perceive it as reliable or superior; others might be on the lookout for something new; and some people might think particular brands speak to them and their way of life. However, what all of these different reasons for purchasing do share in common is a connection with how we understand our own actions and identity in the context of consumer culture. In this chapter, we'll be turning our attention to the various ways in which advertising contributes to our understanding of self-identity and social groups in a capitalist context. While one familiar way of approaching this topic might be to think about the different identity categories that are produced in advertising and the controversies that arise around them – for example, debates around the representation of women in advertising – we'll be pushing our investigation further to consider a range of possible interrelations between advertising, audiences and identity. For example, even before an audience interprets an ad, their identity is already being shaped in relation to it: this is because from the perspective of media companies audiences are commodities to be bought and sold.

We'll begin by introducing a hugely influential historical account of how advertising produces a stupefied, conformist audience, before thinking in more detail about how the audience might be considered as a commodity and the ramifications of such a perspective. We'll then turn our attention to the historical shift from a mass audience to a fragmented audience, and consider what advertisers have to gain from separating society into different segments and how such separation draws on pre-existing structures of social distinction,

Finally, we'll consider how online advertising might be ushering in an age of the audience-of-one as we move from fragmentation and then close with a reassessment of how the changing nature of the advertising audience matches or departs from the predictions of cultural conformity. As is hopefully clear from the last chapter, advertising performs an important cultural and social role beyond the provision of information about particular products, and part of that larger role of advertising involves producing what we will refer to as consumer identity. As we explore the different ways that advertising helps construct consumer identity, you'll be introduced to a range of perspectives regarding the relationship between advertising, its audiences and its ability to appeal, steer and even shape your sense of who you are.

The audience as commodity

One of the fundamental truths of advertising is that its purpose is to sell goods and services. Even if a given ad isn't directly selling you something, then it will still be engaging you with the purpose of selling you something further down the track or setting you up to make a particular purchase decision. What this means in terms of identity is that first and foremost the relation between advertising and its audiences is premised upon a perception of the audience as people who might buy things. Along the way, the audience can be entertained, informed, shamed, excited, enthused, frightened or bewildered, just as is the case with other media texts. However, in the case of advertising, the audience will always also be addressed as an audience composed of potential consumers: a group who are being asked to spend their money in particular ways. This is what separates advertising from other forms of communication: the manner in which advertising assumes its audience to be potential consumers.

'Advertising turns into terror'

This foundational fact of an audience for sale informed some of the earliest and most critical accounts of advertising's potential effects upon its audience. Writing in the 1940s, Max Horkheimer and Theodor Adorno were worried that advertising was going to lead the way into a terrifying cultural dark age. At the heart of their concern was the fear that the profit motive would become so overwhelming that all forms of culture would collapse into an undifferentiated, unthinking and underwhelming ooze that catered only to the lowest common denominator. They referred to this sad state of affairs as the 'culture industry' and suggested that advertising was both the model and the 'elixir of life' for these new mass media forms that were only interested in extracting money rather than contributing to society in the ways traditionally expected of culture (1972, p. 162). Advertising led the way by demonstrating how culture could be planned and made to schedule by groups of technicians cobbling together elements to meet a client's technical brief:

> The assembly-line character of the culture industry, the synthetic, planned method of turning out its products (...) is very suited to advertising: the important individual points, by becoming detachable, interchangeable, and even technically alienated from any connected meaning, lend themselves to ends external to the work. The effect, the trick, the isolated repeatable device, have always been used to exhibit goods for advertising purposes, and today every monster close-up of a star is an advertisement for her name, and every hit song a plug for its tune.
>
> (1972, p. 163)

For Horkheimer and Adorno, advertising had perfected the art of assembling culture for purposes external to itself: not for the sake of expression or argument or illumination, but in order to sell toasters and cosmetics. The consequences for audiences of this race to the bottom is that, according to Horkheimer and Adorno's model, advertising works to stultify and stupefy everyone it comes into contact with. Advertising makes us dumb, because it never expects its audience to work: what little it has to tell us about the world it gives up as easily and obviously as it can. As a form of culture, advertising trains us not to think too deeply or too carefully, but instead to slide off the surface of texts and to be satisfied with flash and novelty, rather than any deeper meaning. Consequently, any truths that advertising offers us are almost necessarily shallow truths designed to satisfy and placate its audience rather than challenge them. From this perspective, to say that advertising doesn't respect its audience's intelligence doesn't go far enough: for Horkheimer and Adorno advertising actively works to make people stupider and rob life of deeper meanings.

This is obviously a very grim assessment of advertising and its relationship to its audience and coming at what, in retrospect, might seem like a very early and innocent moment in the history of advertising it may seem somewhat misguided or even melodramatic. However, we need to be aware of the extent to which arguments like that offered by Horkheimer and Adorno have been central to wider thinking about advertising and its relationship to audiences. While potentially a little over-the-top, the dire predictions of the culture industry thesis crystallise an important and influential opposition to advertising as a site of misdirection and exploitation of audiences that continues to influence contemporary discussions. Advertising has obviously changed a lot since the 1940s, and there's no way Horkheimer and Adorno could have predicted the explosive diversity of contemporary advertising, nor the extent to which it has increasingly invaded every aspect of our lives. Nonetheless, Horkheimer and Adorno's gloomy account of advertising's impact continues to resonate with both academic and popular critiques of advertising, and therefore the first reason their account is still relevant is because it provides us with a solid platform from which to launch an investigation of different takes on consumer identity and subjectivity.

Eyeballs and clicks

As was famously noted by critical communications scholar Dallas Smythe, the audience's status as a commodity means that from the perspective of the advertiser, the audience is not first and foremost made of individuals, but rather units to be bought and sold (1981, p. 242). This, of course, doesn't happen in a material sense – the buying and selling of human beings is after all what we refer to as slavery– but instead takes place in terms of the gathering and sale of audience attention. This perception of audiences as units of attention is perhaps most clearly expressed in the industry lingo of 'eyeballs' or increasingly frequently in terms of 'clicks'. An 'eyeball' refers to a pair of eyes that has seen an advertisement: be it on television, a billboard or a website. A 'click' is a more recent term and refers to the action whereby an online advertisement is clicked on with a mouse by users. Both terms are quantitative measurements of attention that seek to characterise an ad in terms of how many people encountered it and, in terms of clicks, interacted with it in the most basic way.

Both terms also share in common a reduction of the audience to a precise body part – either the eyeball or the index finger – rather than understanding them as a thinking and feeling person. Viewed in such a way, the audience member is simply a pair of eyes and a finger: a representation that leaves out the majority of body parts, perhaps most importantly, the brain. What disappears, then, from this perspective is any activity that would be carried out by the brain: any sense of the interpretation or intention on the part of the audience; any emotional or intellectual response to an ad; even any gathering of information about what the product is and why we might buy it. When thinking in terms of eyeballs and clicks, the advertiser does not care how much attention you actually paid to the ad, if you did or didn't like it, whether you were offended by it or even if you clicked upon it accidently. Such responses are factored into the process according to statistical models (Smythe, 1981, p. 235). All that matters is the fact of encounter between the audience and the ad, removed from any other context. To understand the audience in terms of eyeballs and clicks is thus to understand them not as people but as elements of raw data. This is a somewhat dehumanising and potentially dispiriting way to think about yourself: not as an empowered consumer, but as an indistinguishable looking and clicking machine. In this sense, the earlier comparison with slavery is a little bit telling, because while the economic quantification of attention is clearly light-years away from forced labour, our society still tends to be uncomfortable with calculations that blatantly present human life in economic terms.

Of course, all this leaves a very important question unanswered: who is doing all this buying and selling? In the context of advertising, we are usually accustomed to thinking about the audience as the potential buyers and the advertisers as the potential sellers. However, as stated at the beginning of this section, the audience is not here figured as the buyer, but rather as the commodity: the thing to be bought and sold. The secret to this transformation of the audience lies in the logic of eyeballs and clicks that allows for the advertising audience to be easily abstracted from their specific contexts and counted. Once the audience is converted into a standard interchangeable unit (i.e. a commodity) the so-called consumer can now be sold by media programmers to advertisers, and by advertisers to their clients. This relation is premised on a small but radical shift in how we think about the purpose of advertising, which is as much about delivering audiences to companies as it is about delivering messages to audiences. This is important enough to bear repeating: advertising is not just about selling products to consumers; it's also about *selling audiences to companies*. Under this arrangement, audiences are lured by the 'free lunch' of entertainment and information and then sold to advertisers by media programmers (Jhally, 1990, p. 67). Thus, it is not simply that there exists an 'implied bargain', whereby audiences accept advertisements in exchange for free entertainment and information (Sinclair, 2012, p. 53), but the audience is being gathered up and sold on to advertisers. Once we understand this point, a whole new way of conceptualising advertising opens up.

The consequences of clicks

The transition from a vague 'eyeball'-based system to a measurable click-based system has had several notable impacts on the form of internet content and the economics of online advertising. Whereas in the past the tools available for measuring audience exposure to any given advert were necessarily crude, digital advertising allows for the gathering of precise data so as to not only know how often a keyword forms the basis for a search, but how many people then click on the ad to access the advertised website or product. The ability to measure 'clicks' means that advertisers no longer have to rely on media statistics, or assume that viewers will pay attention, but instead can see exactly when and where an advertisement is generating attention and interest. This threatens one of the most fundamental and, until now unmeasurable, assumptions regarding advertising - that if you put advertising out there, people will pay attention to it.

In terms of form, it has created an economic incentive for 'slide-show' style webpages where users have to click through a series of images or pages as part of a list or story. Such sites are colloquially referred to as 'click-bait' because they require the user to click multiple times while reading, which provides space for multiple ads and increases the amount of measured traffic on the web page. Click-bait also refers to intentionally polemic or controversial content on websites, which increases user traffic and therefore desirability to advertisers, even if site visitors do not engage with the material at any length. Such techniques of using controversy to generate interest and therefore profit certainly preceded digital advertising, but are being exacerbated under new online conditions. It's also worth noting that click-based systems also create new opportunities for exploitation as media producers create programmes to either artificially inflate the amount of clicks on their website in order to increase their desirability in the eyes of advertisers, or to increase clicks on the advertisements of rivals (as click advertising often involves a contract whereby companies pay for each additional click, rather than paying a lump sum in advance, this technique can bankrupt a rival's advertising budget [Spurgeon, 2008, p. 31]).

The price of an audience

Probably the most immediate manifestation of the audience of commodity can be seen in the relative prices paid for advertising time in media like television and billboards at different times and in different places. It is no secret that the most expensive advertising time in the world is during the Super Bowl, the annual final of America's National Football League competition: this fact is trumpeted every year during the news media coverage of the Super Bowl and its advertising, with the astronomical sums (with predictions of a five million dollar price tag for a 30-second slot in 2016 [Ourand, 2015]) serving as a rationale for the attention paid. It is also not a secret that, even beyond major sporting events, a 30-second television slot during primetime is more expensive than the same section of time at midnight or noon, or that it costs more to advertise on billboards along major roads and highways than in bus shelters in the suburbs. However, despite the obvious common sense (one might even say 'ideological') nature of these calculations, the implications of the underlying logic are not always so clear, particularly as they relate to advertising audiences. This is because while it might seem that advertisers are purchasing the rights to particular instances of time and space (i.e. five million for 30 seconds) they are actually purchasing the rights to audience attention, which is measured in terms of the eyeballs and clicks. Advertisers don't buy time on television or space in magazines, rather they buy the audience associated with the time and space. The larger the audience, the larger the price that can be charged for a unit of time (in broadcast media) or space (in print and outdoors media). Thus, even before the audience is addressed by an advertisement, and regardless of the actual content of the advertisement, the audience is bought and sold. This means that they are not people or interpreters of meaning, but rather commercial units and, in the first instance, the audience of advertising is being thought of by advertisers as a commodity rather than a community.

Viewed from such a position, it thus becomes possible to grasp the importance of advertising, and the role of the advertising audience in particular, to the wider structure and purpose of the mass media more generally. Advertising is not just an interruption in between television and radio broadcasts or articles and stories in print, neither is it a slightly awkward intrusion in films, video games or sporting events, nor simply the background clutter of online and outdoor spaces. Advertising is actually the reason why most of those media and material spaces operate in the way that they do, and in some cases the reason why they exist at all. This is particularly well documented in the case of television, where advertising isn't simply an afterthought for broadcasters: it is the reason that the infrastructure and institution of television exists in the first instance (Smythe, 1981, pp. 236–240).

Consequently, from the perspective of the audience commodity, the regular hierarchy of advertising and media content is inverted: it is not advertisements that interrupt television shows or web browsing; it is television shows and web browsing that interrupt the ads. Such a way of approaching advertising flips our normal understanding on its head: TV does not exist to show us programmes with ads getting in the way; TV exists to show us ads, and programmes are the bait to get us there. Hence, while we might be offended or concerned when we hear stories about advertisers exerting direct pressure on television producers to exclude or include certain content, such reactions fail to appreciate that such actions are not deviations, but just the regular business of media production, where advertising comes first and programming second. As such, the moral shock that often accompanies revelations of advertiser interference (such as news media failing to report on the failings of a major corporate advertiser) can be considered an analogue to Jean Baudrillard's contention regarding Disneyland: that it exists to hide the fact that the entire world is a land of corporate-controlled make-believe (1994, pp. 12–13). In the same way, scandals around advertisers exerting control over programme content hide the fact that such control is simply an expression of the foundational logic of capitalist media production. Television programmes and other media content only exist in the first place in order to deliver audiences to advertisers.

What this all means, then, is that at the end of the day, 'the purpose of the mass media is to produce audiences to sell to the advertisers' (Smythe, 1981, p. 242). The audience (or more particularly audience attention) is a commodity that is produced by media content providers and sold to advertisers for an amount that depends upon the quantity of eyeballs, clicks or other quantitative measures of audience 'engagement'. It is because of this fact – because of the role of the advertising audience as a commodity – that media content is always driven to attract the largest number of eyeballs or clicks. One of the consequences of this arrangement is that the goal of media content is to attract the largest possible audience to sell to advertisers, and therefore there exists a possible tendency towards unsophisticated and unchallenging media content bemoaned by Horkheimer and Adorno. Thus, we can see that when the advertising audience is reduced to the status of a commodity, the ramifications of this political economic logic can seem very grim indeed. Moreover, despite what might appear to be the overly bleak nature of the predictions that arise from the audience-as-commodity, we nonetheless need to acknowledge the explanatory power of this model and how it explains and predicts most of the patterns and tendencies around the buying and selling of advertising. And that is why when we are considering the nature of the advertising audience, this is the first fact we must take on board: in the context of advertising, audiences are commodities to be bought and sold.

Breaking down the audience: Fragmentation, segmentation and distinction

At the time that Horkheimer and Adorno were originally writing – during the advent of the modern era of advertising in the 1940s and 1950s – the commercial logic of advertising meant that most advertisements were still aimed at what we might consider a 'mass audience'. In the first half of the twentieth century the main purpose of most ads was to gather as large an audience as was possible. As we saw in Chapter 2, the resulting advertising was formulaic, safe and conservative in its presentation and address because it placed a higher priority on avoiding offence than distinguishing one product from another. Given the relatively under-developed nature of consumer capitalism at the time, this approach to advertising made sense: not only were people unaccustomed to sorting themselves via their purchases, but the percentage of the population with enough wealth to engage in consumer capitalism was much smaller than it is today. As such there was no effort on the part of the advertising industry to break down the potential consumer base into different groups for different product. Instead, the goal of the majority of advertising was to appeal to as many consumers as possible across as wide a social span as possible in order to reach the largest audience for any given product.

We must remember, though, that despite the conception of this audience as a 'mass', the widespread, socially determined opinions of the time meant that in the majority of cases consumers were presumed to be white, middle-class and male (with limited acknowledgement that women might also be interested in purchasing particular sorts of specifically gendered goods like cleaning products and kitchen aides). In contrast to its aspirations to universality, the mass audience of early advertising did not encompass everyone in society, but rather a very particular segment who were deemed to be only able and desirable participants in the new forms of consumer culture. Consequently, ads were overwhelmingly sexist and racist in their exclusionary address to white men, and also occasionally in their content. For example, an infamous ad for Schlitz beer which has had a prominent afterlife on the internet depicts a suited man comforting his crying wife by telling her 'Don't worry darling, you didn't burn the beer!' Yet, regardless of this tunnel vision with respect to possible audiences – which at that time was characteristic of most forms of the dominant media culture and in no way limited to advertising – within the scope of their own limited perspective, advertisers were trying to reach all of a potential audience at once. This approach to advertising would not survive the following decades though, as an expansion in the consumer population would combine with increasing competition between different products and brands to produce a series of fractures and fragmentations in the advertising audience.

The fragmented advertising audience

As we know from experience, contemporary advertising no longer addresses all of us as one undifferentiated mass – rather, advertising addresses us as members of specific groups and communities. There is advertising for young girls, teenage boys, suburban parents, corporate types, retirees, those on a budget and those with little concerns regarding money, those with aspirations towards sophistication and those who consider themselves to be beyond such material concerns. Depending on who you are and what you're being sold, you might be confronted by images of verdant nature or inner-city graffiti, suburban comfort or rural toughness, imaginary conquest or everyday drama as part of a finely wrought effort to appeal to your particular preferences and proclivities (or what a marketer has decided are most likely to be your preference and proclivities). Such distinctions are commonly referred to as demographics or demographic profiling: terms that are no longer restricted to advertising discourse, but have increasingly found their way into everyday consciousness as ways of thinking about different social groups. As a result, the division of the advertising audience into demographics is no longer something that happens behind closed doors, but rather is something of an open secret. In the twenty-first century, very few people are surprised, let alone offended, to discover that they've been placed into a particular category by marketers and advertisers in order to more effectively sell them goods.

The breaking down of the advertising audience into particular demographic groups defined by interests and identity markers such as age, race, wealth, level of education and gender is known by many names, including fragmentation, segmentation and nichification.

These different names emphasise different aspects of this transformation: segmentation and fragmentation focus on the dividing up of the previous mass audience, whereas nichification presents this as a constructive process whereby new forms of identity and community are identified or in some cases even constructed from scratch. The definition of niche, in this sense, follows the ecological meaning of the term which refers to a particular set of behaviours adopted by a species in a given environment. In marketing terms, a niche refers to a group of potential consumers defined by a particular set of interests, needs and consumer demands. Whatever name we give this process, it is the reason that different ads are played during daytime talk shows, evening news, sports games and animated comedies. Each of these different television genres attracts a different audience, which is attractive to different advertisers selling different products. Thus, we are sold cleaning products during the day, banking and financial products during the news, luxury goods during the golf and energy drinks during animated comedies (in New Zealand, we also have the added bonus of being sold farming supplies during the rugby!). This process also works within products – some brands of cosmetics will target different age groups and class backgrounds by advertising with different approaches in different media spaces. Similarly, different beer brands will advertise during major sporting games, late night news and current affairs or comedy shows depending upon how they wish to position themselves to particular consumers. For example, generally speaking, major domestic brands sponsor sports, imported beers will target news programming and niche sports, and low-cost brands will target youth-orientated programming. This process of carving up audiences into smaller and smaller audiences is the result of a confluence of social, economic and technological changes.

Constructing advertising niches

In technological terms, nichification has been enabled first by technological developments such as cable and satellite TV, which allowed for a proliferation of channels based on different viewer interests. Hence, rather than just a few major networks showing programming that was relatively similar in content and delivery, cable and satellite distribution systems allowed for specialised channels focusing on interests such as sports, cooking, history and animals, or demographics, such as young men, middle-aged women, children and queer communities. This increased diversity was also matched in other media forms, such as magazines, where word-processing software meant that it was possible to produce content targeted to much more precise audience segments. More recently, the advent of online distribution for audio, video and 'print' media has meant that content options have increased exponentially. Whereas several decades ago advertising space was at a premium, with only a handful of television channels, radio stations and major print publications, the widespread adoption of internet-based media has meant that the possible time and space for hosting content – and therefore hosting advertising – has increased to the point where they are almost infinite. Whereas space in which to advertise was once limited by media platforms, the internet means that there is always more content which can be monetised through the inclusion of advertising (though not necessarily more audience attention to go around!). The consequences of this expansion is both an ability to pinpoint precise audience niches and a changing economic situation, where an increase in supply of space in which to advertise potentially leads to a decrease in the cost of advertising in some of those spaces. As a result, in multichannel and online environments it is now possible and profitable to target advertising to groups defined not just by gender or age but also by their interest in medical ethics, retro video games or gluten-free cooking.

However, advertising nichification should not be considered simply a result of changing technologies. It also needs to be understood as a consequence of the economic process of audience commodification, which values efficiency and segmentation as organising principles. This is an important revision of the audience-as-commodity, which Horkheimer and Adorno feared would result in the reduction of everything to the same undifferentiated sludge. That their grim prediction (arguably) failed to eventuate is not because their fundamental model of advertising was wrong, but rather because they could not foresee how changing technologies would create a new environment: one where larger profits can be extracted by conceptualising the audience in terms of difference and separating it out accordingly. Thus, just as time and space were rationalised into discrete units during the Industrial Revolution, 'nichification' rationalises the mass audience into discrete groups in order to more efficiently extract profits by ensuring that targeted messages only reach appropriate audiences and thereby eliminating unproductive and costly waste. 'Waste' in this sense is waste eyeballs or clicks: advertiser spending that reaches audiences who are unlikely to buy the product or service being advertised. For example, every audience member who views an advertisement for Heineken but who cannot or does not drink beer, or who has no desire to pay a little more for beer, amounts to wasted advertising spending. By focusing their messages at particular niches, advertisers cut down on wasted advertising spending represented by appealing to groups who are not inclined to purchase the advertised product. This also means that advertising messages can be tailored so that they appeal to the particular targeted audiences with, for example, fun and silly advertising during comedies and serious and sophisticated advertising during current affairs shows.

Fragmented society

It is necessary to note, though, that in distributing their advertising in this way, advertisers are not only reflecting and responding to social differences, but also constructing and reinforcing these beliefs and assumptions about their audience. As Iain MacRury suggests 'consumer research is not, as it might seem, an act of discovery – a light shone to reveal the hitherto unseen or unacknowledged. Instead research can be understood as an operation which, in the act of "description", functionally constructs its objects' (2009, p. 70). The search for markets therefore becomes some of a self-fulfilling prophecy: advertising doesn't just reflect the fragmentation of the audience; it attempts to reproduce and perpetuate audience fragmentation in order to generate profit. Timothy deWaal Malefyt and Brian Moeran even suggest that advertisers are responsible for the creation of social groups such as 'yuppies, guppies, generation X, [and] early adopters' (2012, p. 16). This process can have real social consequences, where differences between different sectors of society are emphasised and barriers to communication and interaction are formed. It's also relevant to note here that in a further extension of the logic of audience commodification, different groups are worth different amounts of money. Thus, although televised golf commands a relatively small audience, that audience is disproportionately white, male and wealthy and therefore desirable to advertisers of luxury goods, like first-class air travel and designer watches, that do not wish to reach a mass audience who cannot afford their product. Given the central role of advertising in financing broadcast media, this is the reason why there are more television channels dedicated to golf than to more popular sports like football or basketball. Media programmers can charge the same and sometimes even more for advertising which reaches small wealthy audiences with more discretionary income than large, but relatively less wealthy, audiences.

Therefore, while the logic of advertising nichification may lead to an expanded range of media options, we need to understand that this increased range is still driven by the central conception of audience as commodity. As a result, there is a distinct disparity with regards to the new audiences opened up through nichification, as media content that is thought to appeal to wealthy consumers is prioritised over content that might appeal to other audiences. If we understand this point with an eye to the wider disparities of capitalist society – where economic privilege often aligns with other markers of social advantage, such as education level, urban locations and skin colour – then it becomes apparent how the apparent increasing diversity of niche programming is actually rather narrowly focused. Certain niche interests, such as arts and crafts, literature, home décor, travel and technology, are catered for extensively: in such instances, there is also the added 'bonus' that they easily lend themselves to the marketing of related products. It is more difficult to point towards those activities that are excluded by this logic, because the lack of profitability means that they have not crystallised into easily identifiable 'activities', although we might think about DIY reality programming as indicative of one potential audience that receives relatively minimal attention in televisual and online media spaces. The diversity that arises out of nichification thus needs to be recognised as a diversity that is driven by profit and therefore excludes many groups and interests as a matter of course. Certain profitable groups have access to a range of media content designed to expose them to particular advertising, while other sections of society are largely excluded. At its extremes, the logic of the niche audience can call into question the viability of programming that meets the desires, interests and world views of larger, but less wealthy, audiences.

Conspicuous consumption

It is obviously not true that advertisements only target wealthy consumers. While a narrow focus on nichification might make it seem as if advertising only ever addresses precisely formed audiences, our own personal experiences should remind us that a great deal of advertising still addresses us en masse, whether it be during the nightly news, on busy streets, subway platforms or prominent ads on major websites (smaller ads on prominent websites are another matter again, as we will consider near the end of this chapter). Yet, just because an advert is placed in a context where it can be viewed by many people, it doesn't necessarily mean that it's for everyone. On the most basic level, not all products are for all consumers, and some ads rely upon audience knowledge and interest that will not be present in all audience members. Differences within and between groups can also be used to advertise and sell products. On a more advanced level, we can also think about how – as is the case with nichification – advertising can also create new separations and groups in order to move products. One of the major ways in which advertising does this is through the production and mobilisation of 'distinction': a social force or set of ideas that judges, classifies and sorts society in terms of a hierarchy of cultural interests, likes and dislikes.

Distinction and taste

Perhaps the simplest mode of distinction is conspicuous consumption: a term coined by Thorstein Veblen to describe the purchase and display of goods in order to communicate one's social status (2000, pp. 194–195). In more colloquial terms, we might refer to this as 'keeping up with the Joneses', and it is certainly an important and relevant aspect of consumer society, where the consumption of certain goods can be used to indicate personal wealth and economic power. The more one is seen to consume and own, especially in terms of discretionary and wasteful spending, the more one's economic power is communicated. Conspicuous consumption has played a long and central role in advertising, with products being pitched as a way to indicate one's power and success in life. Advertisements emphasise how the consumption of certain products can help the consumer stand out and communicate their superiority to other members of their community. Examples of such advertising might include luxury cars, imported beer, high fashion: anything that can stand as an implicit marker of wealth and status. Conspicuous consumption, however, is a relatively simplistic idea and fails to account for how often our purchases don't reflect owning more goods or more expensive goods, but owning classier or cooler or just 'better' products. Rarely do products present themselves as simply more expensive. Instead they are more sophisticated or classy (and they just happen to be more expensive!). This more complicated understanding of the desirability to certain products, and their relation to different social groups, can be approached in terms of the idea of taste.

Taste refers to the sense of what you like, dislike, enjoy, despite and seek out on both a sensual and intellectual level. While taste might appear to be a natural thing – we all like what we like – in a ground-breaking series of influential studies during the 1960s and 1970s, the French sociologist Pierre Bourdieu traced the relationship between upbringing, education and taste in order to draw out how our reactions to different texts, products and art forms can tell us a lot about social stratification. At the heart of Bourdieu's model is the idea that 'taste classifies and it classifies the classifier' (1993, p. 6). With this complicated phrase, Bourdieu articulates two aspects of the social operation of taste: first, the way in which we exercise our taste to establish categories and assign different objects to those categories: second, we can tell a lot from the way in which we judge objects and texts and exercise our taste. Thus, we distinguish ourselves by the distinctions we make, or, in other words, we can tell a lot about a person from the way they judge cultural objects. Bourdieu is particularly interested in how taste is distributed across different social classes and can even work to legitimise and naturalise those class distinctions. For example, those raised in a wealthy and privileged environment are more likely to seek out cultural and consumer goods that are presented as sophisticated, classy and refined, whereas those brought up in working-class environments are more likely to seek out cultural and consumer goods that are presented as authentic, down-to-earth and satisfying. Note that neither category constructs itself as inferior: both understand their preferences as inherently desirable and superior.

What, though, does this have to do with advertising? Well, advertising is the central site in our society for the formation, mobilisation and perpetuation of taste. This is true of not only the products being sold but also the advertisements themselves. This means more than just images of luxury and excess, and can also take the form of experimental or artistic advertising. The famous VW 'Think Small' campaign can be understood as a process of marking the productive as desirable, not through images of luxury but through a defiance of aesthetic conventions. In many cases, despite fundamentally similar or even identical products, advertisements will represent those products in wildly different ways. For example, goods can attempt to situate themselves as refined and artistic through an advertising campaign that draws on markers of sophisticated taste.

As the markers of what constitutes high or sophisticated taste are constantly changing (and by their very nature often localised) it can be difficult to pin down exactly what this means, but Heineken's global 'The Man of the World' campaign from the 2010s serves as a pretty good illustration. 'The Man of the World' includes commercials such as 'The Date', 'The Switch', 'The Express' and 2014's 'The City'. This last example is almost a blow-by-blow account of an attempt to capture 'high-class': in an attempt to return a lost wallet to a mysterious women, a man travels the back alleys of Hong Kong visiting several stylish locales. Along the way, he receives a high-end haircut and shave and a tailored suit, learns to dance, wins a horse race and plays in a piano bar, before locating the missing woman, with whom he shares a Heineken while riding in a private gondola above the city's skyline (he also refuses to enter one location: a yoga studio). Multi-cultural, multi-talented, brightly coloured, tastefully outfitted but not precious, 'The City' is an excellent example of a particular vision of aspirational taste: one that is not only markedly urban, but also urbane. With a shared aesthetic of tailored suits, jazz-inflected soundtracks and mini-narratives revolving around a secret knowledge of urban cool, the 'Man of the World' campaign presents a coherent vision of cosmopolitan, globalised sophistication, which continues into other branding such as bottles marked with the names of global cities like New York, Shanghai and Berlin and a website which tells you 'What's hot' in your city. Such advertising thus not only embodies cool sophistication but also promises to extend that sophistication to its consumers.

Taste in beer advertising

Such taste markers don't work in isolation, however: they only make sense in relation to a wider regime of taste. Sticking to beer examples, we can consider an example like Dos Equis' 'Most Interesting Man in the World' campaign, which first aired in the USA in 2006 and has since gained global reach and been widely shared and reproduced online. The ads, which relate the adventures of the titular most interesting man, are on the surface quite similar to the Heineken ads with a similar presentation of tailored suits and crazy adventures. However, the ads are also more openly comic than the Heineken campaign, with the exploits of the interesting man tending towards parodic excess: he does not simply navigate back alleys and charm strangers; he displays superhuman powers and steers world history. Such understated comic irony is often another indicator of sophisticated taste, but relative to the slick presentation of the Heineken campaign the tendency towards clownishness arguably mocks as much as celebrates the pretension to sophistication and epic coolness. Consequently, we can understand the 'Most Interesting Man in the World' as a bit closer to down-to-earth functional taste than 'The Man of the World'.

It is more difficult to locate globally distributed beer ads that are pitched in less 'high-class' terms: by their nature, globally distributed beer brands tend towards images of refined and stylish presentations. Instead, it is national beer brands that usually make appeals based on authenticity and down-to-earth qualities. For example, in New Zealand, Speights beer advertising features farmers, DIYers and those that reject big city life as unmasculine or immoral, while Tui beer presents images of mischievous larrikins who enjoy a laugh and a prank. In Canada, Molson trades on patriotic imagery, whereas in the USA, Budweiser presented the sentimental story of a lost dog in a 2015 super bowl commercial and otherwise draws on representations of friends watching sport, hardworking 'anti-micro' brewers and burgers. In their different ways, all these examples reject the appeals to sophistication seen in international campaigns as being effete, false or otherwise disconnected with the real lives of real people and instead appeal to different consumers by presenting themselves as obvious and unpretentious. In doing so, such advertising demonstrates how ads can successfully appeal to what Bourdieu called the 'popular disposition' as well as high taste (1984, p. 5), in order to sell products.

What we need to remember, though, following Bourdieu, is that these distinctions between sophisticated and authentic, high and low taste are never natural. Rather they are part of larger struggles regarding inequality and dominance expressed here through cultural forms and their relation to different senses of taste. Advertising mobilises existing taste formations and attempts to reinterpret products in terms of different tastes in order to make certain products appear more desirable to different sectors of society. The different modes of address that we can see in ads for brands like Heineken compared to national beer brands not only appeal to different people, but they do so on the basis of well-established and entrenched structures of taste that tend to correlate closely to wealth and upbringing. Moreover, in appealing to those different ideas of taste, such advertising also works to reproduce and reinforce those structures: helping to perpetuate and even exaggerate taste distinctions. Thinking in terms of these distinctions, we can see that advertising therefore not only presents different identities to its consumers, but does so in a way that taps into larger cultural hierarchies. According to Bourdieu's account, this explanation inverts cause and effect because, although refined tastes might appear to be a result of natural superiority, they are actually cultivated through the leisure time and privileged access to culture afforded to the wealthy. Those in a position of privilege have the opportunity to indulge in practices with delayed, difficult or complicated pleasures – such as hypothetically chasing a mysterious girl through the streets of Hong Kong – because of the spare time made possible by their economic wealth. As Bourdieu demonstrated with a series of wide-ranging empirical studies, 'good' taste therefore reflects economic privilege, rather than natural aesthetic aptitude. Taste is therefore not simply a point of difference, but a means for constructing and maintaining social privilege.

From nichification to personalisation

This tendency towards increasing specificity has only intensified with the advent of online and digital advertising to the point where we now encounter the possibility of advertising tailored for an audience of one. New advertising technologies mean that where advertisers once sought to identify particular groups and market segments, they can now aspire to zero in on individuals and appeal to them on a personal level (however, this is not simply a result of new technology, but rather the ways in which new technologies are shaped by the social and economic context into which they emerge [Deuze, 2007, p. 128]). One of the promises of the digital environment is that it enables advertisers 'to leverage information they have on their audience and deliver more personalised advertising, customisable and relevant to them. Personalisation involves consumer data generating content tailored to the individual' (McStay, 2009, p. 34). The use of personal information has resulted in a heated debate around this topic, with some welcoming the advent of more personalised advertising as a break from irrelevant advertising information, while others voice concerns about loss of privacy and the ability of corporations to decide in advance what information, services or products users might be interested in. Joseph Turow, one of the leading scholars in the new world of online advertising, refers to this growing shift towards personalised advertising as 'one of history's most massive stealth efforts in social profiling' (2011, p. 1): a process that is defined by both its promise to provide individually tailored advertising content and the threat of unparalleled levels of surveillance. This transformation has been enabled by new data gathering and online tracking technologies which are simultaneously both a delivery mechanism for advertising and a means for advertisers to build up detailed personal profiles of individual consumers. The changes have been driven by an ever greater focus on targeting and the elimination of advertising 'waste' that we encountered in the initial growth of fragmentation and niches (Turow, 2011, p. 88).

Online data gathering

At the heart of this process is the proliferation of personal data in online spaces. Perhaps the most obvious examples are social media platforms like Facebook. As most readers are probably aware, social media platforms like Facebook (or whatever has replaced Facebook by the time you are reading this!) provide a space for users to construct personal profiles, communicate with friends and families, share photos, links, videos and other online content, and set up events. The social media platform 'closely monitors all ... contacts, communications and data, selling this information to companies, which then send targeted advertising to [users]' (Fuchs, 2012, p. 145). Social media sites thus analyse and process user data in order to build 'reputation profiles' of users that can be used for marketing purposes (Turow, 2011, p. 123). In the immediate context of social media, users will then receive targeted advertising in their social media profile (in the case of Facebook, the precise placement and form of these ads are changing all the time as part of a long-running and ongoing tug of war between Facebook and its users as regards the appropriate visibility of advertising in that space). It is important to note that this data also extends beyond the information gathered as part of a Facebook profile. Not only does Facebook also gather data from its subsidiary platforms, including WhatsApp, Moves and Instagram, all of which are owned by Facebook, but it also encompasses all those websites which one can sign into via a Facebook profile. If Facebook has a business partnership from an online store at which you make a purchase (or even browse), that data will be passed onto Facebook in order to inform targeted advertising on the social media platform (Fuchs, 2011, p. 139). Similarly, Google gathers data from web searches, Gmail content and the use of other Google applications. Whenever a website offers log-in via an existing Facebook or Google profile, it means that those companies are also able to gather data related to your browsing and clicking activity on those websites.

The upshot of all this data gathering is that companies like Facebook and Google are able to construct an increasingly detailed picture of individual consumers which they can then pass on to advertisers for a price. Social media sites thus serve as an updated form of Smyth's audience-commodity: they gather users through 'free access to services and platforms' and then sell their identities and produced content to third-party advertisers (Fuchs, 2012, p. 144). Both public posts and monitored private browsing data are thus converted into marketing data in a manner that replicates the logic of the audience-commodity (Fuchs, 2012, p. 147). The consequence of this is that internet users will experience targeted advertising not only in the context of social media but everywhere elsewhere online courtesy of advertisers who have purchased user data from sites like Facebook. For example, those who frequently search for fashion-related terms will get more clothing ads and those who frequently post baby photos on Facebook will receive ads for nappies and other baby products as a consequence of photo-reading algorithms that allow websites to extract information from images as well as words. The connection between social media data and responsive advertising is relatively clear in such cases. However, such data profiles do not remain locked to the online space in which they were first gathered: social media companies do not just gather data for themselves but also sell that data to other advertisers, where it will be also be used to target ads in the context of more general browsing. Companies like Facebook sell the user information that they gather to advertisers, who can then use this data to focus on particular consumers or groups of consumers and to adapt their selling techniques for greater success. Such data is very valuable to advertising and marketing firms, and the process of online gathering through social media has proved much easier and much more comprehensive than older survey-based techniques.

Do you want a cookie?

We can consider such social media practices as an example of 'opt-in' data gathering: users sign up to use a platform and voluntarily contribute information about themselves. However, this is not the only way in which personal information is gathered online in order to generate targeted advertising, and 'opt-in' data is usually supplemented by information that is gathered through the use of 'cookies' and device fingerprinting. A cookie is a small piece of HTML data that a website sends to a web browser that then sends back information to the site about the user's browsing habits (McStay, 2011, p. 7). Cookies were originally designed to help store data for administrative functions, but they are increasingly being used to gather data for advertising purposes. Most websites will send cookies to your browser which will then monitor your subsequent browsing activities, including search terms and sites visited, even when you leave the original site. Even Google – the almost inescapable organiser of the Internet – uses cookies to gather user data which it then passes on to advertisers, as is explained deep in the bowels of their 'terms of service' agreements (Fuchs, 2012, pp. 45–46). If this were not enough, there are also a rising number of 'third-party cookies', which marketing firms pay sites to host. For example, if you were to search Dictionary.com, the website would upload several such 'third-party' cookies to your browser (the administrators of which would have paid the site for the privilege) that would then report back to marketing companies on your subsequent browsing habits (Turow, 2011, p. 121). Most contemporary web browsing applications have the ability to block these third-party cookies, but this blocking function must be turned on by the user, making this an example of 'opt-out' rather than 'opt-in' online information gathering.

Nor are cookies the only means of 'opt-out' data collection. In the case of smartphone and other mobile internet technology, users often access the internet through apps, which do not support cookies like a browser does. To get around this problem, several companies have begun to introduce 'device fingerprinting', in which a device directly 'transmits bits of information about its properties and settings when it connects to the internet' (Turow, 2011, p. 152). Such techniques, which can also be applied to traditional laptop and desktop computers, not only get around the limitations of cookies, but also have the potential to collect other data in order to further develop the user profile. This additional data includes location-based information on the user collected via the GPS function now standard on most devices, all payments made using in-built 'near-field' payment technologies and even voice recognition (Turow, 2011, p. 193). Such information can then be used to target advertising to consumers depending on exactly where they are, with companies providing advertising based upon local services and shops (Manzerolle, 2010, pp. 462–465). Moreover, with the increasing popularity of web-based TV and radio services, individual viewing and listening habits can also be integrated into the profile. Indeed, there is probably very little online activity that is not the target of information-gathering by advertisers.

The upshot of all this data-gathering is an unheralded ability for advertisers to target advertising to individuals rather than audiences. This is true on multiple levels and includes not only the ability to deliver particular advertisements to particular individuals, but even the ability to generate individually targeted ads that address people by name or that make use of language, design and colour schemes that are calculated to be more persuasive for certain people. On most websites, the advertisements are determined not by that site, but by an external advertising network that uses the cookies stored in a browser to sort the user into a precise or even personalised category and generate advertising based on that profile (McStay 2011, p. 8). User-generated content can be integrated into advertisements, so that ads will incorporate not only names and language, but even images uploaded by users (Manzerolle, 2010, p. 463). In this vein, the company Teracent offers a service which tailors the formal properties of digital advertising in real time so that even people receiving advertising for the same products at the same time will encounter different advertisements (Turow, 2011, p. 120). As a consequence, everything from the actual content you encounter online to the products advertised and the way they're advertised can be constructed just for you. There is even a growing tendency to use online data in order to personalise the price of products, so that different users will be shown different prices for the same goods from the same store (Turow, 2011, p. 108). Moreover, while most consumers are not particularly happy with the potential for differentiated pricing, for many the rise of personalised advertising is welcome if it means more relevant advertising. However, Turow warns that increased relevance can also be understood as a narrowing of options and the increased possibility of social discrimination (2011, p. 89). While many of us are apparently comfortable with giving our information to advertisers, he cautions that most people don't realise the amount and type of the data they are handing over, nor how such processes don't so much put control in the hands of individuals, but rather enable companies to gather, sort and profit from the surfeit of new individual information that is available online.

Same but different?

With the rise of individually targeted advertising, we might now seem a world away from the concerns expressed by Adorno and Horkheimer over 50 years ago. After all, if advertising speaks to us as individuals, there would seem to be little reason for concern that advertising will usher in a culture of conformity, would there? Such might be our conclusion if we were to naïvely accept the claims of the advertising industry, where advocates of the new era of digital advertising repeatedly assert that old models and fears around advertising no longer apply in this new era and worries about the detrimental consequences for advertising audiences are therefore outdated. However, before we too quickly accept such claims, we should stop and think how much has really changed, particularly with respect to the social and cultural role of advertising in relation to its audience.

While it is true that advertisers increasingly have access to data that allows them to tailor advertisements to our individual preferences and interests, what often goes unremarked is that the personalisation of advertising messages continues to be driven by persistent political economic trends. What this means is that while you may receive ads for beer or cosmetics depending on who you are, and those ads may be tailored to appeal to your particular interests, at the end of the day it is still the same product being advertised, and the same laws of profit determining who is being advertised to. As a result, while the mode of address might change, even if you receive a different advertisement it's still selling the same product. Horkheimer and Adorno referred to this phenomenon as 'pseudo-individualisation'. The prefix 'pseudo' literally translates as 'false', so what this term means is the constructing and presentation of false individual identities. These individual identities are false because they are not based on actual difference, but instead emerge out of false differences and identities, which hide the fact that the products are all minor variations on common, repeated themes. Thus, rather than manufacturers producing different products, advertisers produce difference in consumer markets: designing and divvying up society into demographic groups. As a consequence, however targeted it might get, advertising is not about distinguishing between different products, which are effectively identical, but about 'classifying, organising and labelling consumers' and ensuring that 'something is provided to all so that none may escape' (1972, p. 123). Hence, while advertising might target us individually, this is less a question of recognising our individual uniqueness as creating fake differences through minor shifts in advertising appeal. Viewed from such a perspective, the turn towards individualised advertising appears less as a radical break from the past and more as refinement of a long-standing tactic in advertising.

The production of difference with Dove

A good example of this phenomenon is the advertising for Dove toiletries, which offer an identity that ostensibly rejects beauty myths and seeks to empower women and girls, especially with regard to body image. The Dove brand is owned and administered by Unilever: one of the world's largest and oldest consumer goods companies. The Dove brand began in 1955 with a soap, or 'beauty bar', that was first advertised with a slogan devised by the famous David Ogilvy: a slogan that it retains to this day: 'Dove won't dry your skin like soap can'. In 2004, Dove's branding underwent a major shift with the launch of the 'Dove Campaign for Real Beauty', followed by the launch of the 'Dove Self-Esteem Fund' in 2006. In terms of their advertising, these changes manifested with a shift towards advertisements that feature 'real women': representations of women who are presented as departing from traditional notions of feminine beauty with regard to weight, age and other factors. In doing so, Dove created a brand identity that seeks to align itself with authenticity and quasi-feminist messages around body image and unrealistic social standards around women's appearances. Consumers were thereby offered the opportunity to construct an identity that 'rejects' the messages of the cosmetics industry and advertising more generally by purchasing Dove products. Interpreted in terms of the cultivation of different advertising audiences, we can understand such a move as an attempt to target a particular audience who are concerned with issues such as body image and the social influence of advertising. The fact that such an audience are statistically more likely to have engaged in higher education, and therefore have increased purchasing power, suggests why such a mode of address might be desirable.

In an ironic move, then, we can see how Dove works to construct a brand identity defined in opposition to the objectification and judgement of women's bodies for the purpose of selling moisturiser, shampoo, deodorant and skincare products, i.e. commodities whose main reason for existing is to reproduce and derive profit from consumers' attempts to attain social standards of beauty. Furthermore, such advertising needs also to be understood in light of the fact that the Dove brand is part of the international consumer goods company, Unilever, who also own Lynx, TRESemme and Rexona. The advertising that Dove is responding to and criticising is therefore produced by the same company that makes Dove – a situation that ensures that Unilever can sell products and extract profit from both those who are okay with conventional images of female beauty and those who oppose them. This is certainly a case, then, where 'none may escape': even opposition and critique is re-appropriated as a means to classify and then market to a particular subject position.

The superficiality of Dove's commitment to critical and sensitive representations of women can be seen in the brand's recent fate in the Chinese market. Dove was first introduced to China in the mid-2000s under the guidance of Ogilvy and Mather: the agency responsible for Dove in the USA since the 1950s. At first, the Chinese campaign reflected the 'Real Beauty' branding that had come to define Dove in Western contexts. Initially, advertisements featured pregnant abdomens with slogans asking parents to accept their baby daughters regardless of body concerns such as flat noses and small breasts, and Chinese women were encouraged to share their 'beauty stories' online (Sauer, 2013). However, despite the relatively greater dedication to beauty culture in China than in the West, this approach proved unsuccessful because, in the words of Mike Bryce, Unilever's Asia regional brand development manager for Dove, '[in China] a model on billboards is something that women do aspire to, and feel is attainable' (Hollis, 2009). Faced with such difficulties Unilever even financed the production of *Chou Nu Wu Di*, a four season adaptation of the Colombian telenovela *Yo Soy Betty, La Fea* (adapted in the USA as *Ugly Betty*): the show not only featured wall-to-wall product placement for Dove (and other Unilever products on the side) but was also set in an advertising agency where the title character learnt to use Dove products to realise her own unique beauty (Fowler, 2008). However, despite what would be considered unusually extreme advertising interventions, any remnant of the 'Real Beauty' campaign was eventually dropped from the Chinese market. As of 2016, the website for Ogilvy and Mather China no longer features information regarding empowerment or authenticity regarding Dove: instead the campaign since 2010 has been based on the premise that Dove is 'Better than Milk' (Ogilvy and Mather, 2014). Instead of the ostensibly everyday women who popular Western Dove ads, in China models compare their skin after washing with Dove or bathing in a bath filled with cow's milk. This rapid transformation is indicative of the fact that the central mission of Dove is to sell hygiene products, not to empower women, and the idea of 'Real Beauty' is simply a means to distinguish itself in a market. When there is a conflict between positive messages and moving units, Unilever has no qualms about washing its hands of any progressive or critical messages.

What, then, might this final example of Dove say about the relationship of advertising to its audiences in the final instance? While the intended audience of particular advertising has changed and narrowed over the years, taking advantage of new media platforms and possibilities to tailor advertising to niches and then individuals, one thing we can see is that the central economic rationale of advertising has stayed the same. As a result, although advertising might be able to hone in on ever smaller audiences, we shouldn't mistake this for some sort of trend towards a perfect fit between a product pitch and its intended recipients. This is because, as has been discussed in this chapter, advertising always relates to an audience first and foremost as an economic unit. All the information about likes and dislikes, hobbies, preferences, family and friends cannot and does not change that central fact. Consequently, despite all the different ways that advertising can and does address you as an audience in our contemporary mediascape, one thing is constant: advertising will always address you first and foremost as a consumer and a commodity.

CHAPTER 7

Advertising agencies: Organisation, agency and internal conflict

In the previous section of this textbook, we have focused on understanding advertising as part of the larger social and economic systems of capitalism. In order to do so, we've focused upon different aspects of Marxist-influenced theories of capitalism and culture and taken up a number of key concepts in relation to advertising, including political economy, ideology, consumerism, commodities, fetishism, profit and distinction. The key advantage of approaching advertising in this way is that it allows us to make sense of how and why advertising works the way it does by situating it in a wider historical and social context. Looking at advertising through the lens of capitalism helps us to appreciate the reason that advertising exists in the first place, the reason it persists despite complaints about its ubiquity and doubts about its effectivity, and how the odd quirks and overblown claims of advertising as a media form can make complete sense when taken in the context of capitalism. Consequently, when we approach it by way of capitalism, we're able to develop a conception of advertising as not just an idiosyncratic form of cultural practice but also as a necessary part of the larger context of our everyday lives.

The limits of abstraction

However, while offering powerful analytic methods for making sense of advertising and its relation with other aspects of society, such sweeping theories of advertising are not without their limitations. One particular problem is that such theories tend to offer a monolithic account: one in which advertising appears as a singular and all-powerful social force that unstoppably obliterates everything that stands in its way. Although providing a powerful model for explaining what advertising is and how it operates, such a perspective tends to reduce all explanations to the profit motive. At their most totalising, such accounts of capitalism in general, and advertising in particular, can present a world where everything is determined in advance by the oppressive force of capitalism and where there is therefore no chance for change or resistance. This is a grim picture indeed!

Moreover, not only is this approach to advertising potentially depressing, but it also can be difficult to reconcile with all the experiences we have of advertising, especially if you or someone you know works in the industry. After all, advertising isn't made by faceless robots dedicated to the final triumph of capitalism; it's made by real people who have lives and families and different motivations, morals, politics and values. If we are to understand advertising in all its complexity, it is essential, then, that we account for the ways in which it departs from and challenges the Marxist model that has so far guided us. To be absolutely clear: the purpose is not to discount those critical accounts of advertising, but to acknowledge the potential limitations of those models and to consider the ability of advertising to mean and circulate in ways beyond and even contrary to the capitalist over-determination frequently presumed by critical accounts. The turn to industry perspectives therefore doesn't mean abandoning the Marxist perspective, but in this chapter involves taking into account the advertising industry's discussions and descriptions of its own practice. In the words of the sociologist Anne Cronin, who has studied the practices and beliefs of those who work in the industry: 'Advertising is not an infallible commercial machine, inexorably generating and disseminating consistently persuasive promotional tools' (Cronin, 2004, p. 57). Instead, she suggests, advertising is a much more complicated and piecemeal practice where the people involved are constantly working to justify themselves and their products in response to wider cultural changes.

Consequently, one of the goals of this third and final section of the book will be to question and nuance (though certainly not necessarily reject) the Marxist account of advertising as an unstoppable cultural tool for the reproduction of capitalist society and investigate the ways in which advertisers and audiences complicate any easy equation of advertising for capitalist ideology. To that end, the three chapters in this section will consider alternate approaches to three different aspects of advertising: in this first chapter of the section, we'll be looking at the production of advertising.

The human touch

One of the things that you might have noticed is missing from the Marxist account of advertising is a consideration of the people who make advertising. This is a bit of an oversight for an analytic approach that is so often concerned with the means of production and the social conditions under which economic production takes place: given our concern so far with how commodities are made, it also makes sense to think about how advertising itself is made. Accordingly, in this chapter we'll be turning our attention to the people, processes and practices that are involved in the actual production of advertising, with a particular focus on those who work in the 'creative' departments. In particular, we'll be looking at the corporate entities that make most advertising: advertising agencies. We'll begin with a brief theoretical account of how and why such an approach differs from the Marxist and critical approaches to advertising that we've been talking about so far: this will be discussed in terms of the sociological concepts of structure and agency. We'll then move onto a look at the structure *of* agencies. This will involve a consideration of the different sections of a historically typical advertising firm and the changing makeup of agencies in the new era of globalisation and digital advertising. We will then follow this with a look at the actual people who make advertising by looking at some of the most famous first-hand autobiographic accounts of the industry and more recent ethnographic research into the real lives and beliefs of advertisers. Those involved in advertising have many different opinions about what exactly they are doing, how effective it is and the larger meaning of advertising as a practice: this means that the way that advertising represents itself can change depending on who is talking and who they're talking to. We'll therefore close up the chapter by thinking about the different sites of conflict and cooperation within advertising agencies and how internal power struggles reflect external pressures places upon agencies.

Structure and agency in advertising

The word 'agency' appears here in the guise of a (pretty weak) pun, where 'agency' refers to both the widely used term for those businesses involved in the creation, planning and placement of advertisements and a central sociological term that finds its complement and opposition in the idea of a 'structure'. For our purposes, however, the connection between the two runs deeper than simply sharing a word in common. Instead, in this case, our investigation of the actual practices of advertising agencies in this chapter is motivated by a desire to better account for the notion of agency (in its sociological sense) and how it complicates the Marxist model we have so far addressed. You might therefore say that we are concerned with accounting for the agency of agencies.

The concept of agency refers to the ability (or a belief in the ability) of either humans or collective groups of humans to act in a conscious and reflexive manner to enact change in the world (Ritzer and Goodman, 2003, pp. 378–379). The complementary term of agency is structure: sets of rules and resources that shape human behaviour in particular ways (Slattery, 2003, p. 272). The relation between these two aspects can be considered a form of a chicken-or-the-egg argument: on the one hand, structures are the product of the actions of human agents; while, on the other hand, the behaviour of agents is determined and shaped by structures. Depending on which side of this binary we emphasise, we will have a rather different take on how and why societies (and advertising) work the way they do. From the perspective of a researcher who focuses on recording the beliefs and behaviour of individual actors, it would appear that agency is the master term: but for those who look at society from the perspective of statistics, trends and patterns, then it is the structure that dominates (Pickering, 2008, p. 20). This conflict between structure and agency is one of the foundational debates in sociology and has concerned many of the key thinkers of contemporary sociological theory, including Anthony Giddens, Pierre Bourdieu and Jurgen Habermas (Ritzer and Goodman, 2003, p. 80). Although each of these thinkers approach and present the relation between structure and agency in their own way, all three share a common awareness that these terms are best understood in tension rather than resolved in favour of one or other. As Giddens phrases this there is a 'mutual dependence of structure and agency' (1979, p. 69). Consequently, when assessing the usefulness of structural or agential approaches to advertising we need to recognise that the apparent opposition of the two terms is not something we can simply resolve for either side. It is therefore important to keep both sides in mind when conducting an analysis and consider how they can inform, expand and complicate one another to produce richer, more informative analyses of advertising.

The political economic approaches to advertising which we've been looking at up to this point can be considered to be examples of structuralist thinking: this means that they place more emphasis on structures as a way of explaining and understanding the world, rather than agency (Giddens, 1979, p. 52; Ritzer and Goodman, 2003, pp. 452–453; Slattery, 2002, pp. 267–268). The main structure of concern in this case is capitalism, which is treated as an overarching and over-determining structure that is too large for any individual to stand up to or resist. From this perspective, capitalism is the structure that determines the content and function of advertising, and indeed culture, society and politics more generally. However, this is not the only way to assess the role of advertising. We can also focus on agency – the ability of individuals to exercise free will and make their own decisions – in order to highlight the ability of social actors to resist or reinterpret existing patterns in advertisings. In part, this is a long way of saying that advertisers are people too. Yet, while this might seem like a rather obvious piece of common sense, it was useful for us to come around the long way to this point via structuralist theories. The rationale behind this is that rather than seeing the agency of advertisers as an automatic given, when we approach it from the vantage of critical structuralist accounts, we are then much better prepared to consider how the (hardly surprising) fact that advertising is made by people can have larger ramifications for our understanding of the social, cultural and political role of advertising.

Coming from this perspective, we are intellectually equipped to examine the ways that advertising might reflect the interests and aspirations of the people and institutions that make it, and to therefore appreciate the importance of agency as a concept, rather than a given. This does not mean, however, that we should simply reject structural accounts of advertising as somehow incorrect. Instead, we need to appreciate how the questions of structure and agency as they relate to advertising are not simply a matter of *either* structure *or* agency. Rather, it makes more sense to consider *both* structure *and* agency: to acknowledge the ability of those who produce advertising to make decisions, but not to mistake this for some sort of pure freedom that invalidates approaches that explain advertising in terms of capitalism. Considering the agency of advertisers doesn't mean jettisoning critical and Marxist accounts of advertising, but it does mean that we need to look in more detail at the actual practices and processes of the advertising industry. In doing so, we can get a sense of how advertising not only works to reproduce, reinforce and rationalise capitalism but also functions in other more subtle ways.

The organisational structure of agencies

The advertising agency is the central corporate entity involved in the planning, production and placement of advertising. Agencies come in a range of shapes and sizes: at one end are small boutique agencies catering to local markets and local solutions, while at the other are massive transnational mega-corporations that can incorporate multiple departments and constituents around the world. These agency holding companies, or 'mega-agencies', which include companies like WPP, Omicom, Interpublic and Publicis, have arisen from the merger of previously distinct companies in order to match the scale of contemporary 'mega-clients', such as Unilever, Microsoft, Coca-Cola and Nestle (Sinclair, 2012, pp. 32–42). Such umbrella corporations can include a number of smaller companies with names possibly more familiar to those acquainted with the history of advertising, including Ogilvy and Mather (owned by WPP), Doyle Dane Bernbach (DDB) (owned by Omnicom) and Saatchi and Saatchi (owned by Publicis). Such is the pace of the international advertising industry that it is difficult to predict which of these companies will continue to operate in a few years' time and under what particular name: one of the indications of this complexity is that the name of the world's largest advertising company (at the time of writing), WPP, originally stood for Wire and Plastic Products. Originally, the company manufactured wire baskets, until it was purchased in 1985 by a former financial director of Saatchi and Saatchi and transformed into a holding company through which to launch hostile takeovers of existing agencies (Sinclair, 2012, p. 35). This transformation can be considered indicative of the dynamic corporate environment in which advertising agencies operate and where the long-term existence, let alone success, of any given agency cannot be guaranteed.

The different parts of an agency

Historically, the typical form of the advertising agency has been what is referred to as a 'full service agency': a complex entity that unites the multiple jobs associated with advertising under one roof (Fill, Hughes and De Francesco, 2012, p. 188). Although some regard 'advertising and promotion agencies [as] slightly mysterious places,' and the actual process by which advertising is produced can be rather vague (Fill, Hughes and Francesco, 2012, p. 105), it is nonetheless possible to identify some commonalties between different agencies and how they function. Within full service agencies, we can thus identify five main divisions between which the different tasks involved in advertising are usually assigned:

- 'Media,'
- Account Management (or Handling),
- 'Creative',
- Production, and
- Account Planning.

(Mayer, 2011, pp. 79–84; Nixon, 2003, p. 173)

Each of these divisions plays a discrete role in the production of advertising, although the relative importance and emphasis placed upon the different sections has shifted over time. One of the major consequences of this separation is that the different divisions can potentially develop their own priorities, principles, connections and culture within and between agencies, which can lead to diverging interests or even conflict between the different sections. The advertising that emerges from this process will therefore always be the product of conflict and compromise between these different groups. We will consider the function of each of these divisions in turn.

Media buying Chronologically, it makes sense to consider the 'media' division of the advertising agency first, because the functions of the media division – liaising with media producers and platforms in order to purchase the time and space in which the advertising is to be presented – were the foundation of the first advertising agencies. In the early twentieth century, media buying was the sole focus of agencies, which existed in order to buy and sell space in newspapers for the advertising of goods and services (Leiss et al., 2005, p. 125). In this period, agencies would effectively serve as brokers between newspapers and those seeking to advertise:

> An enterprising young man from the provinces, operating out of a tiny office, persuaded various newspaper publishers to authorise him to sell their space on commission (gradually standardised to 15 percent) to patent medicine manufacturers, dry good emporiums, and anyone else with a need to advertise.
>
> (Lears, 1994, p. 89)

These days, there is obviously a much wider range of media in which to advertise – television, online, product placement, video games and many more in addition to newspapers – and therefore 'media planning' has become an important complement to media buying. Media planning involves the consideration of where to place advertising in order to gain maximum exposure and impact (Davis, 2011, pp. 181–182). This involves not only deciding upon the split between different media forms, but also the choice between different outlets within media: for example, different television shows, print publications or websites. Given that these different media environments can all deliver different audiences at different costs, as well as have ramifications for the content of the advertisements, media buyers and planners have to consider a range of options when deciding upon the optimum media mix for a given campaign or brand. This new complexity in the media environment, in conjunction with the global financial recession, has led some to note a resurgence in the power of media buyers relative to other divisions in the early twenty-first century (Deuze, 2007, pp. 118–119).

Account management Continuing in chronological fashion, the next agency division to achieve prominence was account management: also referred to as account handling, the account men or, simply, the 'suits'. The account manager is most closely associated with the 'business' side of advertising. In the first half of the twentieth century, account management became the most prominent and prestigious division of the advertising agency as a consequence of the growing professionalisation of the industry. When the public thought of advertising during this era, the most likely images to spring to mind were the respectful and staid images of the account men, who were the subject of films such as *The Man in the Grey Flannel Suit* (Frank, 1997, p. 35). As is suggested by the name, the main responsibility of account management is to handle the account, which is another term for the contract to provide advertising for a given client: the company that is commissioning the advertising. The main job of account managers is therefore to keep the client happy: this involves maintaining clear lines of communications as well as supervising the finances, timeline and execution of the overall project. This communication works both ways, with the account manager articulating the client's needs and priorities to other members of the agency and also presenting the agency's ideas to the clients (Mayer, 2011, pp. 78–79). Account managers thus speak alternately on behalf of the agency, the client and between the two parties and must therefore develop strong relationships with clients and work closely with them to ensure that they are included and satisfied with the final advertising products (Malefyt and Morais, 2012, p. 20). On occasion, the close affiliation between the client and the account manager can present problems, because accounts are perceived to put the interests of the client before that of other members of their agency (Hackley and Hackley, 2015, p. 111). The role of account managers tends to be minimised in accounts of advertising from the perspective of cultural studies, media studies and communication, because, of all the different divisions of an agency, they are most closely aligned to the commercial rather than cultural or communicative priorities of the industry.

Creatives As a consequence of their association with the business side of advertising, account managers are often presented as being in conflict with those members who are usually referred to as the 'creatives'. We will consider the larger idea of 'creativity' in advertising and its role in shaping the industry in Chapter 8, but for now we will focus on the people who fulfil the function of creatives within the agency. Traditionally broken down into those who deal with words (copywriters) and images (art directors), creatives are the ones that 'produce and sell ideas' (Hackley and Hackley, 2015, p. 115): they are responsible for slogans, themes and captivating images that drive campaigns and brands and are at the heart of advertising as a cultural form. The creative division of the advertising agency rose to prominence with the 'Creative Revolution' in the 1960s. Since that time, the creatives have most often been the most visible face of the advertising industry and the representatives of what sets advertising apart from other industries. The antics and oddities of creative departments have become the stuff of legend, as we will consider later in this chapter. Consequently, those who undertake creative work in agencies are frequently regarded, and regard themselves, as the heroes of the agency: singled out for praise and attention while other core roles are downplayed or minimised (Malefyt and Morais, 2012, p. 21; Nixon, 2003, p. 39). As a result, there is great demand from people who want to be employed in the creative side of advertising, which leads to a situation that is both privileged and anxious (Hackley and Hackley, 2015, p. 116).

And the rest The final two divisions of a full-service agency are production and account planning. The production division complements the work of creatives: production is where the ideas of the creatives are realised in different media forms. Depending on the size or specialisation of an agency, this might involve graphic designers, film and television directors, web designers and other media specialists. The range of the production division is limited only by the variety of media forms in which a given agency works and can replicate the full range of skills and specialisations used in contemporary media production. Finally, the last division of the agency – account planners – is also often regarded as the most controversial: contrary to what their name might suggest, account planners are largely involved in consumer research, rather than project planning, which is handled by account managers. The main purpose of account planners in an advertising team is thus to provide 'knowledge about the client's target consumers and to develop this into a strategic underpinning for the creative and media disciplines' (Fill, Hughes and De Francesco, 2013, p. 197). Their job is thus to study, measure and account for the perspectives of consumers (Malefyt and Morais, 2012, p. 21). Account planners are often presented as the logical or scientific part of the advertising process, but the validity of their input has often come under scrutiny, however, and scepticism as regards the worth of account planning is often mentioned in industry literature and textbooks (Hackley and Hackley, 2015, pp. 113–114). As a consequence, not all agencies will include account planners and their function will sometimes be merged with that of account managers.

When we take these different factions and departments into account, what should hopefully become clear is that advertising is far from a simple matter of devising an idea for a campaign and a brand and running with it. Multiple voices and perspectives feed into the production of advertising: each with their own insights to share and patch to defend. As a consequence, any given advertisement, and advertising in general, is always the product of multiple competing voices. Therefore, even though we will be focusing largely on the creative side of the industry in the remainder of this chapter – the division that speaks most directly to the media and cultural aspects of advertising – we need to be continually aware of the importance and input of the other divisions. Account managers and media buyers aren't simply addenda to the creative process; they are an essential part of the production of advertising and their input is just as formative and enabling (and limiting) as that produced by those who define themselves as creatives.

The changing agency

The full-service model has been the predominant form for advertising agencies for most of the twentieth century; however, changing conditions in the industry have led to a range of transformations in the ways that agencies do business in response to shifting needs and contexts (Fill, Hughes and De Francesco, 2013, p. 188). Financial recessions, changes in prevailing management theory, pressures towards globalisation and the introduction of new media technologies: all can have an influence on the ways that agencies are organised, and it is therefore difficult to say how any given agency is and will be organised (Nixon, 2003, p. 41). Hence, while the different components of the advertising team have remained largely consistent, what have changed are the business structures of agencies with creative and media functions split off into different companies. Consequently, rather than being all employed by the same agency, it has become more common for clients to hire different specialised agencies to attend to the different aspects of advertising creation. This practice really began to take off in the 1980s and early 1990 as a result of the separation between the media buying and creative-production functions of agencies: a process often referred to as 'unbundling' (Hackley and Hackley. 2015, p. 101; Nixon, 2003, p. 45). The climate of change continued into the twenty-first century, where the advent of online and digital media led to further disruption and change in the advertising industry with the rise of agencies focusing on digital-first advertising methods (Powell, 2009, pp. 14–15). These ongoing transformations – in conjunction with related shifts in consumer behaviour, audience fragmentation and client expectations – have led some academics to suggest that in terms of the agency world itself, such evolutions – not to say 'revolutions' – continue to produce (and require) an ever-increasing number of specialists (Powell et al., 2009, p. 1).

The main result of these shifts has been a rise in what are called 'boutique agencies' or 'media specialists': smaller agencies that offer dedicated services in one part of the advertising production process (Fill, Hughes and De Francesco, 2013, p. 18). Almost by their very nature it is difficult to point towards leading boutique agencies: their small, dynamic nature means that success (or failure) is often right around the corner and the barriers to entry are low enough that new agencies can enter the field at any time. Boutique agencies focus exclusively on one aspect of the production process and stake their reputation on subject matter expertise and flexibility relative to the larger full-service agencies (Deuze, 2007, pp. 122–123). Freed of the potentially conservative influence of the other divisions – such as media buying, planning and account management – creative boutiques present themselves as more responsive and more willing to take risks and push boundaries. Other boutique agencies will specialise in crafting advertising content for one media form. Ten to twenty years ago, this could have meant television, print or outdoors specialists, but increasingly boutique agencies will present themselves as social media and online experts. Eschewing traditional media forms, this new breed of boutiques promise their clients the ability to tap into new forms of informal and networked communication. Thus, regardless of the precise nature of the specialisation, we can see how boutique agencies seek to position themselves as more nimble and savvy than their full-service counterparts.

However, we should be careful not to too quickly buy into either the self-promoting rhetoric of the boutiques or the claims that specialisation is the inevitable future for the industry. Agencies adapt to the wider economic and cultural circumstances in which they operate, so it is difficult to say what the organisation is and will be always (Nixon, 2003, p. 41). After all, the first agencies were almost exclusively concerned with media buying and only later began to develop creative and other functions: a similar transition can be observed with those new media buying companies created by the unbundling of the 1980s and 1990s, which are slowly developing their own research skills and content production (Hackley and Hackley, 2015, p. 101). In the context of economic recessions, agencies tend to become more conservative in both their product and organisation, but usually become more regressive following economic recoveries (Nixon, 2003, p. 43).

If change is one of the few constants of the advertising industry, then we need to remember that change can work towards both specialisation and diversification. Alongside this movement towards comprehensive service on the part of prior specialists, it is also easy to overstate the existing degree of specialisation in the advertising industry: like most large companies, full-service agencies contain a lot of institutional inertia and are slow to respond to trends. This is especially true when parties have a vested interest in existing arrangements. And, at the same time, even now some voices in the industry are calling for increasing consolidation and integration as the way forward (Bruell, 2015; Kawaja 2015). Thus, even as we acknowledge the changing nature of the contemporary advertising agency, we need to be aware that sometimes things that change can stay the same. Even when creative and media buying functions are run out of separate agencies, this does little to change the overall input and direction of the advertising process. For those directly involved, it may seem radically different to work in a small office and alongside contributors from another company, but from the outside looking in, the process still involves a similar balance of the same elements: media buying and planning, account management, creative input, production, and (sometimes) account planning. This is particularly true if we consider the advertising agency from a wider perspective, where no matter how the internal agency divisions are arranged, the social, cultural and political aspects that underpin the larger project of advertising remain largely unchanged.

Advertisers in their own voices

An abstract account of economic circumstances and organisational arrangements of the different sections and functions of advertising agencies can only take us so far, however, in our investigation of the agency of agencies. If we really want to address the finer details of the industry then we need to readjust our focus to get a sense of the personalities and people behind advertising. In order to do so, we have several different sources at our disposal, including ethnographic and interview-based accounts by sociologists and anthropologists who have observed advertisers at work and autobiographic accounts by (in)famous ad men of their own works. Such approaches can complement one another: first-hand musings can provide useful insights into the thought processes and personality clashes that contribute to the production of advertising, while academic observation can correct some of the distortions and exaggerations that almost inevitably arise in such personal narratives. Thus, by taking these two different sources together we can hopefully get an accurate sense of what life is like for those who work in the advertising industry.

From the horses' mouths

Although they should be taken with one if not several grains of salt, first-hand accounts of the advertising industry can provide us with a vivid impression of how the people involved in advertising feel about their craft. Classic accounts of life in advertising – such as David Ogilvy's *Confessions of an Advertising Man* (2004) and Jerry Della Femina's *From Those Wonderful Folks Who Brought You Pearl Harbour* (2010) – are the products of particular historical moments, and consequently need to be understood in the context of their time. They also tend to skew towards the 'creative' end of the spectrum, rather than accounting for the perspectives of account managers or media buyers. Nonetheless, despite these limitations, such contributions continue to exert a powerful influence on both internal and external impressions of the advertising industry: a fact that is borne out by the near constant reprinting of those books since their initial publication. The ongoing circulation and popularity of these works suggests that they continue to speak to aspirations of how advertising is imagined, and possibly the ongoing realities as well.

David Ogilvy is probably the most celebrated and influential ad man of the twentieth century. His classic book, *Confessions of an Advertising Man,* is part memoir, part 'how-to guide', and presents the world of advertising as a cross between the Wild West and a repressive gentleman's club. In such an environment, the hard-nosed advertising man must use his tireless sense of personal industry and spirited cunning in order to outwit a sea of buffoons, bullies and cowards who would stifle his challenging ideas or water down his vision with puffery and fluff. The 'confessions' of Ogilvy's title are really a set of rules for principled success that extol the reader to live a life that is brave and principled: an advertiser must be prepared to take risks, but also must only advertise products which he believes in. Throughout *Confessions*, Ogilvy sings the praise of virtues such as a positive outlook, faith in the individual over the committee, pragmatism over flair, generosity towards rivals, personal integrity and a commitment to sell products rather than entertain (2004, pp. 93, 94, 96, 103, 127, 142–143). It is therefore against the foreground of this checklist of virtue that the state of the industry appears in relief: as dominated by those who lack morals or scruples, who are scared of new ideas, and who would exert a tyrannical authority over those who serve them. Ogilvy assures his reader, however, that with sufficient discipline, hard work and good sense it is possible to beat the rogues at their own game and transform advertising into a legitimate and worthwhile service to the public good, while getting rich at the same time. This is the advertising agency as a proving ground for heroes and good men: a site of conflict, but also a fair and essentially honourable practice once you have accounted for the scoundrels.

In contrast, Jerry Della Femina may well be one of those scoundrels denounced by Ogilvy. His autobiography of the 1960s New York advertising scene, *From Those Wonderful Folks Who Brought You Pearl Harbour*, presents advertising as a never-ending debaucherous party and freak-fest that is frequently cited as a chief inspiration for the TV show *Mad Men*. The title of the memoir is taken from the author's apparent off-colour pitch to representatives of the Japanese electronics giant Panasonic that suggests something of the irreverent, even potentially obnoxious, account of the industry the memoir presents (2010, p. 113). Thus, while his book begins with caveats that the industry is nowhere near as caught up in sex and drinking as is often presumed by outsiders (2010, pp. 16–22), by the time Della Femina comes to chapter 8 claims to probity have melted away as he describes the creative process in terms of:

> The profanity, the screaming, the yelling, the carrying on, the drinking, all at the same time – it's one tight crazy little room that explodes, and it's a very exciting process. To me, this is what advertising is all about because everything follows from that little room.
>
> (2010, p. 168)

In contrast to Ogilvy, Della Femina presents agency life as a flurry of craziness and weirdness that is populated by 'the lamed, the drunks, the potheads, and the weirdos' (2010, p. 71), all of whom are motivated by intense fear regarding the safety and stability of their jobs. As a consequence, he asserts, 'everybody in advertising is mixed up – but especially the creative people' (2010, p. 129).

Between the anecdotes of drunk and hungover meetings and the people who dream up ads with talking cars because they actually talk to cars, a picture emerges of the advertising industry as a crazy and maybe even desperate industry. On the one hand, driven by anxiety, creatives will procrastinate and goof off as they try to find the necessary motivation, while, on the other hand, the opulence and luxury used to woo clients distorts the standards and values of account managers who become 'hooked on the expense-account way of life' (2010, p. 107). The overall impression one comes away with is an industry perpetually on edge and struggling to hide the depths of the weirdness that underpins the heights of its genius.

Sitting somewhere between these two perspectives is Luke Sullivan's *Hey Whipple, Squeeze This!* (2012). Sullivan's book differs from the other two in that it is more recent (originally published in the early 2000s) and much more directly presented as a guide to creating successful advertisements; however, it still presents a particular vision of the advertising world and the personalities, priorities and problems one is liable to find there. Nonetheless, despite the distance in years, there are still many similarities with the industry as presented by Ogilvy and Della Femina. As with Ogilvy, Sullivan touts the personal thrill of crafting responsible, engaging and successful campaigns. He savages the bulk of existing advertisements – '95 percent of advertising is poorly written' (2012, p. 93) – and then provides a litany of tips, rules and tricks for different media and aspects of the business. The cumulative message of this advice is similar to that of Ogilvy's: if you work diligently and with integrity, if you respect your client and their product as well as the purity and strength of your own artistic vision, then you will find success. At the same time, however, Sullivan's general take on the industry bears much in common with that presented in *From Those Wonderful Fellows*. Like Della Femina, Sullivan attests that the advertising industry is full of eccentric characters, who he refers to as 'knuckleheads. All the people just slight left of centre ... oddballs, artists, misfits, cartoonists, poets, beatniks, creepy quiet guys, and knuckleheads' (2012, p. 337). Thus, although in slightly more reserved terms than Della Femina, we are assured that, 30 years on, advertising remains a refuge for the weird. The continuities between Sullivan's and Della Femina's accounts of agency life thus belie Della Femina's lament in his 2010 foreword that 'to paraphrase Mr. Ogilvy's comment in 1968, the lunatics are back in their cells, dead or retired ... The bottom line is now the only line in advertising' (2012, p. 9).

The possible prematurity of such remarks can also be read from a final example of advertisers in their own voices, the documentary *Art & Copy*, which also brings us close to the present day. Released in 2009, *Art & Copy* features a number of noted luminaries of advertising, including George Lois, Mary Wells Lawrence, Lee Clow and Dan Leiden, explaining the industry and how it operates. In keeping with previous representations, most of the contributors cast themselves as mavericks and geniuses, with Lois and Clow particularly distinguishing themselves as a foul-mouthed, straight-talking maniac and an archetypal California surfing hippy respectively. This effect is only magnified as we are whisked around the production spaces of top agencies, with their basketball courts, immensely cluttered desks, indoor bird nests, beautiful sun-lit architectural offices and gargantuan goof-off projects (the employees of Weiden + Kennedy make a giant mural that spells out 'Fail Harder' in relief using only thumbtacks). Thus, contrary to Della Femina's lamentation of the end of advertising weirdness, the cumulative effect of this parade of spectacle and excess, narcissists and visionaries, clearly united in their love of advertising as an expressive cultural form, is to reaffirm the ongoing existence of agency life as a hotbed of unbridled creation and pleasure in work. In the eyes of its practitioners, it would seem that, over 50 years on, the Creative Revolution on the 1960s is still in full swing and the advertising industry remains equal parts lunacy, exuberance and vision. Advertising apparently remains, following Della Femina's famous phrase, 'the most fun you can have with your clothes on' (2012, p. 270).

Advertisers as demographic

Given the extent of our examination so far, however, it would seem remiss to simply take advertisers at their own word. After all, this is an industry dedicated to image management and defined by its ability to make things appear as attractive as possible: it is therefore almost inevitable that advertisers are 'selling' their own industry. Therefore, while it would be a mistake to completely dismiss such representations, we can also gain some additional insights into agency life and practice by turning to academic and outsider accounts of the industry. At the very least, such observations help counteract some of the hype and spin that advertisers construct around themselves and their profession.

A key insight regarding the industry that emerges from academic reports is the relatively homogenous nature of those employed in advertising – particularly in creative departments – as a 'predominantly young, well-resourced, well-educated and fashionable, urban elite' who have high levels of cultural and aesthetic knowledge (McFall, 2004, p. 22). Although no comprehensive statistics are available for the entire global advertising industry, studies of particular companies and locations can provide piecemeal insight into the demographic make-up of the agencies themselves. For example, in the UK context, 80 per cent of advertising employees are aged below 40 years old, and 50 per cent are aged below 30 years old (Nixon, 2003, p. 95), while in the American context, Mark Deuze reports that 'the numbers of [non-white] minorities are still extremely low in the industry' with black employees making up only 2 per cent of senior positions (2007, p. 135). Moreover, it has been well documented that those employed in advertising tend to come from similar backgrounds. For example, British agencies tend to hire staff from prestigious tertiary institutions and senior staff tend to be graduates of 'elite universities', while creative departments are relatively more inclusive: those working in creative areas are 'more likely to come from lower middle class or working class backgrounds, [and they therefore form] a distinct social grouping within the industry' (Nixon, 2003, p. 64). However, even while creative departments have a higher proportion of participants from the lower middle class and working class than comparable occupations, they still tend to possess university-equivalent diplomas in design, fine arts or generalist humanities and social sciences (Nixon, 2003, pp. 60–61). Such studies of contemporary UK advertising match up with the more impressionistic claims of Della Femina's writing about the American context, where 'most copywriters have the same background: middle class to lower middle class' (2012, p.129). The picture that therefore emerges out of these different accounts is an industry that is (in the USA and UK at least) dominated by a group that is younger, whiter and more highly educated than the wider public.

As a result of the relative similarity of those working in the industry there always exists the possibility that they can end up 'living in a media bubble' to quote the title of a report into the New Zealand advertising industry (Nielsen NZ, 2014). What this means in practice is that while advertisers might be up to date with the latest digital technology and pop culture trends, they may overestimate the extent to which the wider public shares their knowledge and interest. Such informal knowledge can then determine the assumptions and priorities that go into the creation of advertising and even shape the construction and interpretation of more formal consumer surveys (McFall, 2004, pp. 25–26). In other words, the world of the advertising agency can be substantially different to the world around them, so that they become out of touch with the interests and reference points of the people to whom they advertise. In some contexts, this insularity can manifest itself in small but significant ways – the industry's enthusiastic turn towards digital platforms can be understood in terms of exceptionally high levels of smartphone and tablet ownership among advertisers (Nielsen NZ, 2014) – or in terms of major disconnections from the wider population. Writing in an Indian context, William Mazzarella wrestles with the fact that not only are the air-conditioned agency offices a world apart from the chaotic streets of Bombay (Mumbai), but that most consumers have no way to afford the goods being advertised (2003, pp. 57–58). Such discrepancies point towards the need for us to be aware of how the tastes of the people behind the advertising – their interests, passions, likes, dislikes and cultural references – can often shape the content of advertisements more than the feedback of any focus group.

The other striking insight that emerges from observational studies of advertising personnel is the extent to which the industry is male-dominated. This does not necessarily mean, though, that most people employed in advertising are men – in fact, 54 per cent of employees at the major agencies are women – but rather that men occupy senior management and executive positives within the agencies (Deuze, 2007, p. 135). This is even truer of the creative divisions, where women are massively under-represented, in the British context at least, making up only 18 per cent of the workforce (Nixon, 2003, p. 96). In his study of British advertising cultures, Sean Nixon argues that this preponderance of men feeds into what he refers to as a culture of 'laddishness' in creative departments that is defined by a celebration of irreverence and oddness, lewd and obscene conduct and intense competitiveness (2003, pp. 98–102). The testosterone-dominated atmosphere of advertising creative departments has several consequences for life in the agency: most immediately, as Nixon notes, the masculine atmosphere leads to the marginalisation and exclusion of female creative employees, who are sometimes even thought to threaten the ability of men to be properly 'creative' (Nixon, 2003, p. 105). Nor is such a situation conducive to the success of shy and retiring employees, 'shrinking violets' in Nixon's terms, who are marginalised and have little chance of success (2003, p. 114). However, the most significant corollary in Nixon's account is the intensely competitive atmosphere that is fostered in the masculine environment as competition is valued over collaboration.

In such a context, creative teams are encouraged to compete with one another for prestige and recognition within an agency framework that rewards thick skins and combative natures. Drawing on interviews with managers, Nixon traces the ways in which prevalent agency management styles 'create the conditions in which assertiveness and the ruthless pursuit of self-interest became the attributes most required by teams to succeed' (2003, p. 112). At its most extreme, this competition can translate into a contempt for the work of others and even for the industry as a whole as creatives aggressively reject the contributions of their peers as failing to live up to vague and ill-defined notions of 'creativity' (Nixon, 2003, pp. 78–79). Moreover, the aggression that underlies the competitive nature of creative advertising is potentially compounded by what Mark Deuze refers to as 'frustration' at the lack of recognition compared to other cultural industries. Whereas those who work in television, film, journalism, popular music and other similar endeavours are acknowledged in credits and by-lines, advertisers remain largely anonymous to the general public (Deuze, 2007, p. 114). Instead of public credit for their work, creative competition in advertising is therefore largely based around a series of industry awards like the Cannes Lion awards, which become the major site of recognition within the industry (Nixon, 2003, p. 88). These awards become particularly important in the context of an industry where reputation plays a central role in promotion and financial success. Denied the outlets for recognition available in other cultural industries, but spurred to competition by management strategies, creative departments can therefore become driven by their pursuit of such awards, and the industry kudos that accompanies them, in ways that eclipse any desire to increase sales for their client.

Conflict and compromise in the agency

This observation – that some creative teams are more motivated by a desire to win awards than to help sell their client's products – does not always sit well with clients; nor does the wider point that creative departments are not necessarily motivated by a drive to increase sales, but instead act according to their own desire to create and be recognised as successive cultural producers. As we saw earlier, David Ogilvy, a renowned figure in the industry, was particular clear on this point: arguing that selling the product should always take precedence over entertaining or pursuing other artistic agendas. In doing so, Ogilvy sought to intervene in what Daniel Miller identifies as the 'the key structural tension ... in advertising agencies internationally' (Miller, 1997, p. 163): that between the competing artistic and economic demands of the industry.

Miller is not alone in his diagnosis of the importance of the creative–accounts conflict: Nixon, for example, argues that creatives often define themselves in opposition to the commercial imperatives of accounts (2003, p. 67), Chris and Rungpaka Hackley suggest 'the tension between the two cultures of art and commerce ... lies at the heart of the fascination of advertising' (2015, p. 144), and Timothy de Waal Malefyt and Brian Moeran point towards the different priorities within the agency, with account planners and the creative team focusing on consumers, while account managers are more concerned with pleasing the client who pays for the ad (2012, p. 5). Similarly, Mark Deuze also acknowledges the possibility for disagreement, but more optimistically argues that it can be best understood in terms of 'creative tension' rather than out-and-out conflict (2007, p. 137). These differences even play themselves out in terms of fashion, with creative departments favouring 'casual styles of self-presentation' (Deuze, 2007, p. 142) while, befitting their nickname of 'the suits', account managers opt for formal business wear in the manner of those employed in legal and finance services (Deuze, 2007, pp. 142–144). Regardless of how it is understood to function, this internal tension within the agency reflects wider discourses about advertising's position at the crossroads of business and art, with the conflicting impulses given form in the two different departments – creative and accounts – within the agency.

Finally, this structural split is further compounded by differences in opinion as to what constitutes success for the agency. Whereas from the point of view of creatives advertising succeeds when it captures the attention of consumers, from the perspective of accounts, advertising is successful when it pleases the client who paid for it to be produced. Viewed in this way, 'advertising's primary aim may not be that of persuading consumers to buy the product' (Cronin, 2004, p. 61), but rather of persuading the client to continue to fund the agency. This task is made more difficult by the fact that there is very little proof that advertising actually increases sales (Cronin, 2004, p. 60)! Faced with such a dilemma, account managers have been documented using a range of tactics to keep clients on their side. These range from the underhanded – fostering paranoia regarding competitors (Miller, 1997, p. 166) – to the subservient – allowing clients to control the creative process – and the pandering: wining and dining executives in order to build personal connections. In practice, some have argued such relationship building can have a greater impact on an agency's ability to gain and keep clients than the actual advertising produced (Malefyt and Morais, 2012, p. 19). Anne Cronin argues that agencies actually expend more effort persuading clients than they do consumers (2004, p. 64): an aspect of what she refers to as the 'political economy of truth' of advertising. At the heart of this concept is the constant struggle from both in and outside of agencies to define how advertising works and how powerful it is. Cronin's interviews with advertisers suggest that rather than considering themselves powerful manipulators of public opinion, most are incredibly anxious about their ability to influence and spend most of their time '*talking advertising up*' (Cronin, 2004, p. 61, emphasis in original).

Agency as form from chaos

In practice, then, we can see how the final advertisements that emerge from agencies are born out of complicated processes. Not only are individual agencies always subject to wider economic forces, but within agencies multiple divisions and departments compete for attention and priority. This splitting of responsibilities means that no single person or department has to weigh up the competing priorities: instead, those priorities become a potential battleground between different aspects of the agency and different people. Divided into separate constituencies, the struggle between creatives and accounts is played out in terms of a 'struggle for relative autonomy. The former need to claim that it is creative and exciting adverts that sell products, the latter assume it is emphasis on product itself and brand that ultimately counts'

(Miller, 2003, p. 80). As a result of such conflict and tension within the agency, it becomes difficult to sustain the notion that an ad campaign is the realisation of a singular creative vision that emerges from a clear unbroken line from conception to execution. Making ads is therefore almost always a challenging task because 'the process of researching, planning, producing and editing a television commercial is fraught with difficulties, and there are no assurances that the completed advertisement will be either an artistic or a commercial success' (Cronin, 2004, p. 59). The content, form and delivery of advertisements begin to appear less as textual expressions of either capitalist ideology or individual creativity and more as the result of compromise and conflict between different parties. Thus, when we begin to map out the relations between the different parties involved in the agency, we can begin to see how the 'semiotics [of an advertisement], and even the degree to which the commodity is subject to over symbolizing, is itself closely bound up with the internal tensions and imperatives of the agencies in their relationships with their clients' (Miller, 1997, p. 182). What we can learn by considering the inner workings of an agency and the people employed there is that finished and final advertisements are therefore never straightforward expressions of pure ideas, but messy contingent and compromised texts made by human beings (some of whom just might be drunk).

CHAPTER 8

Advertising as art: From creativity to critique

In his foundational essay 'Advertising: The Magic System' Raymond Williams describes advertising as the 'official art of capitalist society' (2010, p. 207). Williams isn't paying advertising a compliment here though; he isn't suggesting that advertising belongs in a gallery or should be understood as a work of beauty or genius. Instead, the emphasis in this phrase is implicitly on the *capitalism*, rather than the *art*. Williams' point is that advertising commands the majority of our image-makers and wordsmiths and is the ever-present visual presence of our capitalist world. His phrase should therefore not be read as an endorsement of advertising's artistic merits, but as a declaration that it is the most direct cultural expression of capitalism: the site at which the economic base manifests directly as words, images and sounds. Advertising is not so much art, as art has become entirely capitalist. However, just because Williams did not deign to consider advertising a form of art, it does not mean that such an interpretation is beyond the bounds of all possibility: what would it mean, then, if we were to take Williams' statement at face value? What would it mean to treat advertising like it was art?

In the other chapters in this section, we considered how the actual lives of advertisers and the engagement and opposition of audiences can complicate straightforward applications of the political economic model. However, our discussion so far has failed to address a crucially important aspect of advertising: the advertisements themselves, which have remained a media manifestation of the material organisation of capitalism: a crude demand to buy or a straightforward attempt at persuasion. As both the people who make advertisements and those who consume them are reconfigured as possible sources of complexity and resistance, why should the texts of advertising not also be subject to a re-evaluation? In order to address this oversight, in this chapter we will turn our attention to examining the ways in which advertisements might be considered as more than simply vehicles for the development of fetishism and the delivery of capitalist ideology. This does not mean forgetting the role of advertising within capitalist systems: it is important when we consider advertising as art that we also maintain an awareness of the inescapable implication of advertising within capitalism, but that we also consider how that might not mean that advertising is only ever a question of economics. We will be carrying out this investigation by way of a particular provocation: the suggestion that advertising could be accurately considered a form of art. Transfigured in such a way, what aspects of advertising would such a perspective help bring into view and how might it lead us to rethink the social, cultural and political work of advertising? In order to explore the consequences of such questions, we will begin with a consideration not of art, but of the affiliated notion of 'creativity': a term that currently receives a great deal of attention in the advertising industry and beyond, and in many ways might appear as a synonym for art. Our examination will begin with a consideration of the rise of 'creativity' as an idea, its applications to advertising and the limitations of it as a concept. The discussion of creativity will then lead us to consider how the older idea of 'art' might speak to those limitations and therefore potentially provide a more productive way to think of advertising. To conceive of advertising as art is to think about how it might be a form of cultural production capable of doing more than simply selling a product and reproducing capitalism. Such a suggestion necessitates that we, in turn, consider the different ways that art has been defined and the ramifications of extending those different models to the study of advertising: if advertising is indeed a form of art then what does this mean for how we understand its social, cultural, economic and political roles?

Advertising and 'creativity'

Creativity is something of a buzzword in our modern world, and while it's not always immediately clear what is meant by the term, it's always inevitably something which people want and value. In a somewhat vague sense, 'creativity' seems to invoke a sense of artistic production and the making of new things and therefore can even seem to function as a more up-to-date or even more democratic variant on the idea of art or culture. If you are interested in working in the advertising industry, then there is a good chance that 'creativity' has something to do with that interest. The idea of creativity certainly appears central to advertising, whether it's the essential work of 'creatives' that we looked at in Chapter 7, the pivotal role of the 'Creative Revolution' in the historical narrative of the advertising industry as we looked at in Chapter 3 or the importance of advertising in discussions of the 'creative industries'. Indeed, so important is creativity to advertising that in 2011 one of the major industry award shows was renamed from the Cannes Lions International Advertising Festival to the Cannes Lions International Festival of Creativity. Wherever one looks in advertising, there are declarations of the importance of creativity (McStay, 2013, p. 1), and approached through the lens of creativity, advertising texts promise to be more than just vehicles for capitalist ideology: instead they appear as expressive, aesthetic acts of invention and production. Consequently, not only is creativity 'the one commodity advertising agencies feel that they own, above all other marketing and media disciplines' (Hackley and Hackley, 2015, p. 103), but it has also been referred to as the 'lifeblood of advertising' (Stotesbury, 2005, p. 118): the central, defining force that provides the impetus and purpose of the advertising industry. In the face of such an enthusiastic and assertive embrace of creativity it is difficult to deny that advertising is deeply invested in the notion of the 'creative'.

While the advertising industry is certainly one of the most ardent supporters of creativity, it is far from alone in this celebration of all things creative. Indeed, advertising's promotion of itself as the home of creativity is best understood in light of the wider economic and cultural turn to the creative across the capitalist world. As has been noted in both celebratory and critical accounts, since the 1980s the concept of creativity has become increasingly important in discussions of economic development (Brouillette, 2014, pp. 441–447). The rise of creativity in this sense has been linked, in part, to the decline of the manufacturing sector in places like Western Europe and North America, where the rise of global production and supply chains led to a loss of jobs to factories in Asia: the result of these shifts was an increase in unemployment in what came to be seen as 'post-industrial' economies (Lash and Urry, 2002, pp. 194–195). In order to address the resulting decline in economic fortunes, new policy initiatives were developed, particularly in the UK, which advocated for the establishment of 'creative industries' that drew on local talent in order to replace heavy industry and manufacturing with a new source of income that was less vulnerable to capital flight (Gibson, Carr and Warren, 2015; Prince, 2010, pp. 120–121). Advocates of this new model declared that 'the industries of the twenty first century will depend increasingly on the generation of knowledge through creativity and innovation' and held up creativity as the key to urban renewal (Landry and Bianchini, 1998, p. 12) Thus, the new 'creative industries' paradigm promised to revitalise moribund economies by providing support to a range of industries that were identified as belonging to the newly identified 'creative' sector: a broad category that included publishing, broadcasting, software, architecture and advertising (Prince, 2010, p. 123). As a result, in much of the English-speaking world there has arisen a seeming consensus that the leading industries of the twenty-first century are going to be creative industries, and 'creativity' has been embraced as one of the most desirable attributes in contemporary society. Or, in other words, 'creativity is the new black' (Peck, 2007).

The problems with defining creativity

Hence, although it predates the most recent surge of interest and investment in creativity, the advertising industry's conception of itself as inherently and exceptionally creative has aligned well with larger trends in economic policy and government priorities. It should be little surprise, then, when considering an industry whose primary purpose is to help other companies present themselves and their products in the best way possible, that advertising has taken advantage of this overlap in order to double-down on declarations of its own creativity: as we see in the renaming of the Cannes Lions festival, for example. However, despite the apparent centrality of the concept in both advertising and the wider 'creative industries' discourse, there is one significant problem with the idea of creativity: no one seems quite to know what it means. It is for this reason that David Hesmondhalgh and Sarah Baker declare that '"creativity" is an even looser word than [the notoriously slippery] culture' (2011, p. 560), while Ann Markusen et al. refer to creativity as 'fuzzy' and 'popular but problematic' (2008, pp. 24–25). This problem is potentially even more prevalent in advertising industry discussions, where the long history of association with the term has not led to any clear or stable sense of its meaning. Thus, even though there appears to be broad industry consensus regarding the importance of creativity to successful advertising, there is no such agreement about what it actually is or how it might be recognised.

The lack of a coherent definition of creativity in advertising is not for a lack of trying. Almost every guide to advertising offers its own take on this term, but the consequence is not an increasing consensus, but rather a constant expansion of possible meanings. Senior figures in advertising differ wildly in their conceptions: Sir John Hegarty defines creativity as the nebulous 'expression of self' (2014, p. 51), Jeremy Bullmore evokes the 'mad inventor' and discourses of disorder, gambling and the unknown (2006, pp. 19–20), while the approach of Bill Bernbach, the central figure of the Creative Revolution, is usually understood in terms such as authenticity, honesty, intelligence and humour (McStay, 2013, p. 21). As a result of this diversity, in place of any stable definition of creativity there is an ever increasing litany of hazy and imprecise descriptions and attributes by which it might be identified. Some react to this ambiguity by generating lists that proliferate ostensibly associated attributes. Chris Fill, Graham Hughes and Scott De Francesco, for example, offer a table addressing the different 'dimensions' of creativity, which are listed as 'originality', 'flexibility', 'elaboration', 'synthesis' and the particularly vague 'artistic value' (2013, p. 124). Similarly, Chris and Rungpaka Amy Hackley generate an extensive list of 'advertising creative appeals', including 'social status', 'family values', 'fear', 'humour', 'happiness', 'ambition' and 'celebrity endorsement' (2015, p. 137), while the Institute of Practitioners of

Advertising demonstrate that wooliness can also be found in industry contexts: in 'Judging Creative Ideas' – their guide for helping clients assess agency output – they suggest there is a 'ten-piece jigsaw' for making sense of creativity that can be summarised as knowledge, enjoyment, the client brief, empathy, clarity, questioning yourself, questioning the idea, reflection, refinement and relaxation (Institute of Practitioners, 2006, pp. 8–16). While such lists might appear to hold out the possibility that a definition can be arrived at through an ever-expanding catalogue of other words, in practice they tend to just add to the definitional deficit through an expansion of possible meanings and forms, rather than helping us zero in on a useful and precise meaning.

Perhaps the most frequently evoked definition identifies creativity as involved with originality or novelty: variations on this description in relation to advertising include creativity as the 'violation of expectation' (Fill, Hughes and De Francesco, 2013, p. 124), the 'out of the ordinary' (Stotesbury, 2005, p. 119), or Raymond Rubicam's famous advice to 'resist the usual' (Tibbs, 2010, p. 15). However, as Sean Nixon points out, this understanding of creativity is undermined by the fact that such claims towards radical difference are not really borne out in actual advertising: 'despite the grandiose claims often made about the work they did or would liked to have done, we might profitably interpret the rhetoric of creativity mobilised by creatives as an extrapolation of quite small differences or degrees of differentness' (Nixon, 2003, p. 77). Appeals to creativity as difference therefore ring somewhat hollow in practice, leaving us with little sense of any final meaning. Faced with this situation, some authors even embrace this lack of definition even as they argue for its relevance: Fill, Hughes and De Francesco make a strong declaration for the importance of creativity while simultaneously disavowing any attempt to define the nebulous term: 'Whatever it is, creativity matters' (2013, p. 124). Similarly, in a subchapter titled 'What is It [Creativity]?' Roger Stotesbury advocates strongly for the indispensable nature of creativity, but pointedly fails to answer his own question (2005, pp. 118–119). Across textbooks and industry documents the same pattern repeats itself: creativity is absolutely vital to successful advertising, but no one can say exactly what it is. Consequently, the definition of the concept is prone to shift depending upon who one consults in a manner that suggests not so much a productively flexible concept as a term that can be made to mean anything that the speaker wishes it to mean.

The problems with creativity

Despite the promises that 'creativity' holds out, the fundamental hollowness of the concept rules out any practical or productive application. The term is used 'vaguely and imprecisely, and sometimes in quite contradictory ways' (Negus and Pickering, 2004, p. vi). Creativity thus appears to function overwhelmingly as a 'cant word' (Nixon, 2003, p. 9; Williams, 1988, p. 84): a form of language that obscures rather than clarifies meaning. If this is the case then this raises the prospect that to repeatedly declare the importance of creativity in advertising might be, in effect, to repeatedly say nothing at all. Overstretched, the concept of creativity is drained of its credibility as 'the adjective "creative" is liberally applied to products and works that involve negligible amount of novelty. Alternatively the term creativity ends up trapped within a closed system as a completely self-referential concept' (Hartley et al., 2013, p. 67). Subject to such semantic abuse, creativity becomes an empty cipher that stands in for battles over prestige and power or as a clumsy catch-all for unrelated subjects. Nixon characterises this scenario as a 'cult of creativity' in advertising, where invocations of creativity work to legitimate a 'social fantasy' of success as a product of innate talent, more akin to rock stars than regular business (2003, p. 88). So transformed, creativity offers to resolve the ideological contradiction between the critical, disruptive, artistic aspirations of those who make advertising and the inescapable fact that pretty much all advertising is service work for corporations: creativity as a way that advertisers assure themselves that they are not 'hacks' (Nixon, 2003, pp. 76–78). It is little wonder, then, that faced with such an incoherent concept, the founding fathers of contemporary advertising were dismissive of the term. David Ogilvy declared that he was 'ashamed' to have ever used the word, which he likened to 'the originality of incompetence' (2004, pp. 118–119). Perhaps even more damning, Bill Bernbach, the original 'creative revolutionary', once lamented that 'I fear all the sins we may commit in the name of "Creativity." I fear that we may be entering an age of phonies (Bayers, 2011)'.

Rejecting creativity

Creativity, then, is repeatedly seen as damaged conceptual goods, a position that is also reflected in the wider critical literature on the topic, where commentators have increasingly come to 'creativity' as not simply incoherent but also tied up in economic reforms that actually undermine artistic freedom and working conditions (Cazdyn and Szeman, 2013; Hesmondhalgh and Baker, 2011; McRobbie, 2011; Negus and Pickering, 2004; Turner, 2012). A central part of this is the commodification of art and culture, which in terms of creative industries becomes reduced to sources of potential profit and high-end consumption, rather than sites of experimentation, representation and discussion (Peck, 2007). Produced for profit and separated from traditional ideas of deep thought and reflection, 'in the new cultural economy [creativity] is encouraged to be increasingly populist, noisy, easy, thin' (McRobbie, 2011, p. 85). Moreover, such work is often carried out in exploitative conditions, where workers are overworked and under-compensated for their labour on the basis that the opportunity to work in 'creative' ways is a reward in itself (Hesmondhalgh and Baker, 2011, pp. 6–8). As a consequence, the triumph of creativity seems to be achieving the opposite of what it promises: rather than offering a celebration of human expression and liberation from corporate priorities, it fundamentally subordinates human creation to the demands of the capitalist market. The lack of definitional clarity creates a void which is filled by the common sense platitudes of dominant capitalist ideology.

Thus, while on the surface creativity promises an alignment of the priorities of business and the arts, in practice it manifests as the complete capture of the latter by the former (Turner, 2012, pp. 105–107). This is perhaps best captured in the work of Richard Florida – one of the most celebrated advocates of the creative industries model – who states in a non-ironic and non-condemnatory way that 'human creativity is the ultimate economic resource' (2002, p. xiii) (a remark that is conspicuously absent from later, re-edited editions of the book, *Rise of the Creative Class*, in which it first appears – perhaps indicative of Florida's own retreat from such a blatant statement of economic priorities!). Such a perspective thus undercuts one of the main discursive roles of creativity in the context of advertising: to mark its purposes and practices as distinct from those of purely commercial work (Nixon, 2003, pp. 77–8). Instead of defining the 'creative' side of advertising in opposition to that carried out by the suits in accounts, creativity would instead seem to be an alternate manifestation of the same underlying economic impulses: a 'redefinition of business as art' (Cazdyn and Szeman, 2013, p. 96). For all the talk of inspiration and expression, creativity overwhelmingly seems to refer to a description of culture reduced to an economic resource, like oil or steel, something which can be bought and sold.

Advertising and art

So much for creativity, then: the promises that the concept offers in terms of reimagining advertising as a productive, inspiring media form are undermined by its lack of clarity and meaning that make it instead a vehicle for at best, lazy thinking, and at worst, a form of capitalist false consciousness. However, the abandonment of creativity as a critically useful term does not necessarily mean that advertising is simply a form of ideology delivery and nothing more: simply that creativity does not provide an adequate framework through which to make sense of this expanded concept of advertising. In place of creativity we therefore need a more coherent framework for making sense of advertising, which is why we now turn to 'art': an idea which seems to float around the fringes of discussions of creativity like its discarded former packaging. Indeed, the ideas of art and creativity have been historically closely linked (Williams, 1988, p. 41). The reason we turn to art at this juncture is because, unlike the poor abused notion of creativity, it retains a sense of what Eric Cazdyn and Imre Szeman refer to as 'the political' or even 'the world in general' (2013, p. 89). What this means is that whereas creativity seems to function as an almost inevitably self-contained concept – one is creative for the sake of being creative – art retains the possibility of 'challenging the limits of our ways of thinking, seeing, being and believing' (Cazdyn and Szeman, 2013, p. 99). Art can therefore *be* for other things beside itself: art is potentially, though certainly not always, linked to the wider world in political ways; whereas creativity, or at least the form it takes in current advertising discourse, only ever seems to link back to its generative context in terms of profitability and money. By shifting the terms of discussion from creativity to art, it becomes possible to emphasise coherent ways in which to rethink the cultural role of advertising beyond a reduction to economics.

This turn to art as an explanatory framework might seem unusual to some readers because, on the one hand, art often appears to be a traditional, conservative, even outdated idea that is a world apart from the fast-paced advertising industry: while on the other hand, art might be accused of also suffering from a similar overabundance of possible definitions as that found with creativity. There is a grain of truth to both points. Nonetheless, in contrast to the discourse around creativity, the multiple competing definitions of art have coalesced into a number of well-established and developed theoretical positions, the most relevant of which we will explore shortly. Moreover, the suggestion that art is an 'older' idea that does not align perfectly with advertising can be read as an advantage, because – provided we can account for the potential sites of tension and incompatibility – then the unlikely overlap should be able to help us see advertising in new and productive ways. Looking through the lens of an older idea like art can help us make sense of the phenomenon of contemporary advertising. However, in order to accomplish the substitution of art for creativity in a productive way, and not simply repeat the circuitous and spurious reasoning that characterises much of the thought around creativity, it is imperative that we define art in a careful and detailed fashion.

What is art? (and why should we care?)

Defining art can be a tricky job. There are not simply a few books on the subject: there are enough books to fill shelves, libraries even, with intelligent, thoughtful people grappling with the question of 'What is Art?' Furthermore, since this is a book about advertising, rather than art, it is necessary that we keep this discussion brief and focused upon the task at hand: how the idea of art might improve our understanding of advertising. As a result, rather than get bogged down in the quagmire of infinite variations upon functionalist, anti-essentialist, institutionalist, historical and neofunctionalist definitions (Stecker, 2000, pp. 46–47), we will focus on three particular ways of conceiving of art that can help illuminate what advertising is, what it does and what it doesn't do: a sociological-institutional definition, a formal-aesthetic definition and a critical-aesthetic definition. Each of these definitions speaks to a key site of interaction and tension between advertising and the art world and the potential power of advertising conceived as art.

One of the more common ideas about art is that it is entirely subjective: art is simply whatever you, I or anyone says it is. There is a certain democratic charm to this notion, but sadly it misses the important role that power plays in relation to art. You and I can declare any and everything to be a work of art – a picture painted by my kids, for example – and it really doesn't change anything. The drawing will remain stuck to the fridge. However, if a 'senior art world representative' were to share our opinion that those things constitute art, then the situation could certainly change: gallery doors would open, auction prices would rise and art critics would pay attention. It's a basic fact that in the world of art, some people's perspectives matter more than others in such discussions, and those people have the 'power to proclaim some things works of art and not others' in ways that have real consequences (Mulholland, 2007, p. 18). Such people don't have this power by virtue of some innate talent, but rather because they are part of a larger set of structures and organisations that constitute the art world: these include institutions (such as galleries and museums), rules and rituals (such as openings and exhibitions), categories (such as sculpture, impressionism and superflat) and appointments and designations (such as artists, critics, curators and academics). It is by dint of their sanctioned knowledge and informed engagement with those structures and organisations that particular persons are permitted to say what is art and what is not, in ways that others invested in the structure take notice of. Such an account of art is usually associated with sociologists, like Pierre Bourdieu, who understand the world of art as a 'field' that is organised according to key criteria, institutions and rules (1993, pp. 29–73). To view art in this way is to take an 'institutional' approach that arises from the sociological tradition and which sees art not as an objective category or a subjective opinion, but as part of a system of rules somewhat akin to a giant game (Mulholland, 2007, pp. 27–28). For advertising to qualify as art in this model, the object has to participate in the game of art such that it gains the approval of the right people in the right places. The reward for acceptance into this world is the greater economic, social and even potentially moral value afforded to 'art'.

At perhaps the opposite end of possible definitions is the formalist-aesthetic definition of art. Instead of seeing the category of art as a product of a system of rules and rituals, this definition would see it as a category which particular texts and artefacts become part of by virtue of specific properties that they contain. Such a definition follows in the tradition of the eighteenth-century German philosopher Immanuel Kant, who has probably had more influence over our contemporary idea of art than anyone else. Kant argued that in order for something to be seen as art, it has to 'reject all functionality' (Fenner, 2008, p. 7). A work of art is therefore worthy not because of any advantage or utility it offers us, or premised in rational calculation, but because of the pleasure we find in the encounter with its fundamental lack of purpose, or purposelessness (Kant, 2000, pp. 167–169). Separated from the demands and rules of the rest of the world, art is free to experiment and create in ways that are not tied to achievement of any particular end. From this Kantian beginning arise a whole series of influential arguments around art: that art is a matter of form rather than content (not what is represented, but how it is represented); the art should be for 'art's sake', rather than for any external forces; that art is a site of 'free play'. These arguments are usually understood as questions of aesthetics, which refers to the formal and sensual qualities of the art work. Such a position also informs assumptions that art is inherently inspiring or represents a higher form of truth, because freed from the determining factors of everyday life it can engage in pure sensual experimentation and speak to larger aspects of the human condition. This is not entirely separate from the sociological definition – indeed members of the art world evoke formalist-aesthetic models of art in order to justify their practice – but the two definitions can operate in isolation. From this perspective, art does not need to be sanctioned by the art establishment: it needs to arise out of the context of formal aesthetic freedom.

The final definition with which we will concern ourselves builds out of and on top of the formal-aesthetic definition. To think about art in critical-aesthetic terms is to accept the premise that art arises from an attempted separation from the world, but to argue that the separation is always only ever partial: that art can never be entirely separate from the society that creates it and it has the power to influence that society and change the way we understand it. Moving beyond the ideas of individual genius and inspiration that inform the formal-aesthetic model, the critical-aesthetic model thus seeks to understand art as something that always exists at a social and cultural, we might even say ideological, level. Aesthetics are therefore not simply a matter of form but also an important part of how an artwork communicates meaning and ideology. This perspective arises largely out of the Marxist tradition, with thinkers such as Theodor Adorno, Raymond Williams, Frederic Jameson and, most recently, in the work of Jacques Rancière. You hopefully might remember these names from earlier in this book (and this chapter!) as critics of advertising who have stridently proclaimed that advertising is a herald of cultural decline and the death of the liberatory potential of aesthetics. Indeed, this tradition often imagines art as the indirect opposite of advertising, where the ability of art to enact positive change in the world is measured by its distance from the market capitalism in which advertising is based. Indeed, this is true of all three definitions, where art is usually imagined as separate from, if not entirely opposed to, the monetary dealings of capitalism. This therefore potentially presents something of a problem if we try to interpret advertising as art in light of this model; an objection that we will address shortly by considering how exactly we can understand the aesthetic aspects of advertising.

Advertising inside the institutions of art

It might appear as a simple matter of fact that advertising is not welcome in the institutions of the art world. There certainly appears to be a clear line between those images, videos and sounds that are exhibited in galleries and the use of the same to sell fast food and flat-screen TVs. However, this distinction between the two worlds has not always historically been so stark and may actually continue to be more fluid and unstable than is often acknowledged. As Andrew McStay notes, 'the idea that art and advertising exist in different domains is ... problematized by the history of creative advertising and poster art in particular' (2013, p. 39). A historical case in point is the close relation between painting and early advertising in the earliest moments of advertising in the nineteenth century: when the rights to John Everett Millais' oil painting, 'A Child's World' were infamously purchased by Thomas J. Barratt, the chairman of A&F Pears, and became the basis for the famous 'Bubbles' advertisement for Pears Soap through the addition of the product's logo that effectively 're-anchored' the image. Although, the appropriation of the painting attracted some controversy at the time, it was also the subject of praise by those who thought the integration of fine arts into advertising would help raise the standard of the latter (Iskin, 2014, pp. 225–6; Twitchell, 1997, pp. 184–186). Nor was this an isolated example: the 'move was immediately emulated by the company's competitor, with use of a painting by William Frith' (Gee, 2013, p. 129). Such appropriation was indicative of the ease with which texts might cross the fine line that separated art and advertising at the time: the resulting uproar can be read as a desperate attempt to shore up that division, which seemed under threat from some practices, as much as a statement of any widespread opposition to the appropriation.

Indeed, such crossovers between advertising and art persisted throughout the nineteenth and twentieth centuries with remarkably porous boundaries between the two. Notable examples of cross-pollination include the Poster

Movement of late nineteenth-century Paris, where Jules Chéret received great acclaim for his advertising posters inspired by the Rococo art movement and Japanese woodblock print-making (Gee, 2013, p. 130). The work of Chéret, who is often referred to as the 'father of the modern poster' (Clifford, 2014, p. 13), won great acclaim, even at the time: his advertisements were gathered into print editions for international collectors and were celebrated as 'exemplar[s] of reformed, democratic art' (Gee, 2013, pp. 130–131). Such a definition points us towards a wider understanding of advertising as an art form that brightens the lives of everyday people and helps give their world colour, vibrancy and even enchantment. Understood in this way, advertising is a practice that fills our lives with artwork that bring narrative and splendour to otherwise dull environments.

The work of Chéret and other French pioneers, such as Toulouse-Lautrec, in turn inspired other artist-advertisers across Europe, who developed their own styles incorporating the aesthetic innovations of the day. The Czech artist Alphonse Mucha was a key proponent of the Art Nouveau style, whose most influential contributions took the form of advertising posters, while the Beggarstaff brothers in the United Kingdom pushed the boundaries of public taste with their abstract compositions (Gee, 2013, p. 132). In the first half of the twentieth century, poster makers across Europe incorporated the formal styles of avant-garde art movements and brought them to the wider public: Frank Brangwyn embraced the jagged lines of Expressionism; Tom Purvis incorporated the flat colour planes of post-Impressionism; Edward McKnight Kauffer used cutting-edge collage techniques and Cassandre popularised the fractured forms of Cubism. The art world, in turn, accepted and legitimated the work of these advertisers: both Mucha and Chéret are the subjects of numerous books reproducing and celebrating their work, and advertisements by Brangwyn, Purvis, Kauffer and Cassandre can be found in the collection of New York's Museum of Modern of Modern Art, which has done much to integrate these materials into the mainstream of the art world (Bogart, 1995, p. 122). Such free passage between the worlds of art and advertising suggests that the two spheres experienced substantial overlap and there was less of a stigma of advertising in the art world than we might expect.

It was only with the rise of American advertising techniques following the end of World War Two that this close-knit relationship of art and advertising began to unravel in an international context. In contrast to the artistic styles and forms that had been gaining recognition in European contexts, the American style emphasised realist representation of commodities accompanied by generic photographic images of suburban life (Gee, 2013, p. 136). The ascendancy of the American style as the new global norm in advertising in the 1950s therefore led to an increasing separation of the domains of art and advertising.

However, this was not the end of a connection between the two realms, but simply the beginning of a new phase: in the 1960s, art turned to advertising for 'inspiration', just as advertising had earlier turned to art. Any discussion of the permeability between advertising and art worlds would be incomplete without a consideration of the Pop Art of Andy Warhol and his contemporaries, who took the raw material of everyday commercial life, including advertising and brands, as the raw material for their art. One of the most influential artists of the twentieth century, Warhol worked as a commercial illustrator earlier in his career and took advertising imagery as one of his key sources of inspiration (Fallon, 2011, p. 15). Perhaps his best-known work is his series of paintings of Campbell's Soup cans that directly reflect the object-orientated illustration of advertising, while Warhol also incorporated silk-screening processes, normally associated with advertising, into his artistic practice. In these ways, Warhol's art undermined clear barriers between art and advertising in terms of content, form and method. Like Marcel Duchamp before him – who courted scandal in 1917 by attempting to exhibit a urinal in an art show – Warhol directly challenged the boundaries of what those invested in the field of art considered appropriate for inclusion in gallery and museum spaces by introducing advertising into the sanctified institutions of art.

Other artists working in the Pop Art movement also contributed to the blurring of lines between advertising and art: Warhol's contemporary Richard Hamilton assembled collages from cut-outs of advertisements, and many artists would follow in Warhol's footsteps: Richard Prince's 'Cowboys' series (1980–1992) reworked material from Marlboro cigarette commercials in order to interrogate American masculinity. Indeed, following Warhol, the divisions between art and advertising can seem very thin, from Absolut vodka's Warhol-themed branding and art awards, to a figure like Charles Saatchi: not only a founder of global advertising agency, Saatchi and Saatchi, but also a leading international art collector and patron. In the post-Warhol world, such crossovers are much more common than might be thought, as advertising increasingly circulates in sanctioned display spaces previously reserved for fine art and discussed in terms of aesthetics and appreciation that previously would have been off-limits. Museums and galleries will have exhibitions of advertising works, and publishers of art books will produce volumes dedicated to advertising. Thus, while not all ads are automatically considered the equal of Van Gogh, there are areas of meaningful intersection and cross-pollination that illustrate how advertising can certainly be accepted in terms of the 'game' of art. From such a position, the only thing separating art and advertising is the acceptance of art's in-crowd, which is increasingly extended to advertising. In such terms, the nature of the particular text does not matter, as much as where it is displayed and who comes to see it.

Aesthetic advertising

However, for advertising to be accepted into the realms of art on institutional-sociological terms is not particularly consequential in a wider sense, because when understood in these terms, the designation 'art' is little more than a tautology signifying that the object in question has successfully navigated the rules and systems of the art world. Such acceptance therefore says little about what advertising as art might do or be; only that it has sometimes been awarded the title of art and the cultural status that accompanies it. This could even be interpreted as more of a statement about the 'decline' of the art world, rather than anything about advertising. Therefore, if seeking to really reappraise the artistic status of advertising it is necessary to consider not just its acceptance into the art world, but whether how it measures up in terms of the formalist-aesthetic model of art. As discussed above, at the heart of the formalist-aesthetic formulation of art is the concept of purposelessness: the idea that art is produced and consumed for no practical or utilitarian purpose and therefore expresses some sort of fundamental freedom from the mundane world. This attribute of art has been expressed in multiple ways, including the phrase 'art for art's sake', by which its advocates sought to reject the use of art for educational, political or moral purposes, and the concept of art's 'autonomy', which sought to ring-fence art from the rest of the world, so that it could develop according to its own aesthetic priorities. However it is expressed though, this criterion would seem to immediately rule out the inclusion of advertising, which has been described as 'an art with a *purpose*, namely to make what happens in the marketplace interesting to consumers on a permanent basis' (Leiss et al., 2015, p. 414, emphasis added). Advertising always, by its very definition, has a purpose – to sell – and it is that purpose, rather than any particular convention, style or tradition, that makes advertising advertising. This objection on the grounds of inalienable purpose would therefore seem to disqualify advertising from being art in formal-aesthetic terms.

There are, however, two potential challenges to advertising's non-acceptance as art: the first is on historical grounds, the second is conceptual. In his history of the avant-garde – a series of influential art movements in the late nineteenth and early twentieth centuries, including Cubism and Expressionism – Peter Bürger argues that the autonomy of art is not an eternal truth, but rather the result of historical processes. Prior to the nineteenth century, art was certainly not produced for its own sake, but rather was part of religious devotion and proselytising, or for the glory of monarchs and feudal courts (Bürger, 1984, pp. 46–48). Consequently, some of the most famous and inspirational examples of art were not made as 'art' but rather as sacral artefacts or demonstrations of courtly power. Moreover, even though it presented itself as such, avant-garde art was not wholly autonomous, but has been widely recognised as tethered to the demands of patrons and the art market 'by an umbilical cord of gold' (Greenburg, 1957, p. 101). Claims to complete autonomy are therefore undermined by the basic fact that artists need to eat, and therefore they have always needed financial support, whether from a patron or the market, in order to make art for a living. When we pay closer attention to the material conditions of art production we begin to notice that 'many artists specifically produce things to be sold, [and] artist's letters from the past are full of references to monetary matters' (Schroeder, 2000, p. 39). Consequently, the fact that advertisers are paid to do their jobs does not necessarily make them that much different from those often held up as the paradigmatic examples of autonomous art in light of the 'the commission-caging stunts of the old masters, and their apparent willingness to accommodate clients' demands' (Brown and Patterson, 2000, p. 15). Most artists, like most advertisers, are tied to the world by brute economic facts.

Recognition of the material-economic aspects of art implied by an historical account does not necessarily mean though that the autonomy of art is simply a myth, but rather that autonomy is not as pure and all-encompassing as the more abstract definitions might suggest. Instead, Bürger suggests that it is a particular aspect of art – the aesthetic – that is autonomous (1984, pp. 40–41). This conception of art, autonomy and aesthetics is potentially productive in terms of advertising, because it allows us to consider how – although advertising is obviously tied to capitalism – the aesthetic aspects of advertising might nonetheless be considered autonomous. When we speak of the aesthetic aspects of advertising we are interested in its form, style, palette, rhythm, narrative and structure, the use of colour, sound and words, the stories told and the images presented, the combination of different sensual elements that is always more than just the presentation of a commodity. We know the 'what' of advertising – it sells us things – but a concern with aesthetics redirects us to consider the 'how' of advertising.

Advertising as art?

Such elements are particularly apparent in an example such as Sony's 2005 ad for its Bravia range: 'Bouncy Balls'. Widely celebrated at the time of its initial release, the ad remains widely available online and is a continuing reference point in discussions of the expressive and artistic potential of advertising. The ad's central concept is strikingly simple: thousands of brightly coloured bouncy balls cascade down the steep streets of San Francisco to the soundtrack of Jose Gonzales' acoustic version of 'Heartbeats'. The camera cuts quickly between different shots and perspectives, but the film nonetheless feels slow and dreamlike due to the use of slow-motion footage, unhurried shifts of focus between the different visual planes and the relatively relaxed speed of the editing compared to the rapid bouncing. The result is a visually captivating play of colour that is simultaneously fast and slow, amazing and everyday, and which demonstrates the ability of artistic work to transform an ordinary space into a site of wonder. These qualities of the ad are not so much a matter of what the ad is about – it lacks any real sense of subject or even message – but rather the manner in which it presents itself. The central purpose here is visual wonder, which certainly ties into a sales pitch for the product in question, but the power of which cannot be entirely explained or argued away simply by virtue of its status as an advertisement.

Such an example is therefore indicative of how advertisers were (and are) capable of aesthetic experimentation in ways that can approximate the 'free play' historically reserved only for sanctified artists. Indeed, inspired by avant-garde artists, many advertisers actively and explicitly sought to use advertisements as their canvas on which to create new ways of seeing the world by 'yok[ing] formal innovation to thematic predictability and experimental techniques to familiar scenes' (Lears, 1994, p. 302). As we explored in Chapter 7, creatives often regard themselves as unbeholden to pressure from clients and the profit motive and seek to freely express themselves and entertain and challenge their audience, as much as sell a product. Thus, while clients may not always appreciate formal innovation and aesthetic experimentation, and indeed can actively block campaigns they feel distract from their goals, there always exists the potential for advertisements to offer aesthetic experiences in the small spaces of freedom carved away from client's briefs. While such freedom is far from the norm, the possibility that it exists, indeed almost the inevitability that it must exist somewhere at some time, opens the door for the interpretation of advertising along formal-aesthetic lines.

Advertising changing the world

It would be a mistake, however, to think that the artists associated with the avant-garde were only interested in painting, sculpting, writing and composing in new ways. Rather their artistic efforts were part of a larger, bolder project: to recreate the world by creating new ways of imagining, interpreting and understanding it (Rancière, 2004, pp. 29–30). This bolder set of claims aligns with the critical-aesthetic tradition, where aesthetic freedom in art is regarded not as an end in itself, but as a meaningful contribution to political change. Thus the visible, stabbing brush strokes and vibrant, clashing colours of Expressionism aspired to speak fundamental truth through art in order to reflect a new epoch for mankind (Kandinsky and Marc, 2011, pp. 36–37), the distorted, multiple viewpoints of Cubism represented fractured and fracturing perspectives on space and time (Gleizes and Metzinger, 2000, pp. 10–14), while Suprematism sought to represent a world beyond the organising categories and familiar forms of human thought (Malevich, 2011, pp. 106–125). In the work of the avant-garde, the potential distance between aesthetics and social norms allows art to comment on and potentially alter the perception of what is politically desirable, socially possible and even of reality itself (c.f. Adorno, 1997, p. 2; Bloch, 2002, p. 22; Brecht, 2002, pp. 74–75).

Before we get ahead of ourselves, we should probably slow down though: such bold claims may well seem out of place in a discussion of advertising. After all, even the most experimental agencies were after formal innovation but not the 'political and cultural convictions' associated with the avant-garde (Lears, 1994, p. 340). However, as discussed above, it is precisely through the use of form that the critical-aesthetic model of art understands the political force of art to operate: the aesthetic aspects of advertising may therefore convey specific meanings or complicated messages regarding consumerism. Thus, the fact that as early as the 1960s, major advertisers like Pepsi were incorporating aesthetic techniques – such as 'rapid-fire clustering of images' (Lears, 1994, p. 343) – initially pioneered by the avant-garde should give us some pause before we write off the critical potential of advertising aesthetics. In fact, a great number of the aesthetic techniques that characterise contemporary advertising were initially pioneered in the context of avant-garde aesthetics. From the fourth-wall breaking dialogue of 'The Man Your Man Could Smell Like' ads for Old Spice, which recall the Epic Theatre of Bertolt Brecht, to the familiar sight of talking animals and inanimate objects, which draws on Surrealist traditions, our advertising is defined by forms of presentation that emerge out of experimental aesthetic traditions rather than traditional realist or simple declamatory forms. Even the utterly banal practice of cutting between shots based on theme or tone, a technique that is the absolute norm in advertising, rather than the exception, finds its origins in the experimental film-making of Sergei Eisenstein rather than any mainstream cinema or TV practice. Nor were any of these aesthetic practices developed simply for ornamental purposes, but rather as ways to bring the audience to certain political understandings through their experience of the artwork. Recounting his work as art director for the pioneering agency Papert, Koenig, George Lois declares that 'I hated the system, I hated the status quo, we were changing the system and everyone respected it. They really understood you were changing the culture and making political, graphic statements ... I was always trying to sell the product but I was also making a point – I think advertising can be, should be and at times has been revolutionary, subversive' (quoted in Pray, 2009). While Lois is far from the norm, the existence of such sentiments in the advertising world certainly suggests some potential or at least aspiration towards critique.

The central question, then, is whether such practice is possible through advertising, or is a figure like Lois deluding himself? Does the aesthetic still have the ability to bring about changes in awareness and understanding once it is incorporated into the everyday practice of advertising or are aesthetic innovations reduced to gimmicks by the shift in context? This is a larger and more useful question than whether advertising qualifies as art, instead asking us to consider whether the cultural role of advertising as a media form is completely over-determined by its function to sell. Writing of the relation between advertising and the avant-garde, Jackson Lears suggests that when incorporated into advertising, such techniques are reduced to 'technical brilliance' because they lack the 'authenticity' of art or a commitment to 'telling some difficult truth about human experience' (1994, p. 343). Similarly, Williams argues that the 'special insensitivity of the trained and assured technicists' of advertising reduces the disconnection techniques of modernist art to commercial iconography (2007, p. 35). Such an argument is indicative of the position that the aesthetic power and protest of the avant-garde becomes neutralised when incorporated into the dominant structures of capitalism. In this interpretation, advertising can never carry the same aesthetic challenge to existing power structures as the work of the avant-garde because its conditions of production mean that it always operates in the service of the dominant ideology of capitalism.

In contrast, others have argued that the integration of aesthetic dissent into advertisings makes it potentially more, rather than less, disruptive because of the 'wider circulation, constant repetition and, most importantly, "not art" status' of advertising (Brown and Patterson, 2000, p. 13). This alternative interpretation thus argues that advertising not only exposes a wider group of people to forms of aesthetic critique in a more consistent way, but that they are more effective because their audience don't see them coming in the same way. Whereas audiences of avant-garde art expect to be shocked, enthralled or challenged as a matter of course, and are therefore inured to such provocations, advertising audiences do not as a rule expect to be confronted in the same way, so in those instances when such an aesthetic encounter does occur it is all the more profound for being unanticipated. To permit the possibility that a critique of current ways of life, and indeed of capitalism and consumerism, might emerge from advertising is therefore to suggest that the capitalist context does not always completely over-determine the potential for culture, and for aesthetics in particular, to offer a different vision of the world. In this model, advertising isn't simply a straightforward expression of capitalism, but rather an attempt by companies to capture and control a form of artistic expression that exists outside capitalism, and therefore can potentially (but certainly not always, or even frequently) give voice to alternative ways of understanding and engaging in the world (Gilbert, 2008, p. 109).

The stakes of advertising as art

At stake in this argument is the question of whether the capitalist context always over-determines the power of advertising, and commercially produced culture more generally, to say meaningful and even critical things about the society that produces it. Does the fact that something is made for profit mean that it cannot challenge the idea of profit as the basis for society? This question cannot be answered in any final sense here, indeed it should not, because the answer to this question changes depending upon the context in which it is asked and the examples which are available. Therefore, rather than saying once and for all whether advertising can be or not be art, with all the values, privileges and implications that attend to that term, we should instead consider whether and how does advertising work as art here and now, in the context that we are living in and attempting to make sense of. This does not mean that we simply return to the idea that 'art' is simply whatever you and I say it is, nor is it a return to the ultimately empty conceptual free-for-all opened up by the idea of 'creativity': instead, it means thinking carefully about how particular instances of advertising might fit one, all or none of the three definitions of 'art' that we have explored in this chapter and what that means for how we understand the social, cultural and political role of advertising. To refer to advertising as art thereby becomes more than a statement of appreciation; it becomes a means by which to conceptualise a whole new set of possibilities for the social work of advertising. Thus, while advertising has often been referred to in glib or dismissive ways as the 'art of capitalism', if we take this statement at face value then it opens up potentially powerful new ways of understanding advertising. To consider the aesthetic aspects of advertising is therefore not so much to discount or supplant its status as an expression of capitalism, but rather to complicate and nuance our understanding of advertising's important relationship to art, culture, politics and capitalism.

CHAPTER 9

Empowering consumers: Engagement, interpretation and resistance

In the autumn of 1956, audiences at the Fort Lee movie theatre in New Jersey, USA, were subject to one of the most infamous experiments in advertising history. Unbeknown to movie-goers, over a six-week period screenings of the 1955 film *Picnic* were interspersed with two messages that were flashed on screen for 1/3000 of a second every five seconds. The first message read 'eat popcorn'. The second message read 'drink Coca-Cola'. As a result of these flashed messages, the man responsible for the experiment, James Vicary, claimed that popcorn consumption increased by 57.5 per cent and Coca-Cola consumption increased by 18.1 per cent. The good people of Fort Lee had been part of one of the first and most famous demonstrations of what would come to be called 'subliminal advertising'.

There is, however, one problem with this story: *Vicary's experiment was a sham.* Given the subsequent confusion around central details, there is some doubt as to whether it even took place and if it did its effects were almost certainly massively exaggerated. At the very least, the experiment lacked a control group, and therefore had no way to measure the apparent effect against an audience not exposed to the messages. In his retelling of the Fort Lee experiment, Charles Acland, on whose account the above description is based, describes how due to a proliferation of different versions and renditions of the event very few facts of the incident can be confirmed (2012, pp. 91–94). For example, in some reports the location of the movie theatre changes, the movie in question was not named until two years after the experiment apparently took place and by Vicary's own later testimony the results were overstated, if not invented outright. Such public overstatement was typical of Vicary, who by this stage of his career had shown a gift for self-publicity and was fast becoming a public face of the new 'science' of marketing research

(Acland, 2012, pp. 96–101). Yet, despite the profound lack of evidence around the experiment, this particular incident would go on to serve as one of the founding myths of subliminal advertising: a form of communication that ostensibly implants thoughts directly into the human brain by operating at a level below normal perception.

The reason that we open this chapter with a discussion of subliminal advertising is because it draws our attention to the relationship between advertisements and consumers and prompts us to consider how much power advertising has over its audience. To be clear, subliminal advertising does not work: despite extensive industry and scientific attempts to replicate Vicary's experiment, researchers have known since the 1960s that there is absolutely no proof that stimuli are more effective when they are imperceptible (Acland, 2012, pp. 17–20). By looking at subliminal advertising, we are therefore reminded of the need to not overstate the power of advertising and give audiences sufficient credit as regards the ability to question, as well as accept, advertising messages. In contrast to the assumptions of the subliminal model, the realities of audience–advertising interactions are much more complicated and much more interesting. Audiences discuss, judge, criticise, love, hate, ignore and resist advertising: sometimes they even make their own. In this chapter, we will take up the notion of agency explored in the chapter 7 and apply it to audiences as we did to advertisers: this will involve a consideration of the different ways in which audiences use, interpret, reject and resist advertising messages. Thus, just as advertisers are more than faceless robots seeking to reproduce capitalist ideology, we will consider how advertising audiences are more than just passive dupes who absorb and accept instructions to consume. In doing so, I hope to respond to Daniel Miller's call to 'rescue the humanity of consumers from being reduced to a rhetorical trope in the critique of capitalism' (2001, p. 234). Not only does an appreciation of audience agency better respect the intelligence and critical capacities of the audience, but once we understand that advertisements don't directly inject meanings into the brains of consumers, we are better placed to assess the ways that advertising is actually taken up by audiences.

The active advertising audience

In its exploration of the ramifications of the active audience, this chapter will begin by considering how that idea informs both critical and industry studies approaches to advertising. In the context of marketing and consumer studies, such an approach to audiences leads to a consideration of the ways in which audiences can use advertising to meet their own social, cultural and personal needs: as the basis for forming communities of common interest, as resources by which to define their identity or as part of their online presentation of self. Taking up a different angle, in the context of media and cultural studies, the active audience usually forms the basis for examining how audiences often resist advertising messages and consumerism more generally. In its more extreme forms, such resistance can often take the form of activism, and we'll also look briefly at some prominent forms of anti-consumerism. This will then lead us into a consideration of how advertising responds and adapts to these different forms of resistance by incorporating political and anti-consumerist language or by adopting non-traditional methods for delivering advertising messages. Finally, the chapter will conclude with a discussion of how, taking the complicated dance of audience resistance and advertising response into account, we might conceive of the politics of audience's responses to advertising.

At what we can consider the opposite end of the scale to the subliminal model of advertising – where advertising exerts influence on an audience without their knowledge or consent – is the notion of the active audience. A dominant research paradigm in a number of different disciplines concerned with advertising studies, the active audience approach works on the central proposition that audiences do not passively absorb meaning, but are instead 'active producers of meanings from within their own cultural context' (Barker, 2012, p. 326). Building on that starting proposition, there are many different ways in which we can conceive that production of meaning depending on how we characterise the audience's active engagement.

Encoding/decoding and the active audience

In the context of Media and Cultural studies, the dominant conception of the active audience is the Encoding-Decoding model, which is concerned with how audiences interpret the meanings of cultural texts in light of their particular context. This approach to audiences arises out of a working paper authored by cultural theorist Stuart Hall, in which he set out a model for understanding the transmission of meaning in mass media at the points of both production (encoding) and consumption (decoding). For the purposes of studying the active audience, it is the decoding or consumption stage that is the most important. Hall suggests that rather than passively absorb the meaning of a media text (such as an advertisement), the technological, economic and social contexts of the audience will shape how they decode, or interpret, the text (1996, p. 128–130). Different audience members will therefore interpret the text differently based on factors such as by what technological means they access the text and their ideological beliefs. Hall suggests that there are three main stances an audience member can take as regards the text: they can accept it as the producer intended, reject it or, most commonly, 'negotiate' with it to accept certain elements while contesting, questioning or refusing others. By and large, most audiences tend to fall into this last, broad category where they are neither entirely opposed or accepting of the textual meaning. Hall's model allows us to understand how interpretation and interaction is, on the one hand, not completely free or individual, but, on the other hand, is also never completely circumscribed by a single 'correct' meaning (1996, pp. 136–137).

Hall's model has the added benefit of having been empirically tested by David Morley and Charlotte Brunsdon in their 1980 *Nationwide* project, in which he studied audience responses to the *Nationwide* news programme. Morley and Brunsdon's study demonstrated how different audience members interpreted a news story in different ways depending upon their occupation, gender and class position (Morley and Brunsdon, 1999, pp. 257–270; Kim, 2004, pp. 103–104). Unfortunately, given the resources such a study demands and the potential commercial sensitivity of the subsequent information, no similar applied investigation of encoding/decoding has been carried out with advertisements. In the absence of empirical data, the study of advertising decoding has been carried out in more abstract terms: for example, in terms of semiotics and ideological analysis as considered in Chapter 3. Nonetheless, even in the absence of such information it is possible to offer some further development of how audiences might negotiate or resist the meanings of ads. Leiss et al., for example, suggest three main ways in which audiences resist advertising on the level of interpretation: 'ideological resistance', 'modes of address resistance' and 'lifestyle resistance' (2005, p. 506). Drawing on interviews with teenagers about advertising, Leiss et al. suggest all three modes of resistance are active sites in which audiences contest and challenge the meanings of ads (2005, pp. 508–518).

Lifestyle resistance refers to a rejection of the world presented in the ad, particularly in terms of the desirability of the values presented, where 'values' refers to both abstract ethical codes, and very pragmatic values in terms of clothing and hair style. It can be difficult for advertisers to stay up to date with all the subtleties of new fashions, trends and opinions, and this can leave advertisements vulnerable to scorn and rejection when they inevitably fail to accurately capture contemporary taste (Leiss et al., 2005, pp. 508–9). A similarly fraught area is what Leiss et al. refer to as 'modes of address'. This term denotes what can be thought of as the 'tone' of the ad: whether it is being ironic or earnest, comic or serious, enthusiastic or subtle (2005, pp. 515–516). Therefore, while 'lifestyle resistance' refers to whether consumers can identify with the people and promises represented by the ad, resistance in terms of modes of address refers to how the ad speaks to the audience and whether that way of speaking lines up with how the audience likes to be spoken to. Finally, 'ideological resistance' refers to an audience's rejection of an ad because of the assumed worldview it embodies. This most often takes the form of an objection to advertising representations regarded as racist or sexist (Leiss et al., 2005, pp. 511–512): an important acknowledgement that audiences don't just absorb the ideology of ads, but can also refuse it. In wider terms, ideological resistance can also take place in relation to statements around individuality (Leiss et al., 2005, p. 513) or even consumerism itself. All three forms of interpretive resistance are examples of audiences not simply passively absorbing the meanings of ads, but instead rejecting meanings intended by producers or deciphering them in their own way. Sometimes this occurs intentionally when audiences actively consider and critique an advertisement, but just as often interpretive resistance happens inadvertently due to a mismatch in expectations or experiences between advertiser and audience.

Uses and gratifications (and complications) of advertising audiences

In contrast to the interpretive model, in marketing and consumer research, the dominant conception of the active audience is what is referred to as the Use and Gratifications model (U&G): a theoretical model that is, as the name suggests, primarily concerned with the use to which audiences put advertising and the gratifications they receive from it. U&G is frequently understood, following the early formative work of Elihu Katz, as a concern with 'what people do with media' as opposed to 'what media do to people': 'It is a model of media analysis that envisions the audience as active participants who engage with media in order to consciously satisfy their own needs and wants' (Jensen, 2002, p. 157). As such, audiences are thought to engage with advertising because they make a conscious choice to do so, because of the pleasures and benefits they can gain from such engagement. U&G was most influential in media and communications research during the 1970s and 1980s, but has since fallen out of favour in those disciplines due to concerns about its potential overstatement of the audience's self-control and self-knowledge and the assumption that media exist in order to serve clear, beneficial functions in society. However, despite the recent lack of favour in the more critical disciplines, the U&G model continues to inform much of the research into audience engagement with advertising and consumer culture in the context of marketing studies. The continuing influence of U&G can be seen, for example, in Sergio Cabrera and Christine Williams' analytic overview of recent marketing textbooks where they find that:

> According to the textbooks, the consumers' role is to have boundless needs, wants, and desires for which they turn to the market for fulfilment. It is

> assumed that consumers are seeking to fulfil their needs, wants, or desires while simultaneously maximising the 'value' that they receive from this fulfilment. Influenced by their culture, subculture, values, beliefs, attitudes, lifestyle, personality, life-cycle stage, age, gender, family, and social and reference groups (including class), as well as other psychological factors, the actions of consumers in the market are assumed to be rational and predictable.
> (2004, p. 361)

From this perspective, consumer engagement with consumable goods – and with the advertisements that provide those goods with meanings and values in the context of global capitalism – is a semi-logical process by which those consumers seek to obtain uses and gratifications from those encounters.

I note that this process is only 'semi-logical' in order to highlight that although Cabrera and Williams assert that the marketing model presumes 'rational and predictable' consumers, contemporary research in marketing is particularly concerned with non-conscious behaviour modification from advertising. Indeed, one of the main topics of marketing and consumer research is the way in which consumer decision-making is determined by prior knowledge, priming and cultural expectations (Ariely and Norton, 2009, pp. 478–480). Thus, although the consumer is understood to be rationally self-interested in their pursuit of satisfaction, it is not presumed that they are rational in their assessment of how their own acts of consumption lead to satisfaction. A case in point is a study that shows that consumers who self-identify as preferring Coca-Cola fail to exercise that preference when branding is removed (Ariely and Norton, 2009). Such findings emphasise the central role of advertising in shaping consumer engagement and preference, and – in a manner that recalls the discussions of commodity fetishism and sign-value in Chapter 5 – we can see how audiences' priorities regarding consumption are shaped as much by advertising as they are by the actual material and physiological facts of consumption. The uses and gratifications an audience receive from the purchase and consumption of Coke are more about its brand identity than its mixture of sugar, carbonated water and caffeine. In fact, a comprehensive review of marketing research identifies a large number of such biases and priming techniques that 'serve to shape people's preferences without their awareness' and which can sway consumer preference (Ariely and Norton, 2009, p. 490). The cumulative effect of such research works to trouble the image of the empowered consumer by suggesting that there are persuasive forces at work in advertising that might complicate the notion of autonomous audience decision-making.

However, despite an increasing awareness of such subconscious processes in consumer reactions to advertising, such influences and prejudices are still largely interpreted in light of the active U&G model in marketing research. What this means is that rather than being interpreted as challenges that fundamentally undermine the central assumption of almost-total audience control, the revelation of psychological complications is integrated into existing U&G models, such that they are understood as deviations from an overall pattern of rational behaviour rather than indicative of a fundamental loss of control on the part of the audience. Thus, there still remains the central assumption that people do things with media rather than vice versa, but with the added caveat that the uses and gratifications that audiences find in media are partly shaped by the way those media are presented to them. It is this sense of audience empowerment that is key to the active audience model, especially when considered in relation to the relatively powerless view of the audience that is often explicit in more critical, political economic accounts. Hence, while preferences and even experiences such as taste may not be anchored in a completely material awareness of objects – which recalls Williams' concept of 'the magic system' – they nonetheless are presented as a rational response to the identities, meanings and values presented through advertising. Importantly, this acknowledgement of non-material influences of consumption stops well short of the influence imagined in the subliminal model. Rather, this is an acknowledgment that when considering the ways in which audiences make use of the media, cultural desires are just as real and legitimate as physiological and material desires. In such a framework, advertising audiences remain largely empowered to make their own autonomous choices about their media engagement, with the proviso that audience decisions are affected by influences such as social and cultural context.

What does the audience get from advertising?

Having considered the various complications associated with the U&G model it is perhaps time to consider what, then, are the uses and gratifications which audiences seek from advertising? The simplest answer is that the audience gains information: information as regards goods and services available for purchase. An understanding of advertising as the provision of information is one of the most longstanding assumptions in market research. When advertising is understood primarily in terms of information transfer, then there is a focus upon how audiences interpret advertising in order to learn about products, their features and their cost so that they can make rational choices about how to spend their money. From such a perspective, 'the consumer [is conceived] as someone who is information centered [sic], someone constantly seeking out and manipulating information in order to make choices between consumer goods and services' (McCracken, 2005, p. 162): thus, consumers read, view, interact and listen to advertising so that they can learn information. Moreover, it is the provision of such information that sets advertising apart from the fictional or lyrical forms that constitute the bulk of popular culture: unlike a television show or popular song, advertising makes statements about the world beyond itself that are potentially of use to the consumer trying to maximise their personal satisfaction in a consumer society. Understood in such a way, the use of advertising is clear: it is an informative medium that provides the means for its audiences to successfully navigate the complicated world of contemporary capitalism.

Meaning-transfer in advertising

There is, however, a problem with such an approach to advertising: if you have made it this far through this book, then it is hopefully apparent to you that advertising does much more than just provide information. In fact, many advertisements don't even provide any real information at all: in contemporary advertising, it is extremely common to find no mention of any features or advantages of the product in question. Instead, advertising audiences are frequently presented with cartoon mascots, short stories or evocative imagery that say little to nothing about the actual qualities of the product for sale. Consequently, if you are a consumer seeking to 'use' such advertising for information, then there is little 'gratification' to be gained from a great deal of advertising. This conundrum illustrates the central limitation of what Grant McCracken influentially refers to as the 'information-based model' of advertising (2005, p. 162). McCracken argues that such a model, which seeks to understand advertising in terms of the communication of information, has historically dominated consumer research and, as a consequence, the full cultural and social role of advertising has been overlooked (2005, pp. 166–167). In order to address this oversight, McCracken suggests the need for a 'meaning-based model' of advertising that is concerned with the cultural and social meanings evoked by advertising.

McCracken's meaning-based model has proven influential in subsequent market and consumer research. The meaning-based model expands the notion of audience use beyond the acquisition of information to consider how audiences can use advertising to gain access to cultural reservoirs of images, stories, affects and attitudes. McCracken refers to this as the 'meaning-transfer' model, wherein advertising plays a central role within a larger system of meaning in consumer society (2005, p. 97). According to this model, advertising is one of two key processes by which meaning is transferred from the wider cultural world to particular consumer goods and services (the other being the fashion system). The transfer of meaning – which McCracken explains largely through recourse to decisions made by the creative director – works by establishing 'symbolic equivalence' between the cultural categories and consumer goods; however, it is only when the 'viewer/reader' recognises the 'similarity' between the two sites that meaning transfer is complete (1988, pp. 77–79). The need for this recognition on the part of the audience means that this model is not simply about the imposition of information, but instead requires the active participation of the audience. By interpreting the advertising and engaging with the particular consumer goods, the audience/consumer can gain access to the cultural meanings that have been associated with the product. Thus, in this model, advertising 'is the conduit through which meanings are constantly transferred from the culturally constituted world to the consumer good' (McCracken, 2005, p. 164) and the audience is positioned as an active participant in the unlocking of meaning that advertising encodes into consumer goods.

By taking into account the role of meanings, the audience's use of advertising is expanded beyond the search for information to instead involve the active unlocking and procurement of cultural meanings. Thus, while remaining within the broad framework of the U&G model, the particular nature of those uses and gratifications is expanded to take into account a range of applications beyond the purely instrumental access of information. In this way, the intertwined practices of advertising and consumption are thereby re-envisioned as a socially important site of communication and meanings: the means by which consumers can 'communicate to others their relationships to complex sets of otherwise abstract social attributes (such as status), thus identifying themselves within social structures' (Leiss et al., 2005, p. 230). In other words, in conjunction with consumption, advertising becomes a means by which audiences can mobilise large bodies of cultural meanings that are otherwise very difficult for individuals to directly access: advertising places meanings into goods, which audiences then actively negotiate and take control of through consumption. In the process, the practice on consumption becomes understood as more than just a passive act of absorption, but instead can be regarded as a practice of appropriation or even of production (Sassatelli, 2007, pp. 102–103). However, this still leaves a question unanswered: if consumption is a form of production, then what is being produced?

Constructing consumer identities

The most common answer to this question is that advertising and consumption are used by audiences in the production of their identities. In their book-length discussion of consumers, Yiannis Gabriel and Tim Lang refer to 'Identity [as the] Rome to which all discussions of modern Western consumption lead' (2006, p. 79). Identity is our sense of who we are as a distinct individual: it is that aspect of ourselves that we consider to be a consistent being through time and space and in different contexts and relationships. Comprising various aspects – including gender, sexuality, race, ethnicity, lineage, location, nation and religion – identity is often thought about as something that is stable and pre-given. However, despite the apparent stability of identity in our everyday lives, there is a long history of examination and investigation in disciplines like philosophy, sociology and psychology as to how identity is formed and transformed. Following Anthony Giddens, this notion of identity can be classified as 'life politics': 'a reflexive relation to the self in which the individual is [concerned with] taking control ... of the shape of his or her own life through the negotiation of self-identity' (Lury, 2011, p. 198). In a similar manner, we might think of identity as a 'symbolic product, which the individual must actively construct out of the available symbolic materials' (Elliott and Wattanasuwan, 1998, p. 132). Indeed, whether we think of identity in terms of life politics or symbolic products, much current thinking on the subject considers identity to be not only a product of the intersection of larger social forces but also a dynamic category which we are constantly constructing from the cultural and social resources that surround us (McCracken, 2006, p. 163). According to this model, identity is actively constructed by individual agents rather than given or enforced by social structures: it is therefore less of a fact and more of an ongoing creative project or story we tell about ourselves.

In light of this paradigm (sometimes referred to as a 'postmodern' model of the consumer and consumption), consumerism and consumption have been identified and even celebrated as key sites of contemporary identity construction (Firat and Venkatesh, 1995, p. 260). In a cultural context where older measures of identity – such as kinship structures, political ideology or occupation – no longer carry the weight they once did, then consumer choices can function as replacement sites of identification (Dardot and Laval, 2014, p. 293; Miller, 2001, p. 234). This should come as little surprise, given the effort expended in carefully developing, sustaining and distributing consumer meanings, consumption offers widely available and surprisingly stable sites of cultural meaning across different social groups and geographic locations: for example, with its globally integrated advertising campaigns, McDonald's has become a more consistent site of international cultural meaning than most major churches. In this new consumerist world, 'Consumer goods are [...] essential to the project by which our lives are constructed. Consumer goods, in their anticipation, choice, purchase, and possession, are an important source of the meanings by which we construct our lives' (McCracken, 2005, p. 164). Individual consumers purchase goods and services in order to gain access to their associated meanings and to thereby make statements about who they are and what they believe in. Nor does this process need to be only about the communication with others. Richard Elliott and Kritsadarat Wattanasuwan argue that the consumer-subjects' formation of identity through consumption is not only a way to represent oneself to others, but can also help us to understand ourselves and our deepest beliefs and values. Identity through advertising is thus not just about presentation and appearance, but can also be considered a way in which we try out different social roles and types for ourselves (Elliott and Wattanasuwan, 1998, p. 134). In both inward and outward looking ways, consumer practices have become central to our sense of identity and self.

The construction of identity through consumption should not be understood as something separate from advertising: when consumption serves as a means by which to build identity, then advertising becomes absolutely central to this process. This is because when consumption is interpreted primarily in terms of the construction of self, rather than physical use, then there is a need to emphasise its symbolic aspects: and it is through advertising that consumption is invested with symbolic meanings and value. In the pursuit of identity, consumer desire is thus focused on the 'symbolic rather than material reward[s]' of consumption as consumers purchase goods and services for the stories and meanings invested in them, as much as they do for the practical use of those products (Warde, 2014, p. 283). Thus as we recognise the role of consumption in construction of identity, we need to also recognise the function of advertising in investing goods and products with symbolic and social meanings in the first instance:

> As consumption plays a central role in supplying meanings and values for the creation and maintenance of the consumer's personal and social world, so advertising is recognized as one of the major sources of these symbolic meanings.
>
> (Elliott and Wattanasuwan, 1998, p. 132)

So imagined, the act of consumption becomes a means to unlock and lay claim to the meanings and values invested in a commodity through advertising. Consequently, in an identity-construction model, advertising is recast as more than just the provision of persuasive sales pitches: instead, it becomes the means by which goods are transformed into 'carriers of vivid and powerful images, enabling us to choose them consciously from among many similar ones, promising to act as the raw material out of which individual identities may be fashioned' (Gabriel and Lang, 2006, p. 86). If consumption is a central means by which individuals construct their identity, then advertising is the ultimate origin point at which much of that meaning and identity is produced. Advertising is the means by which meanings are initially crafted and dispersed ready to be taken up by consumer audiences.

From this perspective, the world of consumption appears as a buffet of possible identity choices: the individual chooses who they wish to be and selects an appropriate brand from a plurality of options (provided they have the funds to do so, and can find representations in the world of advertising that speak to their sense of self). Identity can be purchased by individuals, in a similar manner to how companies use branding to define themselves: 'individuals can buy identities off the peg, just as corporations can buy themselves new images, new brands and new identities by adopting new symbols, signs and other similar paraphernalia' (Gabriel and Lang, 2006, p. 84). Nor does self-identity need to be the selection of pre-existing meanings from store shelves: it can also involve the negotiation of meaning. For example, the American beer, Pabst Blue Ribbon (PBR) was originally branded in terms of working-class identity, but in recent years has been taken by hipsters as a marker of ironic consumption. In this instance, brand identity was transformed by consumers in order to meet their own purposes, rather than taken up wholesale. Identity formation thus becomes a creative process of selection, negotiation and combination – drink Heineken to be sophisticated and use Dove to show you're sensitive! – that can be considered similar to the production of a collage: an art style characterised by the combination of fragments of pre-existing images in order to create something new. By assembling the correct collection of brands, consumers can deliberately combine the meanings provided by advertising in order to assemble their preferred sense of self. Viewed in this light, advertising becomes less about persuading consumers to purchase particular products, and more about investing products with meanings in the hope that consumers will choose to consume them in order to add those meanings to their own construction of self. In its most extreme forms, this can lead to the cultivation of the self as if it actually were a brand: a practice that finds expression in a great deal of online activity and social media engagement (Hearn, 2008, pp. 198–200, 201–212). We can therefore add another set of uses and gratifications to our list: audiences use advertisements in order to determine and access the social meanings of commodities and obtain gratification by bringing those meanings into their construction of identity through purchase and display.

Constructing consumer communities

Nor are the social meanings constructed from the raw material of advertising and consumption necessarily restricted to an individual's construction of identity and self; they also play central roles in the construction of communal and group identities. After all, at the most basic level, consumption is never carried out by one person; it is always a communal activity and the uses and gratifications it provides can also be understood on that wider level. At a wider level, then, consumer purchases can be interpreted as a means of self-fashioning in order to align oneself with a 'neo-tribe' (Lury, 2011, pp. 201–203). Straddling the line between a real social formation and a marketer's fantasy, the idea that consumers can be divided into competing tribal formations represents not only the belief that consumption patterns are now the key source of communal identification in the twenty-first century but also that marketing success can be obtained by acquiring enough quasi-anthropological data in order to classify one's target market (see Cova, Kozinets and Shankar, 2007; Caldwell and Brown, 2007). However, despite the element of self-selection that often surrounds neo-tribal rhetoric (with its seeming affinity for online quizzes as a means of identification), such a model is ultimately too premised on a marketing-based desire to segment and target audiences to sit easily with an active audience model. The tribal model thus fits with a view of the audience as commodity (see Chapter 6), rather than an active audience, and to think about the collective manifestation of a uses and gratifications paradigm we will have to instead consider a less sweeping model for making sense of collective audience engagement with advertising and consumerism.

Perhaps the most influential account of such communal engagement is the concept of the 'brand community', wherein 'ordinary people not only actively engage with their favourite products but come to feel a sense of attachment to networks of devotees who admire the same brand' (Warde, 2014, p. 288). This idea of a brand community – a community bound together through their shared commitment to a product – was first developed in the work of Albert Muniz Jr. and Thomas O'Guinn who studied how members of both neighbourhoods and online communities formed bonds around particular products. Importantly, Muniz Jr. and O'Guinn were interested not just in how consumption engenders loose affiliations, but how robust and persistent communities could arise out of shared interests in certain brands, such as Saab and Apple (2001, pp. 415–417). For their purposes, Muniz Jr. and O'Guinn identify three central characteristics of a brand community: that members were conscious of their connection to each other and difference from non-members (2001, pp. 418–421); that members engaged in shared activities based in the celebration of the brand (2001, pp. 421–424); and that members experienced a sense of social obligation towards one another and sought to encourage and assist one another in the use of branded products (2001, pp. 424–426).

Based on these criteria it should be clear that not all brands are the basis of brand communities: only those that inspire unusual devotion on behalf of their consuming audience. Thus, it would not really make sense to speak of

McDonald's as the basis of a brand community – no matter how much the company might want to foster such identifications – because consumers of McDonald's rarely identify themselves as such and there is little evidence of solidarity between McDonald's' customers. As Muniz Jr. and O'Guinn suggest, 'communal feelings' take on less formal organisation in the case of high market share brands (2001, p. 428). However, in the case of a less dominant fast-food brand, such as the American West Coast chain In-N-Out Burger, there are certainly signs that a brand community is operating: customers can and do purchase clothing and accessories with the company's logo and there is a long-standing 'secret menu' the knowledge of which was historically shared by fans by word-of-mouth (but which is now available on the company's website). When consumers choose to openly declare their allegiance to a brand, cement their loyalty through the cultivation and sharing of particular forms of knowledge and encourage others to join them in their brand-orientated identity, as in the case of In-N-Out Burger, then we are operating in the territory of a brand community.

Other, more famous, examples of brand communities include those built around Harley-Davidson and Apple. Harley-Davidson, in particular, is often singled out as a key example of an organic brand community that was originally established by fans and users of the company's iconic motorbikes rather than planned and implemented as part of a marketing strategy. Building on the image of Harley-Davidson as an outlaw symbol that was cultivated by Hollywood films from *The Wild One* (1953) to *Easy Rider* (1969) and manifest in real motorcycle gangs, such as the Hell's Angels, the community has adopted the brand as a symbol of rebellion and freedom. Not only is it possible to purchase an incredibly wide range of Harley-Davidson–branded clothing and accessories or eat at a Harley-Davidson–themed restaurant in Las Vegas in order to demonstrates one's allegiance to the community, but there are multiple semi-formal and non-corporate Harley-Davidson gatherings across the United States and the world. Riders from around the world converge on the Harley-Davidson museum in Milwaukee for official celebrations every five years, and the brand has a strong presence at the annual Sturgis motorcycle rally in South Dakota: an event that attracted over 700,000 attendees in 2015. Indeed, few brands command such loyalty and affection: Harley-Davidson is one of the select few corporate logos that appear as a frequent (and un-ironic) tattoo. As a consumer-created brand community, the Harley-Davidson community is therefore a powerful illustration of the social uses and gratifications that consumers can obtain through interaction with advertising and consumer culture. The Harley-Davidson community cannot be reduced to a marketing stunt (though it has certainly been supported and shaped by the company-driven 'Harley Owners' Group since the early 1980s): it is a legitimate community in which participants receive not only a sense of identity but also a meaningful connection with others on that basis of shared allegiance to common beliefs. Membership in a community, with all the affective and social benefits it brings, here emerges as a central use and gratification of brand engagement.

If the Harley-Davidson community is noted for its passion, then the Apple community might be noted for its reach and scale. Apple is probably the most conspicuous and powerful brand community of the twenty-first century, which is no mean feat to continue to inspire such dedication even after its ascension to ever-present market champion. Furthermore, while Harley-Davidson certainly has some online presence, the Apple community is constituted as much online as it is in physical, face-to-face interactions. This makes somewhat intuitive sense: the enjoyment of a motorbike is rooted in the tangible experience of speed and power, whereas Apple devices gain a large part of their appeal through their connection on online databases. Writing in 2001, Muniz Jr. and O'Guinn point towards the way that online discussions and message boards can act as a repository of stories and information about brand communities, and a way for their members to help one another and proselytise (2001, pp. 417, 421–425). Over a decade later, this aspect of their model has clearly expanded beyond what was conceivable at the turn of the century with the massive expansion of online communication and communities.

Active audiences online

The Apple brand community has been at the forefront of this expansion with the development of a seemingly infinite number of pro-Apple fan productions and how-to guides. Central examples of the ability of brand communities to expand online are websites like cultofmac.com and apple.wikia.com: a user-generated guide to all-things-Apple established in 2005 that has over 1200 fan-generated articles. There are also Apple-dedicated sites on social media platforms, such as Fans of Apple on Facebook with just under a million 'likes' at the time of writing. Such examples are indicative of how the expansion of the online realm into every aspect of everyday life (a development largely enabled by Apple itself) has revolutionised the ability of brands and brand communities to expand their reach and involvement in consumers' lives. Many in marketing circles have seized upon these new forms of interaction as evidence of a new era of activity audiences where 'consumers are empowered and interactive and should be invited to participate in the elaboration of the brand' (Arvidsson, 2006, p. 101) (although as we have discussed so far, audiences were hardly passive prior to the internet). Consequently, whereas when Muniz Jr. and O'Guinn originally coined the term, brand communities were relatively rare beasts – composed of people willing to attend a weekly meeting or to frequent particular physical locations – these days the barriers to entry are much lower and while the membership of brand communities are therefore potentially less devoted, they are also more numerous.

Following the success of brands like Apple in fostering online communities, there has been a virtual stampede of brands and companies seeking to establish a basis for similar consumer engagement. As a result, there has been a marked increase in what we might consider the uses and gratifications that consumers can obtain from the online interaction with advertising and branding. On the one hand, we see low-investment, directly financial interactions, such as the return to the traditional direct-marketing practices of coupons and discounts for those who share advertising materials through social media networks: when consumers 'like' a company on Facebook or interact with the Twitter or Instagram accounts of companies then they are often granted access to special offers and deals in exchange for helping raise brand visibility. On the other hand, there are also websites that invite consumers to actively participate in the production of videos or other online content: for example, many companies have established digital repositories where audiences can share tips and advice about how to best use commodities such as cleaning products or cosmetics. In between there are almost an infinite array of options from branded avatars to interactive advertising campaigns that generate content from user suggestions: notable examples of this latter practice range from Burger King's pioneering 'Subversive Chicken' campaign to Under Armor's award-winning 'I Will What I Will' campaign from 2014 starring Gisele Bundchen. From the perspective of the marketers, the rationale behind such advertising practices is clear: not only are those who actively engage in this manner more likely to demonstrate greater loyalty towards their chosen brand, but they are also doing work to make the brand more attractive by producing additional content and support for other consumers. Thus, when audiences engage with these forms of online brand community they are potentially finding gratification in their engagement with a brand community but also effectively contributing to the value of the brand.

Immaterial labour online

The active involvement of the audience means that consumers are not just involved with brands at the moment of purchase and consumption, but help to build brand identity and value. Audience members are contributing their time, effort and skills in order to enhance the wealth of images, meaning and information that surround the brand in a case of what is called 'immaterial labour' (Lazzarato, 2014, p. 77). Originally coined by the Italian Marxist theorist, Maurizio Lazzarato, immaterial labour refers to:

> The labor (sic) that produces the informational and cultural content of the commodity ... [including] a series of activities that are not normally recognized as 'work' – in other words, the kinds of activities involved in defining and fixing cultural and artistic standards, fashions, tastes, consumer norms, and, more strategically, public opinion.
>
> (Lazzarato, 2014, p. 77)

We can see how the work of online audiences falls into this category: they promote brands, provide information about how to use them and even argue on their behalf in cases where companies and products have come under public censure. In a way, then, consumers come to do the work of marketers and public relations teams, but with one crucial difference: unlike the professionals, members of a brand community don't get paid. Technology theorist Christian Fuchs has argued that this unpaid situation is the equivalent of the 'slave-like exploitation of Internet prosumers on the corporate web' (2011, p. 145).

This form of labour is therefore not just immaterial; from the perspective of the company it is also unpaid: that is to say, it is free. Tiziana Terranova has identified such 'free labour' as a central part of the digital economy, which relies upon the unpaid contributions of volunteers, open source coders and amateur web designers (2004, pp. 73–77). Online brand communities are no different in this regard as they work as figurative machines to transform 'user activity into commodified content' (Arvidsson, 2006, p. 104). This, then, is the less utopian side of brand communities: which are not only providing gratifying social connections for their audiences but also simultaneously exploiting their connection to the product to increase corporate value without having to pay compensation. A key example of such practices are campaigns such as Doritos 'Crash the Super Bowl', whereby consumers are invited to create their own ads as part of a global competition, with the winner being screened during the Super Bowl. However, it should be noted that such practices are not necessarily new or unique to online spaces (Terranova, 2004, p. 79). Every time you wear branded clothing or engage in conversation about a brand you are doing similar work. The difference, however, is that online spaces provide both greater scope for such practices and an easily accessible record of them. As was noted earlier, in the context of U&G derived models of audience engagement consumption is reconfigured as an act of production: what is different from the dominant forms of production in a capitalist economy is that, in the majority of cases, the production of the active audience is not subject to monetary compensation.

There is, however, one more turn of the screw in accounting for the distribution of power in the case of the active audience. While consumer-producers are certainly losing out in stark economic terms, this does not mean that marketers and advertisers are always happy to cede ownership and control over branding. In an odd inversion of the moral dynamics that often inform such discussions, Susan Fournier and Jill Avery lament the empowerment of consumers over marketers in online spaces and caution that 'the [online] social collective is an inherently self-interested entity who activities are not necessarily aligned with the best interests of the brand' (2011, p. 197). Rather than viewing the web as a site of free labour, Fournier and Avery caution marketers about the ability of consumers to critique, parody and 'hijack' online advertising in ways that can hurt brand value and derail marketing campaigns. Thus, through social media and online media sharing, consumers can turn marketing campaigns to their own ends. Sometimes this can be a calculated part of a campaign strategy – such as Skittles bold decision to cede complete control of its website to user-generated content (Fournier and Avery, 2011, p. 196) – but more often it represents an unwanted loss of power on the part of the brand: an infamous example of this is the hijacking of the McDonald's #McDStories campaign on twitter, which devolved into consumers spreading horror stories about their experiences eating at McDonald's. In this new era of 'social empowerment, hyper-criticism, and instant transparency', where online audiences can 'humiliate' brands, Fournier and Avery therefore suggest a need to move from 'brand building' to 'brand protection' in the face of the risks posed by the active engagement of audiences (2011, pp. 202–203). When you are not paying for labour, it seems like your labourers will often depart from the desired and sanctioned scripts.

Activist resistance to advertising

Fournier and Avery's fears mark the point where the active involvement of the audience in the construction and distribution of a campaign begins to fade into a set of practices that work along similar lines but to entirely different ends. Such practices should alert us to the limitations of analytic paradigms which characterise all audience participation as labour, because that label can blind us to the fact that such activities cannot always be accurately characterised as an analogue of formal work (Hesmondhalgh, 2010, pp. 276–278). Activist resistance refers to those practices that seek to disrupt advertising and consumerist messages through direct and public opposition. Activist resistance potentially takes in a very large number of practices – from anti-sweatshop protests to consumer boycotts to the establishment of alternative, local systems of production and distribution – but for our purposes we'll be focusing on a very particular subsection of consumer activism: culture jamming. Christine Harold describes culture jamming as a 'movement [that] seeks to undermine the marketing rhetoric of multinational corporations, specifically through such practices as media hoaxing, corporate sabotage billboard 'liberation', and trademark infringement' (2009, p. 349). Some prominent forms of culture jamming involve the subtle defacement of billboards, such that their meaning is inverted, or the running of false advertising campaigns that bring products into disrepute. For example, a McDonald's ad with the slogan, 'You have about 10,000 taste buds, thrill them all' will be altered to read, 'You have about 10,000 taste buds, *kill* them all'. The subtle change carried out using the same typeface thus reverses the overall meaning of the original through a very small change in the actual appearance of the ad. Audiences engaging with the ad may not even register the change at first, which potentially makes it all the more shocking when they do eventually take notice. In this manner, culture jamming seeks to promote anti-consumerist messages in a non-confrontational and comic manner.

Culture jamming

Culture jamming takes its name from the idea of communications jamming more generally, whereby a communications signal is blocked or distorted: most often culture jamming refers to attempts by activists to use the forms, technologies and techniques of mass media in order to criticise capitalism or private media (Harold, 2009, p. 351). Such activist practices are inspired in large part by the work of the French Marxist philosopher Guy Debord, who devised a whole new itinerary of activist tactics for satirising and critiquing capitalist society and the mass media. Probably the most influential of Debord's tactics is the idea of 'détournement', which involves altering a familiar object of the mass media so that it carries an opposite or oppositional meaning to the original intention (2005). A relatively straightforward example of détournement is the early work of the Canadian magazine, Adbusters, who created parody ads which ridiculed the brands they took as their subjects: Calvin Kline would be switched to Calvin Klone, the Camel cigarette mascot Joe Camel would be changed to Joe Chemo and so on. Adbusters established themselves at the centre of the global culture jamming movement in the 1990s and 2000s, and their work, which poked fun at the materialism and excesses of advertising, is emblematic of activist responses to advertising during that period. By taking on the form of advertising while introducing messages contrary to consumerism, culture jamming is thus indicative of a response to advertising that seeks to engender more critical ways of thinking about advertising and consumer culture. Combining the potential for outright rejection of the media text that we see in the encoding/decoding model with the more active and productive forms of audience activity, activist responses to advertising constitute a virulent rejection of not only specific ads but also the larger cultural and social forces that they represent.

Dealing with such activist responses, it is hopefully quite clear that we are a very long way from the subliminal model with which we begun this chapter. Not only have we considered how audiences can question advertising, but how they can then go on to produce their own work in an outright opposition to the messages of a consumer society. The very fact that such activist responses are not only possible, but take place surprisingly regularly, is indicative of the overreach of the subliminal model and should stand as a stark reminder that while advertising places a formidable role in our society, it is far from all-powerful. In this chapter, we've explored a range of ways in which audiences do more than just passively absorb the meanings of adverts. From the interpretive resistance of the encoding/decoding model to the wide range of potential uses and gratifications audiences can obtain by engaging with advertising, there are a number of reasons for thinking about the audience–advertising relationship as more than just a one-way imposition of ideology. Consequently, when seeking to account for the social role of advertising, we always need to do more than simply assume that the audience reaction to advertising can be read off the ads themselves. Audiences are not empty vessels waiting to be filled, and they are not innocent victims of consumerist conspiracies. They are participants in their mediated world – which certainly includes advertising – and any concerted attempt to understand that world has to take into account the manner in which audiences actively engage in the interpretation, construction and sometimes the rejection of advertising.

CHAPTER 10

The politics of advertising: Capitalism, resistance and liberalism

In this book, we've considered advertising from all manner of different angles: we've looked at its development in historical terms; we've considered its fundamental role in the economics of the media; we've investigated its ideological role in the context of capitalism, its organisational structures and its aesthetic possibilities. Finally, we will conclude our study by thinking about advertising in political terms. By this, I don't simply mean the way in which advertising is used in political campaigns or to communicate government announcements (where advertising increasingly functions as a way of enacting politics and gaining and distributing political attention [Banet-Weiser, 2012]). Instead, we will be looking back over the multiple aspects of advertising with an eye to how they can be understood in light of an expanded concept of politics as 'those processes whereby power relationships are implemented, maintained, challenged, or altered in any sphere of activity whatsoever' (Gilbert, 2008, pp. 7–8). This expanded form of politics – which is how the term is usually understood in the context of Media and Cultural Studies – draws our attention to the wider role of advertising in our society as it shapes our perception of the world, what we regard as natural and normal, and how we understand our own ability to act and change that world.

Such an understanding of the politics of advertising has, of course, been an important aspect of our study of advertising all the way through this book. Although not always directly framed in these terms, in our consideration of the different topics we have always had one eye on how advertising intervenes in larger questions of ideology, agency and the competing priorities of institutions, artists, audiences and financial accounts. Discussions about advertising's relation to capitalist structures of ownership and economic power, the power of producers and audiences to intervene in the practice of advertising or the potential of advertising to help us see the world in new ways: all of these are political discussions insofar as they relate to larger questions about how and why our society operates the way it does. Consequently, much of this last chapter will hopefully not be new to you, but will instead work to revisit and recap material in a slightly different light that, by way of conclusion, will help draw together the different threads of our examination of advertising as a media and cultural form.

The politics of capitalism

The most commonly offered assertion regarding the politics of advertising is that it works in the service of capitalism. Such an argument was at the heart of the second section of this book, where we undertook an in-depth examination of three key sets of concepts in the Marxist analysis of advertising: capitalist ideology, commodities and audiences. Modes of analysis derived from Marxist theory have historically been the dominant means of understanding and analysing the political role of advertising in media and cultural studies. Marxist critics were the first to pay close attention to advertising, rather than simply dismiss it as trivial ephemera, and what commentators like Max Horkheimer, Theodor Adorno, Raymond Williams, Sut Jhally and Michael Schudson perceived in advertising was a media form that worked to reinforce capitalism. Given that the economic structure of capitalism is inherently predicated on the unequal distribution of profits, the celebration of capitalism and consumerism in the context of advertising can be seen as a profoundly political contribution to the continued existence of these material inequalities. Advertising works to produce and maintain power relations by not only leading us to understand capitalism in particular ways but also by implicating the audience into the very systems of exchange that constitute the capitalist way of life.

Thus, by presenting constant consumption as not just the only 'normal' way of life, but as the solution to all possible problems and a deeply desirable and pleasurable way to live, advertising directly contributes to the normalisation and reassertion of the capitalist economic system. The power of this political intervention is only reinforced through advertising's central role in commodification: the transformation of all aspects of life into commodities. Cast free from their original social relations of production, goods and services become reimagined as quasi-magical entities whose existence (and price) is justified through the cultural meanings they embody, rather than their material qualities. Such transformations also have the effect of insulating consumers from the potentially upsetting conditions in which many of our commodities are produced: third-world factories and environmental damage disappear from our awareness to be replaced by dancing models and cartoon animals. This way of conceiving commodities is deeply political because it allows us to remain ignorant – or at the very least maintain a resting state of only dim awareness – of the material structures of global capitalism that often conflict with our own beliefs about how the world should be. Similarly, the Marxist model also suggests that consumers remain largely unaware of the extent of their own exploitation due to advertising: gathered and sold for a profit by media platforms, audience engagement with ads can be configured as labour on behalf of advertisers, while online algorithms harvest huge amounts of personal data in order to segment and target ever more tightly defined demographic groups.

One of the common themes in this Marxist model of advertising is the idea of deception and the implication that advertising audiences and consumers are unaware of the real conditions of their lives. This is a deeply political claim, and also one that it is worth subjecting to some scrutiny. Although, as discussed in Chapter 4, more sophisticated ideological models have moved on from the assertion that ideology is simply a form of 'false consciousness' – a false impression of the world – ideas of deception and deceit continue to inform many ideological accounts of advertising. From a sympathetic angle, we can see that there is a good reason for this, as such accounts allow us to explain why so many people continue to live their lives in a way that would appear to contradict their professed beliefs about how we ought to live our lives and organise our society (or, advertising convinces people that they *do* want to live in a world determined by profit and purchase). However, such a model of understanding requires that we work with the assumption that the audiences and consumers for advertising are defined by a fundamental lack of power and inability to see through such deception. This is a somewhat troubling assumption on which to base our analysis as it would seem to suggest that most people are dolts: an assertion that is (probably) not true, and even if it were, it would make more sense to try to remedy the situation, rather than simply point it out. In repeating this claim without trying to rectify this state of affairs, there is the chance that we might end up not just revealing these conditions but also reinforcing them.

Complicating this political angle even further is the fact that a substantial minority of advertising doesn't reproduce and celebrate capitalism or consumerism in any simple way. Indeed, there exist a number of prominent examples of advertising that appear to criticise consumption as a way of life or promote alternative political visions: from Apple's famed '1984' ad where a lone female rebel challenges an oppressive system to Sprite's 'Obey Your Thirst' campaign that was premised on dismissing sales pitches that offered special abilities rather than material goods. There are always new examples of advertising campaigns that exhort audiences to reject consumption, money and status, in favour of 'nonconformity, escape, resistance, difference, carnival and even deviance' (Frank, 1997, p. 133): more recent examples that challenge the straightforward reiteration of capitalism might include Dove, U by Kotex, Miracle Whip and Old Spice. Such examples adopt a range of approaches from ambiguity to irony to a direct embrace of the language of progressive politics in ways that set them apart from any simple celebration of consumption and purchase.

Nor is this a phenomenon restricted to new or recent advertising. In his study of ads of the 1950s and 1960s, especially those that arose out of the creative revolution, Thomas Frank argues that advertising has long embraced criticism of mass culture and mass consumption: usually through the dismissive equation of consumption with conformity and a celebration of rule-breaking (1997, pp. 55–58). Such ads address their audience as critical sceptics, rather than mindless drones, and therefore seem to suggest the potential for a less monolithic politics of advertising (Frank, 1997, pp. 63–64). Frank, however, rejects such a conclusion and instead reasserts the priority of an economic model of understanding by asserting that the language of revolution and rebellion primarily serves to reinforce the fashion cycle: advertising of this type didn't send the message that *all* consumption was undesirable and would present their own products as being outside or alternative to the systems they were critiquing (1997, pp. 230–231). Overturning the old order thus becomes a reason to consume new commodities, rather than a political goal.

Yet, despite Frank's dismissal, it does not necessarily follow that there are no grounds for a more progressive or liberating politics of advertising. While Frank is certainly not wrong when he argues that advertising's politics of non-conformity align very comfortably with the consumerist demand to constantly purchase, this economic account doesn't completely exhaust the possibilities of advertising's critical potential. While it is likely an overstatement to declare that advertising opposes capitalism, it is also clear from such examples that it can and does do more than simply celebrate the consumerist way of life. In practice, advertising can and does refer to values and ideals that do not fit easily within the demands of our current economic relations, even if it cannot simply change them. Therefore, in our consideration of the politics of capitalism and advertising, we may want to expand our interpretation of advertising's role from just a cultural site that celebrates capitalism, to a place where we, as a society, discuss and think through capitalism. While it would be foolish to deny that most advertising takes capitalism and consumerism for granted, we also should acknowledge that every so often it provides a vehicle for conservations that are more critical of our wider economic context or, at the very least, points towards contradictions, complications and desires that cannot be easily contained or explained within the context of capitalist ideology. Thus, while advertising does almost overwhelmingly work to constantly and consistently reassert capitalist ways of making sense of the world, it also retains the potential to speak in more critical ways about the politics of capitalism.

The politics of agency

The normalisation and reassertion of the capitalist economic system is not, however, the only way in which advertising can be considered political: also important are the competing evaluations of the abilities of advertising producers and audiences to craft, influence, negotiate, reject or reappropriate advertising messages. When we focus on the potential for the individual people involved to put their own spin on advertising – as we did in the seventh and eighth chapters – then we are emphasising the role of agency in these processes. In the second section of the book we shifted from a structuralist model of advertising, which emphasises the influence of overarching frameworks of power and meaning, to a more angential model that sees the world in terms of individual choices and decisions. In terms of the production, we considered how advertising is produced by agencies, which have their own histories, priorities and organisational structures. The people who make advertising navigate a range of competing positions within agencies and constantly work to not just promote commodities but also themselves and their profession. In terms of the consumption of advertising, we addressed all the different ways in which advertising audiences become actively involved in the interpretation, engagement and distribution of ads for their own ends. Audiences don't simply passively absorb advertising messages; they use them to craft identities and communities and potentially can even respond to ads in ways that oppose consumer society.

The shift in focus in these two chapters – from structures to agents – can itself be considered a political act, because it leads us to see the world in a way where individuals are empowered, behaviour is intentional and the resulting circumstances are understood as the outcome desired by the people involved. Consequently, it may appear that this is a much more respectful and hopeful way to make sense of the world and therefore more politically desirable. After all, if everybody has the ability to work out what they want in clear terms and the power to put those desires into practice, then it would seem to follow that the resulting world is exactly the world which everybody most wants. Viewed in this way, advertising would appear to be nothing more than a useful exchange between different groups of people that involves not only the communication of information about available goods and services but also the altruistic provision of cultural resources by advertisers so that audiences can use them to assemble new meanings and identities. Seen like this, advertising isn't about selling products; it's about creating and sharing stories, songs, images and experiences: just another part of popular culture. Yet, while this certainly might be a more optimistic outlook, it doesn't mean that it is necessarily a more accurate account of how the world works. We need to be very careful not to mistake a change in analytic focus for a change in the world, and thereby consider that the world is a friendlier and freer place simply because we have changed our perspective.

Given the positive political conclusions that arise from an emphasis on agency, it's probably no surprise to find that industry accounts tend to emphasise such explanations of their business. After all, such a benign picture of advertising presents the industry in much more attractive terms than those which arise out of the Marxist model. Not only does the concept of agency allow for a reinterpretation of advertisers as creative cultural workers and free spirits, rather than capitalist drones; it also leads to a much more benign account of the audience. When seen as lacking agency, audiences appear as innocent pawns of a manipulative consumerist system: when they are thought to possess agency, audiences are equal partners who are actively involved in the consumer process. An emphasis upon agency thus leads to the diminishment of questions of influence and manipulation in favour of communication and mutual benefit. Yet, at the same time, advertisers also rely upon consumers not having *too much* agency; otherwise they wouldn't be susceptible to their messages. This situation leads to a contradiction regarding how advertisers and marketeers understand their influence over consumers. On the one hand, the practice of advertising is premised on the idea that advertisers and advertisements can exert influence over consumers through an in-depth knowledge of their preferences and habits: on the other hand, industry and scholarly literature in the area often works on the assumption that consumers are sovereign, autonomous and clued-up agents who make rational and reflexive choices about their purchases and therefore can't be easily swayed by marketing tricks and tactics. This, then, is an example of Anne Cronin's 'political economy of truth' referred to at the end of Chapter 7: advertisers walk a delicate line between talking up their own agency – and therefore their ability to persuade and influence consumers – and the agency of their audiences: the prevalence of which ostensibly negates any need for critique or regulation.

The politics of agency are therefore such that when we emphasise it, we create an impression of advertising as a benign practice that is concerned with the exchange of cultural resources and is really no reason for wider concern. An emphasis on agency means that advertising appears increasingly as a non-threatening conversation, rather than as a motivated sales pitch. Such a perspective can prove very useful: it can nuance our understanding of advertising, so that it appears to be more than a giant act of manipulation and deception. By bringing attention to advertising's cultural and social work beyond the reproduction of capitalism, such a model draws our attention to important facts of advertising practice that might otherwise go overlooked if we stay focused on the reproduction of capitalism. In fact, when taken in conjunction with the more directly critical Marxist perspective, the politics of agency permit us to make sense of two competing aspects of advertising at the same time. This is the dialectical approach referred to in the Introduction, whereby we hold two competing conceptions of advertising in our head at the same time even though they seem to contradict one another. These contradictions, however, are not the product of the models we apply, but rather the practice of advertising itself, which contains within itself apparently irreconcilable aspects. By adopting a dialectical approach we can therefore take into account the real contradictions that shape the practices and politics of advertising, which is a site of cultural conversation and capitalist ideology, individual freedom and structural domination, creative expression and clandestine surveillance. By exploring advertising from the perspective of both capitalism and agency, we are able to better grasp its complicated cultural functions without prematurely reducing it to one role or another.

The politics of art

Finally, we can also consider the politics of advertising in terms of ideas of art. In Chapter 9, we considered the relationship between advertising and art, how they have historically been differentiated and what it might mean to consider advertising a form of art. To speak of advertising in terms of the privileged concept of art is to make several political statements, which speak back to those raised in terms of the politics of capitalism and agency. On the one hand, the distinction between art and advertising is strongly informed by a fundamental Western opposition between art and commerce: an opposition that advertising straddles and undermines. This situation gestures to advertising's internal contradictions as a practice that seeks to be both deeply artistic and thoroughly commercial and therefore sits uneasily within the art–commerce binary. Advertising thereby becomes a way for us to think through the power and purpose of that binary and the role it plays in ordering the wider cultural coordinates of our society that inform conceptions of what professions and pursuits are worthwhile, which are frivolous and which are shallow. Consequently, to conceive of advertising as a form of art – and to really consider how advertising might be art in a deep and profound sense – is to potentially challenge the dominance of some deeply held cultural beliefs.

On the other hand, to consider advertising in terms of art is also to revisit the implications of the dialectic of capitalism and agency. This is because when we approach art as an actual material category, rather than an abstract ideal, then we can understand it as a concept that is both grounded in its formative economic context and also capable of gaining some measure of autonomy from that context and offering critical comment upon it. To understand advertising as art is therefore to consider, on the one hand, its role with the context of capitalism and how comprehensively the conditions of its production determine its ability to comment upon those conditions (maybe not as much as the classical Marxist model would suggest?). On the other hand, engaging with advertising as art also leads us to consider the agency of its creator and the formal means by which the advertising text might exert an influence upon its audiences: advertising as art thus operates at the intersection of questions of capitalism and agency while also introducing new particular political possibilities that emerge out of a concern with form in relation to historical context. To look at advertising in this way thus opens up a new set of political questions and possibilities.

The power of advertising

What we can see, then, is that when we consider advertising in political terms, there are a number of different and potentially opposing aspects that we need to consider and keep in play all at the same time. Advertising is a powerful force for the reproduction of capitalism, but it is also an important ongoing cultural conversation that can potentially enact wider and potentially progressive social and cultural changes. Advertising can be addressed as just one of many cultural industries concerned with the production of representations or narratives, or it can be considered a media form that is particularly tied to the operation of capitalism, and therefore it is where we learn to talk about capitalism in a more reflexive and therefore thoughtful manner. Depending on which perspective we privilege, advertising can appear more threatening or auspicious, but what is important is that no matter which aspect we focus upon we try to keep the others in mind so that we can develop and maintain a sophisticated understanding and not simply rely upon a caricature of the social, cultural and political roles of advertising. Advertising plays these multiple roles whether the people involved – be they producers or audiences – are consciously aware of their part, which means that no one involved has a final say in exactly what advertising means: as if that could even be pinned down once and for all. As we've seen throughout this book, the consequences of advertising as a social form have shifted in different historical moments, depending upon context and the people involved, and even between particular advertising texts. As a result, the final consequences of advertising as a social and political form remain up for debate; however, what there should be no doubt about is the central and important role advertising plays in our contemporary capitalist world.

References

Acland, Charles (2012) *Swift Viewing: The Popular Life of Subliminal Influence* (Durham: Duke University Press).

Adorno, Theodor (1997) *Aesthetic Theory*, ed. and trans. Robert Hullot-Kentor (New York: Continuum).

Althusser, Louis (1971) 'Ideology and Ideological State Apparatus', in *Lenin and Philosophy, and Other Essays*, trans. Ben Brewster (New York: Monthly Review Press), 23–70.

Ariely, Dan and Michael I. Norton (2009) 'Conceptual Consumption', *Annual Review of Psychology* 60: 475–499.

Arvidsson, Adam (2006) *Brands: Meaning and Value in Media Culture* (London: Routledge).

Banet-Weiser, Sarah (2012) *Authentic™: The Politics of Ambivalence in a Brand Culture* (New York: New York University Press).

Barker, Chris (2012) *Cultural Studies: Theory and Practice* (London: Sage).

Barthes, Roland (1972) 'Myth Today', in *Mythologies*, trans. Annette Lavers (New York: Hill and Wang), 109–159.

______(1978) 'Rhetoric of the Image', in *Image, Music, Text*, ed. and trans. Stephen Heath (New York: Hill and Wang), 32–51.

Baudrillard, Jean (1981) *For a Critique of the Political Economy of the Sign* (St. Louis: Telos Press).

______(1994) *Simulacra and Simulation*, trans. Shelia F. Glaser. (Ann Arbor: University of Michigan Press).

Bayers, Chip (2011) 'Bill Bernbach: Creative Revolutionary', *AdWeek.com*, August 8, www.adweek.com/news/advertising-branding/bill-bernbach-creative-revolutionary-133901. Accessed 1 November 2015.

Berger, John (1974) *Ways of Seeing* (London: Penguin).

Best, Beverley (2010) *Marx and the Dynamics of Capital Formation: An Aesthetics of Political Economy* (New York: Palgrave Macmillan).

Bignell, Johnathan (1997) *Media Semiotics: An Introduction* (Manchester: Manchester University Press).

Bloch, Ernst (2002) 'Discussing Expressionism', in *Aesthetics and Politics*, ed. Ronald Taylor (London: Verso), 16–27.

Bogart, Michele H. (1995) *Advertising, Artists and the Borders of Art* (Chicago: University of Chicago Press).

Bourdieu, Pierre (1984) *Distinction*, trans. Richard Nice (Cambridge, MA: Harvard University Press).

______(1993) *The Field of Cultural Production* (Cambridge: Polity).

Brecht, Brecht. (2002) 'Against Georg Lukács', in *Aesthetics and Politics*, ed. Ronald Taylor (London: Verso), 68–85.

Brouillette, Sarah (2014) 'Creative Labor', in *Contemporary Marxist Theory*, eds. Andrew Pendakis, Jeff Diamanti, Nicholas Brown, Josh Robinson, and Imre Szeman (London: Bloomsbury), 441–448.

Brown, Stephen and Anthony Patterson (2000) 'Figments for Sale: Marketing, Imagination and the Artistic Imperative', in *Imagining Marketing: Art, Aesthetics and the Avant-Garde*, eds. Stephen Brown and Anthony Patterson (London: Routledge), 4–32.

Bruell, Alexandra. (2015) 'Advertisers are Seeking New Ad Model: But don't Really Know What It Is', *AdAge.com*, 24 August, http://adage.com/article/agency-news/advertisers-seek-ad-model/300060/. Accessed 1 September 2015.

Bullmore, Jeremy (2006) *Apples, Insights and Mad Inventors: An Entertaining Analysis of Modern Marketing* (Chichester: John Wiley & Sons).

Bürger, Peter (1984) *Theory of the Avant-Garde*, trans. Michael Shaw (Minneapolis: University of Minnesota Press).

Cabrera, Sergio A. and Christine L. Williams (2014) 'Consuming for the Social Good: Marketing, Consumer Citizenship, and the Possibilities of Ethical Consumption', *Critical Sociology* 40(3): 349–367.

Caldwell, Jill and Christopher Brown (2007) *8 Tribes* (Wellington: Wicked Little Books).

Cazdyn, Eric and Imre Szeman (2013) *After Globalization* (Chichester: Wiley-Blackwell).

Clegg, Cara (2016) 'As Earthquakes Rock the Region, Kyushu Shinkansen Commercial is More Poignant than Ever', *Rocket News 24*, April 20, http://en.rocketnews24.com/2016/04/20/as-earthquakes-rock-the-region-kyushu-shinkansen-commercial-is-more-poignant-than-ever%E3%80%90video%E3%80%91/. Accessed 5 February 2016.

Clifford, John (2014) *Graphic Icons: Visionaries who Shape Modern Design* (New York: Peachpit Press).

Cova, Bernard, Robert Kozinets and Avi Shankar (2007) *Consumer Tribes* (London: Routledge).

Cracknell, Andrew (2011) *The Real Madmen* (London: Quercus).

Creativity Online (2011) 'JR Kyushu Shinkansen: One Kyushu', *Creativity-Online*, April 27, http://creativity-online.com/work/jr-kyushu-shinkansen-one-kyushu/23062. Accessed 5 February 2016.

Cronin, Anne M. (2004) *Advertising Myths* (London: Routledge).

Dardot, Pierre and Christine Laval (2014) *The New Way of the World: On Neoliberal Society* (London: Verso).

Davis, Martyn P. (2011) 'Advertising Planning and Budgeting', in *The Practice of Advertising*, ed. Adrian Mackay (London: Routledge), 173–189.

Debord, Guy (2005) *Society of the Spectacle* (Detroit: Black and Red).

Deuze, Mark (2007) *Mediawork* (Cambridge: Polity).

Douglas, Norman (1917) *South Wind* (Project Gutenberg), www.gutenberg.org/ebooks/4508. Accessed 15 December 2015.

Duhigg, Charles and David Barboza (2012) 'In China, Human Costs are Built into an iPad', *New York Times*, 25 January, www.nytimes.com/2012/01/26/business/ieconomy-apples-ipad-and-the-human-costs-for-workers-in-china.html. Accessed 8 May 2015.

The Economist (2010) 'Suicides at Foxconn: Light and Death', *The Economist*, 10 May, www.economist.com/node/16231588. Accessed 2 May 2015.

______(2014) 'Little Brother: Advertising and Technology', *The Economist*, 13 September, www.economist.com/news/special-report/21615869-technology-radically-changing-advertising-business-profound-consequences, Accessed 6 March 2015.

Elliott, Richard and Kritsadarat Wattanasuwan (1998) 'Brands as Symbolic Resources for the Construction of Identity', *International Journal of Advertising* 17(2): 131–144.

Engine Film (2011) *News: We Won Some Awards at Cannes Lions* 2011, www.engine-f.co.jp/news/detail/we-won-some-awards-at-cannes-lions-2011/. Accessed 3 February 2015.

Fallon, Michael (2011) *How to Analyse the Works of Andy Warhol* (Edina: ABDO Press).

Femina, Jerry. D. (2010) *From Those Wonderful Folks Who Gave You Pearl Harbor* (New York: Simon & Schuster).

Fenner, David E.W. (2008) *Art in Context: Understanding Aesthetic Value* (Athens: University of Ohio Press).

Fill, Chris, Graham Hughes and Scott De Francesco (2013) *Advertising Strategy, Creativity and Media* (New York: Pearson Education).

Firat, A. Fuat and Alladi Venkatesh (1995) 'Liberatory Postmodernism and the Reenchantment of Consumption', *Journal of Consumer Research* 22(3): 239–267.

Florida, Richard (2002) *Rise of the Creative Class* (New York: Basic Books).

Fournier, Susan and Jill Avery (2011) 'The Uninvited Brand', *Business Horizons* 54(3): 193–207.

Fowler, Geoffrey A. (2008) 'Unilever Gives 'Ugly Betty' a Product-Plug Makeover in China', *The Wall Street Journal*, 29 December, www.wsj.com/articles/SB123051038411338387. Accessed 12 February 2016.

Fox, Stephen R. (1997) *The Mirror Makers: A History of American Advertising and its Creators* (Urbana and Chicago: University of Illinois Press).

Frank, Thomas (1997) *The Conquest of Cool: Business Culture, Counterculture and the Rise of Hip Consumerism* (Chicago: University of Chicago Press).

Friedman, Milton (1982) *Capitalism and Freedom* (Chicago: University of Chicago Press).

Fuchs, Christian (2011) 'New Media, Web 2.0 and Surveillance', *Sociology Compass* 5(2): 132–147.

______(2012) 'The Political Economy of Privacy on Facebook', *Television and New Media* 13(2): 139–159.

Fulcher, James (2003) *Capitalism: A Very Short Introduction* (Oxford: Oxford University Press).

Gabriel, Yiannis and Tim Lang (2006) *The Unmanageable Consumer* (London: Sage).

Gee, Malcolm (2013) 'Art and Advertising – circa 1880 to the Present', in *Advertising as Culture*, ed. Chris Wharton (Bristol: Intellect), 127–142.

Gettins, Dominic (2005) *How to Write Great Copy* (London: Kogan Page).

Gibson, Chris, Chantel Carr and Andrew Warren (2015) 'Making Things: Beyond the Binary of Manufacturing and Creativity', in *The Routledge Companion to Cultural Industries*, eds. Kate Oakley and Justin O'Connor (London: Routledge), 86–96.

Giddens, Anthony (1979) *Central Problems in Social Theory* (Berkeley: University of California Press).

Gilbert, Anthony (2008) *Anticapitalism and Culture* (New York: Berg).

Gilpin, Robert (2001) *Global Political Economy: Understanding the International Economic Order* (Princeton: Princeton University Press).

Gleizes, Albert and Jean Metzinger (2000) 'Cubism', in *Modern Artists on Art*, ed. Robert L. Herbert (Mineola: Dover), 1–16.

Goldman, Robert and Stephen Papson (2006) 'Capital's Brandscapes', *Journal of Consumer Culture* 6(3): 327–353.

Green, Chris (2014) 'Food Giants Target Children with Addictive "Advergames"', *The Independent Online*. 29 March, www.independent.co.uk/news/uk/home-news/food-giants-target-children-with-addictive-advergames-9222302.html. Accessed 12 December 2014.

Greenburg, Clement (1957) 'Avant-Garde and Kitsch', in *Mass Culture: The Popular Arts in America*, ed. Bernard Rosenberg (Glencoe, IL: Free Press), 98–107.

Hackley, Chris and Rungpaka Amy Hackley (2015) *Advertising and Promotion* (London: Sage).

Hall, Stuart (1996) 'Encoding/Decoding', in *Culture, Media, Language: Working Papers in Cultural Studies 1972–79* (London: Routledge), 128–138.

Hardy, Jonathan (2015) 'Political Economy Approaches to Advertising', in *Advertising: Critical Approaches* (London, Routledge), 65–84.

Harold, Christine (2009) 'Pranking Rhetoric: "Culture Jamming" as Media Activism', in *The Advertising and Consumer Culture Reader*, eds. Joseph Turow, and Matthew P. McAllister (London: Routledge), 348–368.

Hartley, John, Jason Potts, Stuart Cunningham, Terry Flew, Michael Keane and John Banks (2013) *Key Concepts in Creative Industries* (London: Sage).

Hearn, Alison (2008) '"Meat, Mask, Burden" Probing the Contours of the Branded "Self"', *Journal of Consumer Culture* 8(2): 197–217.

Hegarty, John (2011) 'Foreword', in Andrew Cracknell, A. *The Real Madmen* (London: Quercus).

______(2014) *Hegarty on Creativity: There are No Rules* (London: Thames & Hudson).

Hesmondhalgh, David (2010) 'User-Generated Content, Free Labour and the Cultural Industries', *Ephemera: Theory and Politics in Organisation* 10(3/4): 267–284.

Hesmondhalgh, David and Sarah Baker (2011) *Creative Labour: Media Work in Three Cultural Industries* (London: Routledge).

Hodapp, Eli (2013) 'Yes, the Toyota Corolla Is Now a Power Up in EA's "Tetris Blitz"', *Touch Arcade*. 11 September, http://toucharcade.com/2013/09/11/yes-the-toyota-corolla-is-now-a-power-up-in-eas-tetris-blitz/. Accessed 28 November 2014.

Hollis, Nigel (2009) 'Dove Teams Up with Ugly Betty in China', *Millward Brown*, 15 January, www.millwardbrown.com/global-navigation/blogs/post/mb-blog/2009/01/15/Dove-teams-up-with-Ugly-Betty-in-China.aspx. Accessed 2 March, 2016.

Horkheimer, Max and Theodor Adorno (1972) 'The Culture Industry: Enlightenment as Mass Deception', *The Dialectic of Enlightenment* (New York, NY: Herder and Herder), 120–167.

Institute of Practitioners of Advertising (2006) *Judging Creative Ideas* (Institute of Practitioners of Advertising) www.ipa.co.uk/Document/judging-creative-ideas-best-practice-guide. Accessed 16 November 2015.

Iskin, Ruth E. (2014) *The Poster: Art, Advertising and Collecting, 1860s–1900s* (Lebanon: Dartmouth College Press).

Jameson, Fredric (2009) 'Ideological Analysis: A Handbook', in *Valences of the Dialectic* (London: Verso).

Jensen, Klaus Bruhn (2002) 'Media Reception: Qualitative Traditions', in *Handbook of Media and Communications Research: Qualitative and Quantitative Research Methodologies*, ed. Klaus Bruhn Jensen (London: Routledge), 171–185.

Jhally, Sut (1990) *The Codes of Advertising: Fetishism and the Political Economy of Meaning in the Consumer Society* (London: Routledge).

Johnny (2013) 'How an Unscripted Train Commercial went Viral and United a Nation', *Spoon & Tamago*, 13 August, www.spoon-tamago.com/2013/08/13/how-an-unscripted-train-commercial-went-viral-and-united-a-nation/. Accessed 2 February 2016.

Kandinsky, Wassily and Franz Marc (2011) 'Preface to *Der Blaue Reiter Almanac*', in *100 Artists' Manifestos: From the Futurists to the Stuckists*, ed. Alex Danchev (London: Penguin).

Kant, Immanuel (2000) *Critique of the Power of Judgement*, ed. Paul Huyer and trans. Paul Huyer and Eric Matthews (New York: Cambridge University Press).

Kawaja, Terence (2015) 'Back to "Mad Men": What the Future Holds for Ad Agencies', *AdAge.com*, 3 September, http://adage.com/article/guest-columnists/back-mad-men-future-holds-ad-agencies/300195/. Accessed 13 September 2015.

Key, Wilson Bryan (1973) *Subliminal Seduction: Ad Media's Manipulation of Not So Innocent America* (Englewood Cliffs: Signet).

Keyes, Ralph (2006) *The Quote Verifier: Who Said What, Where, and When* (New York: St Martin's Press).

Kim, Sujeong (2004) 'Rereading David Morley's *The "Nationwide" Audience*', *Cultural Studies* 18(1): 84–108.

Landry, Charles and Franco Bianchini (1998) *The Creative City* (London: Demos).

Lash, Scott and John Urry (2002) *Economies of Signs and Spaces* (London: Sage).

Lazzarato, Maurizio (2014) 'Immaterial Labor', in *Contemporary Marxist Theory*, eds. Andrew Pendakis, Jeff Diamanti, Nicholas Brown, Josh Robinson, and Imre Szeman (London: Bloomsbury), 77–92.

Lears, Jackson (1994) *Fables of Abundance: A Cultural History of Advertising in America* (New York: Basic Books).

Lefebvre, Henri (2008) *Critique of Everyday Life* (London: Verso).

Leiss, William, Stephen Kline, Sut Jhally and Jacqueline Botterill (2005) *Social Communication in Advertising: Consumption in the Mediated Marketplace* (New York: Routledge).

von Logue Newth, Tom (2013) *The Ad-Makers: How the Best TV Commercials are Produced* (Burlington: Focal Press).

Lury, Celia (2011) *Consumer Culture* (Cambridge: Polity).

MacRury, Iain (2009) 'Advertising Research: Markets, Methods and Knowing Consumers', in *The Advertising Handbook*, eds. Helen Powell, Jonathan Hardy, Sarah Hawkin and Iain MacRury, 3rd edn (Oxon: Routledge), 46–73.

Malefyt, Timothy D.W. and Brian Moeran (2003) 'Introduction: Advertising Cultures – Advertising, Ethnography and Anthropology', in *Advertising Cultures*, eds. Timothy Malefyt and Brian Moeran (Oxford: Berg), 1–33.

Malefyt, Timothy D.W. and Robert Morais (2012) *Advertising and Anthropology* (London: Berg).

Malevich, Kazimir (2011) 'Suprematist Manifesto', in *100 Artists' Manifestos: From the Futurists to the Stuckists*, ed. Alex Danchev (London: Penguin).

Manzerolle, Vincent (2010) 'Mobilizing the Audience Commodity: Digital Labour in a Wireless World', *Ephemera: Theory and Politics in Organisation* 10(3/4): 455–469.

Marchand, Roland (1985) *Advertising the American Dream: Making Way for Modernity 1920–1940* (Berkeley: University of California Press).

Markusen, Ann, Gregory Wassall, Douglas DeNatale and Randy Cohen (2008) 'Defining the Creative Economy: Industry and Occupational Approaches', *Economic Development Quarterly* 22(1): 24–45.

Marx, Karl (2001) *Capital* (London: Electric Book Company).

______(2011) '"Preface" to *A Contribution to a Critique of Political Economy*', in *Cultural Theory: An Anthology*, eds. Imre Szeman and Tim Kaposy (Malden: Wiley and Blackwell).

______(1999) *The Eighteenth Brumaire of Louis Bonaparte*. Marxists Internet Archive, www.marxists.org/archive/marx/works/1852/18th-brumaire/. Accessed 4 July 2015.

Marx, Karl and Engels, Friedrich (1987) *The Communist Manifesto* (New York: Pathfinder Press).

______(1993) *The German Ideology*, ed. C.J. Arthur. (New York: International Publishers).

Mayer, Richard (2011) 'The Advertising Agency', in *The Practice of Advertising*, ed. Adrian Mackay (London: Routledge), 69–91.

Mazzarella, William (2003) 'Critical Publicity/Public Criticism: Reflections on Fieldwork in the Bombay Ad World', in *Advertising Cultures*, eds. Timothy Malefyt and Brian Moeran (Oxford: Berg), 55–74.

McCracken, Grant (1988) *Culture and Consumption: New Approaches to the Symbolic Character of Consumer Goods and Activities* (Bloomington: Indiana University Press).

______(2005) *Culture and Consumption II: Markets, Meanings and Brand Management* (Bloomington: Indiana University Press).

McFall, Liz (2004) *Advertising: A Cultural Economy* (London: Sage).

McMorran, Chris (2013) 'Kyushu Shinkansen Commercial', *Learning Spaces*, 15 September, http://blog.nus.edu.sg/mcmorran/2013/09/15/kyushu-shinkansen-commercial/. Accessed 8 February 2016.

McRobbie, Angela (2011) '"Everyone Is Creative": Artists as Pioneers of the New Economy?' in *Culture and Contestation in the New Century*, ed. M.J. Léger (Bristol: Intellect), 77–92.

McStay, Andrew (2009) *Digital Advertising* (London: Palgrave Macmillan).

______(2011) *The Mood of Advertising: A Critique of Online Behavioural Advertising* (London: Continuum).

______(2013) *Creativity and Advertising: Affect, Events and Processes* (London: Routledge).

Merskin, Debra (2003) 'History: The 1920s', in *The Advertising Age Encyclopedia of Advertising*, eds. John McDonough and Karen Egolf (New York: Fitzroy Dearborn).

Miller, Daniel (1997) *Capitalism: An Ethnographic Approach* (Oxford: Berg).

______(2001) 'The Poverty of Morality', *The Journal of Consumer Culture* 1 (2): 225–243.

______(2003) 'Advertising, Production and Consumption as Cultural Economy', in *Advertising Cultures*, eds. Timothy Malefyt and Brian Moeran (Oxford: Berg), 75–89.

Miller, Mark Crispin (2007) 'Introduction', in Vance Packard, *The Hidden Persuaders* (New York: IG Publishing).

Morley, David and Charlotte Brunsdon (1999) *The Nationwide Television Studies* (London: Routledge).

MSNBC (2010) 'Chinese Factory Asks for "No Suicide" Vow', *MSNBC.com*, 26 May, www.nbcnews.com/id/37354853/ns/business-world_business/?ns=business- world_business#.VoX1oVIwRj8. Accessed 18 November 2014.

Mulholland, Neil (2007) 'Definitions of Art and the Art World', in *Exploring Visual Culture: Definitions, Concepts, Contexts*, ed. Matthew Rampley (Edinburgh: University of Edinburgh Press), 18–33.

Muniz, Jr., Albert and Thomas O'Guinn (2001) 'Brand Community', *Journal of Consumer Research* 27(4): 412–432.

Negus, Keith and Michael Pickering (2004) *Creativity, Communication and Cultural Value* (London: Sage).

Nielsen NZ (2014) 'Living in a Media Bubble: Agency in NZ', *Nielsen.com*, 31 October, www.nielsen.com/nz/en/insights/reports/2014/living-in-a-media-bubble-agency-life-in-nz.html. Accessed 8 August 2015.

Nixon, Sean (2003) *Advertising Cultures* (London: Sage).

Norris, Vincent P. (1980) 'Advertising History: According to the Textbooks', *Journal of Advertising* 9 (3): 3–11.

O'Brien, Sean and Imre Szeman (2004) *Popular Culture: A User's Guide* (Scarborough: Thomson Nelson).

Ogilvy & Mather (2014) 'Better than Milk', *Ogilvy.com.cn*, www.ogilvy.com.cn/portfolio_page/better-than-milk/. Accessed 12 February 2016.

Ogilvy, David (2004) *Confessions of an Advertising Man* (Frensham: Southbank).

O'Reilly, Terry and Mike Tennant (2009) *The Age of Persuasion: How Marketing Ate Our Culture* (Berkeley, CA: Counterpoint).

Orland, Kyle (2013) 'The Newest *Tetris Blitz* Item Is an Obnoxious Toyota Corolla Ad', *Opposable Thumbs*, Ars Technica. 13 September, http://arstechnica.com/gaming/2013/09/the-newest-tetris-blitz-item-is-an-obnoxious-toyota-corolla-ad/. Accessed 5 December 2015.

Ourand, John (2015) 'CBS Price for Super Bowl 50 Spot: $5M?' *Sports Business*, 2 February, www.sportsbusinessdaily.com/Journal/Issues/2015/02/02/Media/SuperBowlAds.aspx. Accessed 5 April 2015.

Packard, Vance (2007) *The Hidden Persuaders* (New York: IG Publishing).

Peck, Jamie (2007) 'The Creativity Fix', *Eurozine,* www.eurozine.com/articles/2007-06-28-peck-en.html. Accessed 16 September 2015.

Pendergrast, Mark (2000) *For God, Country and Coca-Cola* (New York: Basic Books).

Pickering, Michael (2008) *Research Methods for Cultural Studies* (Edinburgh: Edinburgh University Press).

Pope, Daniel (1983) *The Making of Modern Advertising* (New York: Basic Books).

Powell, Helen (2009) 'Advertising Agencies and Their Client', in *The Advertising Handbook,* eds. Helen Powell, Jonathan Hardy, Sarah Hawkin, and Iain MacRury, 3rd edn (New York: Routledge), 13–23.

Powell, Helen, Jonathan Hardy, Sarah Hawkin and Iain MacRury (2009) 'Introduction – The Advertising Business', in *The Advertising Handbook,* eds. Helen Powell, Jonathan Hardy, Sarah Hawkin and Iain MacRury, 3rd edn (New York: Routledge), 1–10.

Pray, Douglas (2009) *Art & Copy* (New York: The One Club).

Prince, Russell (2010) 'Globalizing the Creative Industries Concept: Travelling Policy and Transnational Policy Communities', *Journal of Arts Management Law and Society* 40(2): 119–139.

Rancière, Jacques (2004) *The Politics of Aesthetics* (London: Continuum).

Ritzer, George and Douglas J. Goodman (2003) *Sociological Theory* (New York: McGraw-Hill).

Sassatelli, Roberta (2007) *Consumer Culture: History, Theory and Politics* (London: Sage).

Sasson, Donald (2006) *The Culture of the Europeans: From 1800 to Present* (London: HarperCollins).

Sauer, Abe (2013) 'How Unilever Is Translating the Dove Real Beauty Campaign for China', *Brandchannel,* 15 July http://brandchannel.com/2013/07/15/how-unilever-is-translating-the-dove-real-beauty-campaign-for-china/. Accessed 1 February 2016.

de Saussure, Ferdinand (2007) *Course in General Linguistics,* trans. Roy Harris, ed. Charles Bally and Albert Sechehaye, 17 edn (Chicago: Open Court).

Schroeder, Jonathan (2000) 'Edouard Manet, Calvin Klein and the Strategic Use of Scandal', in *Imagining Marketing: Art, Aesthetics and the Avant-Garde,* eds. Stephen Brown and Anthony Patterson (London: Routledge), 36–51.

Schudson, Michael (1986) *Advertising, The Uneasy Persuasion* (New York: Basic Books). Siltanen, Rob (2011) 'The Real Story Behind Apple's "Think Different" Campaign', *Forbes* 14 December, www.forbes.com/sites/onmarketing/2011/12/14/the-real-story-behind-apples-think-different-campaign. Accessed 22 May 2015.

Sinclair, John (2012) *Advertising, The Media and Globalisation: A World in Motion* (London and New York: Routledge).

Slattery, Martin (2003) *Key Ideas in Sociology* (Cheltenham: Nelson Thornes).

Smythe, Dallas (1981) 'On the Audience Commodity and its Work', in *Dependency Road: Communication, Capitalism, Consciousness and Canada* (Norwood: Ablex), 22–51.

Spurgeon, Christina (2008) *Advertising and New Media* (London and New York: Routledge).

Stecker, Robert (2000) 'Is It Reasonable to Attempt to Define Art?' in *Theories of Art Today,* ed. Noel Carroll (Madison: University of Wisconsin Press), 45–64.

Stotesbury, Robert (2005) 'Advertising Creativity', in *The Practice of Advertising,* ed. Adrian Mackay (London: Routledge), 118–131.

Strasser, Susan (1989) *Satisfaction Guaranteed: The Making of the American Mass Market* (Washington DC: Smithsonian Books).

Sullivan, Luke (2012) *Hey Whipple Squeeze This!: The Classic Guide to Creating Great Ads* (Hoboken: Wiley).

Swedberg, Richard and Ola Agevall (2005) *The Max Weber Dictionary* (Stanford: Stanford University Press).

Terranova, Tiziana (2004) *Network Culture: Politics for the Information Age* (London: Pluto Books).

Tibbs, Andy (2010) *Advertising: Its Business, Culture and Careers* (London: Routledge).

Tomka, Béla (2013) *A Social History of Twentieth-Century Europe* (London: Routledge).

Trefis Team (2015) 'Google Q1 Earnings: Ad Revenues Post Growth Once Again', www.forbes.com/sites/greatspeculations/2015/04/27/google-q1-earnings-ad-revenues-post-growth-once-again/. Accessed 18 December 2015.

Tungate, Mark (2013) *Adland: A Global History of Advertising* (London: Kogan Page).

Turner, Graeme (2012) *What's Become of Cultural Studies?* (London: Sage).

Turow, Joseph (2011) *The Daily You* (New Haven: Yale University Press).

Turow, Joseph and Matthew McAllister (2009) 'General Introduction', in *The Advertising and Consumer Culture Reader*, eds. Joseph Turow, and Matthew P. McAllister (London: Routledge), 1–8.

Twitchell, James B. (1997) *Adcult USA* (New York: Columbia University Press).

Veblen, Thorstein (2000) 'Conspicuous Consumption', in *The Consumer Society Reader*, eds. Schor, Juliet B. and Douglas Holt (New York: New Press), 187–204.

Veldstra, Carolyn and Walters Tim (2004) 'Glossary', in Susie O'Brien and Imre Szeman. *Popular Culture: A User's Guide* (Scarborough: Thomson Nelson).

Warde, Alan (2014) 'After Taste: Culture, Consumption and Theories of Practice', *Journal of Consumer Culture* 14(3): 279–303.

Weber, Max (1961) *General Economic History*, trans. Frank Knight (New York: Collier Books).

Wernick, Andrew (1991) *Promotional Culture* (London: Sage).

Wharton, Chris (2015) *Advertising: Critical Approaches* (London: Routledge).

Williams, Raymond (1988) *Keywords* (Glasgow: Fontana).

______(2004) *Television* (London: Routledge Classics).

______(2005) 'Advertising: The Magic System', in *Culture and Materialism* (London: Verso), 170–195.

______(2007) *Politics of Modernism: Against the New Conformists* (London: Verso).

Williamson, Judith (1995) *Decoding Advertisements: Ideology and Meaning in Advertising* (London: Marion Boyers).

Wilson, Sloan (1955) *The Man in the Gray Flannel Suit* (New York: Simon and Schuster).

Žižek, Slavoj (2012) 'The Spectre of Ideology', in *Mapping Ideology*, ed. Slavoj Žižek (London: Verso), 1–33.

Index